Mirage of Police Reform

Mirage of Police Reform

Procedural Justice and Police Legitimacy

———

Robert E. Worden and Sarah J. McLean

UNIVERSITY OF CALIFORNIA PRESS

University of California Press, one of the most distinguished university presses in the United States, enriches lives around the world by advancing scholarship in the humanities, social sciences, and natural sciences. Its activities are supported by the UC Press Foundation and by philanthropic contributions from individuals and institutions. For more information, visit www.ucpress.edu.

University of California Press
Oakland, California

Suggested citation: Worden, Robert E. and McLean, Sarah J. *Mirage of Police Reform: Procedural Justice and Police Legitimacy.* Oakland: University of California Press, 2017. doi: https://doi.org/10.1525/luminos.30

Library of Congress Cataloging-in-Publication Data
Names: Worden, Robert E., author. | McLean, Sarah J., author.
Title: Mirage of police reform : procedural justice and police legitimacy / Robert E. Worden and Sarah J. McLean.
Description: Oakland, California : University of California Press, [2017] | Includes bibliographical references and index.
Identifiers: LCCN 2017012517 | ISBN 9780520292413 (pbk. : alk. paper) | ISBN 9780520965966 (ebook)
Subjects: LCSH: Police-community relations—United States. | Police administration—United States.
Classification: LCC HV7936.P8 W67 2017 | DDC 363.2/3—dc23
LC record available at https://lccn.loc.gov/2017012517

26   25   24   23   22   21   20   19   18   17
10   9   8   7   6   5   4   3   2   1

To Alissa, for sharing all that life has presented for more than thirty years, and to Chuck, for your partnership and always being a sounding board and source of support

CONTENTS

FIGURES AND TABLES

FIGURES

TABLES

ACKNOWLEDGMENTS

We incurred many debts of gratitude in conducting the research that we summarize in this book. It was supported by Award No. 2010-IJ-CX-0027, awarded by the National Institute of Justice (NIJ), Office of Justice Programs, U.S. Department of Justice, to the John Finn Institute. The initial incarnation of the book was our technical report to NIJ. We must add that the opinions, findings, and conclusions or recommendations in this book are those of the authors and do not necessarily reflect those of the Department of Justice.

We are grateful to the police chiefs who agreed to their departments' participation in the project: Chief Mark R. Chaires (ret.) of the Schenectady Police Department, and Chief Frank L. Fowler of the Syracuse Police Department. Police executives who open their agencies to social research inevitably take risks in the intrinsically political world that they inhabit, since no one can say what findings the research will later yield. But the advancement of knowledge about the practice of policing would be limited indeed if those executives played it safe.

We are grateful also to: Schenectady Chief Brian Killcullen, now retired from that agency, who as the assistant chief of the Bureau of Field Services was a de facto project liaison, and who extended the department's cooperation after Chief Chaires's retirement; and to Deputy Chief Rebecca Thompson, who heads the Uniform Bureau of the Syracuse Police Department and was the project liaison there. For their unstinting assistance in obtaining department records, we thank Matt Douglas of the Schenectady police and Kim Brundage of the Syracuse police, and thanks to Schenectady's Sgt. Robert Brandow (ret.) for all of his work in retrieving video files of Schenectady patrol incidents. We also thank our grant manager at NIJ, Brett Chapman.

Assistance of incalculable value was provided at numerous junctures by the staff of the John Finn Institute: Andy Wheeler; Jen Grella; Marty Deane; Eva Dice; Gabby Vega; Kenan Worden; Caitlin Dole; Cass Davidoff; Jasmine Silver; Kelly Becker; Danielle Reynolds; Melissa Mackey; and Chris Dum. Jake Bratton of JB Research executed our plans for a telephone survey both effectively and efficiently.

Justin Pickett and Steve Mastrofski read the entire draft report to NIJ and provided thoughtful comments. Alissa Pollitz Worden did us the favor of making helpful comments on a previous draft of chapter 2. Two reviews of the NIJ report commissioned by NIJ provided constructive feedback, and so did the reviews done at the behest of the University of California Press; we gratefully acknowledge the anonymous reviewers. Our editor, Maura Roessner, has been as generous with encouragement and guidance as she has been patient with us.

Finally, we acknowledge the memory of Lt. John Finn, of the Albany Police Department, whose commitment to putting social scientific analysis to work in the service of policing is honored by the Institute that bears his name. We think that he would approve of this analysis.

The Procedural Justice Model as Reform

Accounts of the shooting differ. Ferguson police officer Darren Wilson testified that he first encountered Michael Brown and Dorian Johnson as they walked down the middle of Canfield Drive on August 9, 2014.[1] Wilson had just finished a call for a sick baby at a nearby apartment, during which he heard a call go out about a theft in progress at a market on West Florissant Street. Wilson was not dispatched to the theft scene, and he had heard only parts of the communication over his portable radio, but he reportedly knew that the suspect was wearing a black shirt and that a box of cigarillos had been taken. As Johnson, 22, and Brown, 18, walked one behind the other near the double yellow line, traffic flow was paused as cars took turns going around them. Officer Wilson, a large man at nearly 6'4" and 210 pounds, stopped as the young men approached his Tahoe, and when Johnson passed his side-view mirror, Wilson said, "Why don't you guys walk on the sidewalk?" Johnson replied, "We are almost to our destination" and continued walking, and as Brown approached the car's mirror Wilson said, "Well, what's wrong with the sidewalk?" Brown retorted, "Fuck what you have to say," attracting extra attention from Wilson, who then noticed that Brown carried a box of cigarillos in his right hand, and also that he wore a black shirt, matching the description of the suspect in the theft at the market.

Wilson notified the dispatcher that he was "on Canfield with two" and asked for another car, and then he backed the Tahoe up past Johnson and Brown, angling the car across the middle of the road. He started to open the car door and said to Brown, "Hey, come here for a minute," but Brown, 6'4" and 292 pounds, shut the door saying, "What the fuck are you going to do about it." Wilson tried to move Brown back with the door and said, "Get the fuck back," but Brown pushed back, shutting the door, and struck Wilson in the face with his hand. Brown turned to Johnson and handed him the cigarillos, now in Brown's left hand, and said, "Hey, man, hold these," and Wilson grabbed Brown's right arm. As he later explained to the grand jury, he "felt like a five year old holding on to Hulk Hogan" (the professional wrestler). Brown struck Wilson again, and as they struggled, Wilson considered his options: his mace, which he could not readily reach, and which posed the risk of incapacitating Wilson more than Brown; his expandable baton, on which he was partially sitting, making it awkward to draw; his flashlight, on the passenger side of the car, which he considered to be of dubious effectiveness in close quarters; and his firearm. He drew his gun and told Brown, "Get back or I am going to shoot you." Brown grabbed the gun, pushing it into Wilson's hip, and said, "You are too much of a pussy to shoot me." As Wilson pulled the gun up, with Brown still holding onto it as well, he pulled the trigger; after two clicks, the gun discharged on the third pull, the bullet going through the door panel, breaking the retracted window and causing glass to fly out. Both parties were startled.

Brown stepped back at that point, and according to Wilson, "He looked up at me and had the most intense aggressive face. The only way I can describe it, it looks like a demon, that's how angry he looked." Brown came back toward Wilson then, and Wilson tried to fire again, but the gun did not discharge. Wilson racked the slide and pulled the trigger again, and the gun fired, the bullet grazing Brown's hand. Brown turned and ran west on Canfield, and Wilson got out, notifying dispatch that shots had been fired. Wilson gave chase until Brown stopped and turned toward him, whereupon Wilson told him to get on the ground. When Brown started running at Wilson, Wilson started firing. Wilson saw Brown's body jerk and inferred that Brown had been struck at least once, but Brown continued to approach, and so Wilson started backpedaling and resumed firing. He saw Brown flinch but not stop, and "at that point it looked like he was almost bulking up to run through the shots, like it was making him mad that I'm shooting at him." When Brown was eight to ten feet away, he leaned forward as if he intended to tackle Wilson, and Wilson fired again. Brown went down, face first.

According to Brown's companion that day, Dorian Johnson, Wilson's first words to him and Brown were "Get the fuck on the sidewalk," and Johnson insisted that Brown said nothing to Wilson until after Wilson backed his car up to intersect them.[2] Once Wilson backed up, though, he asked them, "What did you say?" Wilson opened his car door and, because they were so close to the car, the door hit both Johnson and Brown, and the door "closed back on him [Wilson], like real fast." Wilson then grabbed Brown's shirt around the neck area. Brown put his hands on the car and tried to pull away. Johnson heard Brown and Wilson talking to one another, "yelling and cussing," and saw them engaged in a "tug of war." Brown was pulling away as Wilson tried to pull him into the car, Wilson's left hand on Brown's right arm. Johnson never saw Brown's hand touch Wilson's gun, nor did he see Brown at any time form a fist or strike Wilson.

Other witnesses provided testimony to the St. Louis County grand jury, and their accounts varied. Some said that Brown was surrendering when Wilson fired the fatal shots; others said that Brown was shot in the back. Several witnesses saw the conflict between Brown and Wilson, and some said that they saw Brown punch Wilson while Brown was partly inside the Tahoe. No camera recording, other than that of the theft at the Ferguson Market, was available. But Brown's blood or other DNA was found inside the driver's door, on the upper left thigh of Wilson's pants, and on Wilson's shirt and firearm. Reaching its conclusion more than three months after the shooting, the grand jury declined to indict Wilson. Announcing the grand jury decision, the St. Louis County prosecutor Robert McCulloch explained that physical evidence and the most credible witness testimony indicated that as Brown charged at Wilson, the officer fired five shots, and then fired another five shots as Brown made a "full charge" at Wilson (Eckholm 2014). A federal investigation into Wilson's actions concluded that his use of deadly force was not a violation of Brown's civil rights.

Ferguson, Missouri, is a small city of 21,000, two-thirds of whom are black. As in many American cities, Ferguson's police, with only four blacks on a force of fifty-three, have historically had a tense relationship with its black community. Michael Brown was black; Wilson is white. The deadly shooting sparked protests in Ferguson the next day, which became violent. Brown's death galvanized the Black Lives Matter movement, which organized a freedom ride to Ferguson (Day 2015; also see Luibrand 2015). Demonstrations continued episodically for weeks and months thereafter in Ferguson and elsewhere, reinforced by a series of incidents in which unarmed black men—and one youth—died at the hands of police, including Tamir Rice, 12, who was shot and killed by Cleveland police as he drew a toy gun from his waistband, in November 2014; Walter Scott, who was shot and killed by police in North Charleston, SC, in April 2015; Freddie Gray, who died as a result of injuries to his spinal cord sustained while being transported by Baltimore police, also in April 2015; and Samuel DuBose, who was shot and killed by police during a traffic stop in Cincinnati in July 2015. Parts of these and other incidents involving deadly force were captured in digital video, either by police cameras or citizens' smart phones.

In late 2014, a presidential task force was charged with formulating recommendations for (re)building public trust in policing, and the short ninety-day turnaround reflected the urgency of its work (President's Task Force on 21st Century Policing 2015). As we write in the fall of 2016, police reform remains a salient issue. The President's Task Force issued its report and recommendations, and it also produced a guide to implementation for police agencies. The Federal Bureau of Investigation is committed to devising a system for collecting data on police use of deadly force, which until now has been reported only as justifiable homicides on a voluntary (and hence unsystematic) basis by police agencies.

But police conduct, and especially police use of force, has been a recurring issue in the United States and other Western countries. It arises with some frequency at the local level and at times on a national scale. Twenty-three years before Michael Brown was killed, the beating of Rodney King by police in Los Angeles attracted national attention. King was a black man who, at the conclusion of a vehicle pursuit, was tased, struck by batons, and kicked by four LAPD officers, while nineteen other officers watched. Much of the incident was captured on video by a citizen and later viewed by people across the United States. Los Angeles Mayor Tom Bradley formed an independent commission to investigate the use of excessive force by Los Angeles police, and the commission's report summarized a broadly conceived inquiry into organizational dynamics that underlay police use of force. Commonly known as the Christopher Commission, after its chairman, Warren Christopher, the report noted that "police violence is not a local problem" (Independent Commission on the Los Angeles Police Department 1991, i), and the reception of the report reflected the national character of the issue. For its part, Congress mandated that the Justice Department collect national data on the use of force by police.

Twenty-three years before the King beating, another commission issued a report. The National Advisory Commission on Civil Disorders, also known as the Kerner Commission, was appointed by President Lyndon Johnson in 1967 to inquire into the whys and wherefores of riots that rocked American cities. The purview of the Kerner Commission included but was by no means limited to police practices. And it found that: "Disorder did not erupt as a result of a single "triggering" or "precipitating" incident. Instead, it was generated out of an increasingly disturbed social atmosphere, in which typically a series of tension-heightening incidents over a period of weeks or months became linked in the minds of many in the Negro community with a reservoir of underlying grievances. At some point in the mounting tension, a further incident—in itself often routine or trivial—became the breaking point and the tension spilled over into violence."

Police actions comprised the "prior incidents" in almost half of the cases, and the "final" incidents in twelve of twenty-four cases. The Commission's recommendations for the police were:

·   Review police operations in the ghetto to ensure proper conduct by police officers, and eliminate abrasive practices;
·   Provide more adequate police protection to ghetto residents to eliminate their high sense of insecurity, and the belief of many Negro citizens in the existence of a dual standard of law enforcement;
·   Establish fair and effective mechanisms for the redress of grievances against the police, and other municipal employees;

- Develop and adopt policy guidelines to assist officers in making critical decisions in areas where police conduct can create tension;
- Develop and use innovative programs to ensure widespread community support for law enforcement;
- Recruit more Negroes into the regular police force, and review promotion policies to ensure fair promotion for Negro officers;
- Establish a "Community Service Officer" program to attract ghetto youths between the ages of 17 and 21 to police work. These junior officers would perform duties in ghetto neighborhoods, but would not have full police authority. (U.S. National Advisory Commission on Civil Disorders 1968)

Contemporary prescriptions for reform bear a fairly strong resemblance to those of nearly fifty years ago. One new development in the reform agenda, however, is an emphasis on procedural justice and police legitimacy. Building trust and legitimacy was the first of the six "pillars" identified by the President's Task Force, around which its analysis and recommendations were organized. Its report stresses that "[b]uilding trust and nurturing legitimacy on both sides of the police-citizen divide is not only the first pillar of this task force's report but also the foundational principle underlying this inquiry into the nature of relations between law enforcement and the communities they serve." Its first recommendation was that "[l]aw enforcement culture should embrace a guardian mindset to build public trust and legitimacy. Toward that end, police and sheriffs' departments should adopt procedural justice as the guiding principle for internal and external policies and practices to guide their interactions with the citizens they serve" (11).

Even before the events that propelled police shootings into national headlines, however, steps had been taken by the Department of Justice to launch the National Initiative for Building Community Trust and Justice, which enlisted six pilot sites, in each of which three interventions are being implemented. One of the interventions is procedurally just policing. Making procedural justice a central plank in the reform agenda rests on a substantial volume of research into citizens' perceptions of and attitudes toward the police.

Can and will reform predicated on procedural justice as the main determinant of public trust succeed? As well grounded in logic and empirical evidence as it appears to be, we are doubtful. We believe that a procedural justice model of policing, which we describe below, is likely to be weakly implemented in police organizations, despite the best of executive intentions, and also that improvements in the procedural justice with which police act in their interactions with citizens are unlikely to yield corresponding improvements in citizens' subjective experiences with police. Moreover, we believe that the prescription for a procedural justice model rests on a misdiagnosis of the fundamental issues.

Some explanation is in order.

POLICE LEGITIMACY AND PROCEDURAL JUSTICE

When people have contacts with the police, the fairness with which police are perceived to act affects citizens' trust and confidence in the police and their sense that the police deserve to be obeyed—that is, the procedural justice that citizens subjectively experience affects the "legitimacy" of the police. A large body of social psychological research demonstrates the strength and consistency of these empirical relationships. Procedural justice, this research tells us, is a matter of treating people with dignity and respect, giving them an opportunity to explain their situations and listening to what they have to say, and explaining what police have done and/or will do, so that it is clear that officers are taking account of people's needs and concerns and basing police decisions on facts. This research further tells us that legitimacy is important, not only for its own sake but because it has consequences. People who believe that police are legitimate are more likely to accept police decisions and comply with police requests and directives, more likely to cooperate with the police, and more likely even to abide by the law.

Legitimacy is, in the context of this social psychological research, an abstract outlook, with both cognitive and affective elements. It is subjective in nature, but as we discuss below, it is affected by citizens' experiences. As the National Research Council's Committee to Review Research has observed: "Legitimacy is the property that a rule or an authority has when others feel obligated to voluntarily defer to that rule or authority. In other words, a legitimate authority is one that is regarded by people as entitled to have its decisions and rules accepted and followed by others" (National Research Council 2004, 297).

The legitimacy of the police is thought to be important for several reasons. First, research suggests that citizens who see the police as legitimate are, in their interactions with the police, more likely to comply with police commands, directions, and requests. In the micro-context of police-citizen encounters, citizens' compliance makes the performance of police tasks easier (Mastrofski, Snipes, and Supina 1996; McCluskey 2003; McCluskey, Mastrofski, and Parks 1999), and can be expected to result in less use of force by police and fewer injuries to both police and citizens. Second, citizens who see the police as legitimate might be expected to more readily cooperate with police and other legal actors, for example, in reporting crime, and perhaps in providing information (Hart and Rennison 2003). Third, citizens who regard legal authorities as legitimate may be less likely to break the law. Research on this question is hardly conclusive, but findings suggest that offenders may be less prone to recidivate when their treatment by the legal system conforms to principles of procedural justice (Paternoster et al. 1997; also see Tyler 1990; Tyler and Huo 2002).

Legitimacy and other attitudes toward the police, extant research suggests, comprise a stock that police can either build or deplete through their performance, though it is also clear that the public's attitudes toward the police are to a significant extent shaped by forces beyond the control of police.[3] Several elements of procedural justice shape citizens' subjective experience:

- People are more satisfied when they have an opportunity to "tell their side of the story"—to explain their situation or behavior to authorities.
- People are more satisfied when they believe that authorities' decisions are based on facts.
- People are more satisfied when they feel that they have been treated with dignity and respect.
- People are more satisfied when they trust authorities' motives, which is more likely when authorities explain their actions in terms that demonstrate that they have taken account of citizens' concerns and needs.[4]

Thus the research suggests that, in the words of the Committee to Review Research, legitimacy is "created" in individual encounters, and is also created in a more general form by the aggregated actions of police: "When a police officer responds to a call or stops someone on the street, what happens affects general feelings that people have regarding the extent to which authorities are legitimate and entitled to be obeyed" (National Research Council, 2004, 298). The effects of each contact on the attitude of the citizen participant are quite modest. The effects may be somewhat greater when we take account of both direct and indirect experiences, as the effects of vicarious experience ripple through circles of relatives, friends, and neighbors (Miller et al. 2003; Rosenbaum et al. 2005). The effects may be greater still as they accumulate across many contacts: in a single year, even in a fairly small city, police handle tens of thousands of calls for service, make thousands of arrests, issue thousands of traffic and other tickets, and have innumerable other contacts with the public. It may be possible to establish a reputation for treating people properly by *earning it,* through behavior that accords with principles of procedural justice. Given the asymmetrical effects of positive and negative experiences, which we discuss in a later chapter, it is easier to establish a reputation for treating people improperly by treating them unjustly, thereby eroding the stock of legitimacy. But the evidence base on which these expectations rest does not withstand close scrutiny, as we explain in later chapters.

A PROCEDURAL JUSTICE MODEL OF POLICING

Translating this body of research into police practice is not straightforward, however. With the voluminous research on procedural justice and legitimacy as a point of departure, Stephen Schulhofer et al. (2011) describe a procedural justice model of policing (also see Tyler 2004; Meares 2009). They make the important point that outcomes—say, whether or not the citizen is ticketed, searched, or even arrested—are not determinative of citizens' subjective experience; people can be satisfied with their encounter with police even when the outcomes are unfavorable for them, so long as they believe that they were treated justly. The implication is, as they emphasize, that police need not choose between "toughness" and "fairness." Police can be both "tough" and fair when they take enforcement action with cognizance of procedural justice: "Instead of seeking to instill fear or project power, officers would aim to treat citizens courteously, briefly explain the reason for a stop, and, absent exigent circumstances, give the citizen an opportunity to explain himself before significant decisions are made" (Schulhofer et al. 2011, 352). Thus the procedural justice model does not prescribe nonenforcement. It is about *how*, not *whether*, police authority is exercised. The procedural justice model is long on the forms that procedurally just policing takes at the street level, and its rationale, but rather short on the managerial measures that police departments should take in order to implement the model. One such measure is to establish procedures for procedurally just policing. Schulhofer et al. suggest that

> In connection with street stops, operational guidelines within each department could formalize appropriate steps, such as the need for courteous treatment, the obligation to give the citizen a reason for the stop, and a chance to explain the circumstances. . . . . Such steps could be made a routine part of every officer's behavior on the beat. . . . officers could easily carry and give to those they stop a card containing a short statement of the rules that govern police stops. The card would enumerate the rights that must be respected (including the right to have the reasons for the stop explained and the right to tell their side of the story before decisions are made) and the procedures for complaining about unfair treatment. (Schulhofer et al. 2011, 354)

We might suppose further that police departments that adopted such a model would establish and enforce expectations that their officers exercise their authority with procedural justice. Their chief executives would make procedural justice an explicit priority, and their expectations would be embodied in departmental policies and procedures. They would train their officers in proper police-citizen interaction (see, e.g., Schuck and Rosenbaum 2011; Skogan, Van Craen, and Hennessy 2014). They would monitor the available indicators of police performance, such as complaints and use of force, and recognizing the limits of these indicators, they would make supervisors responsible for spot-checking the quality of police-citizen encounters. They might even develop more systematic measures of such performance, conducting periodic surveys of citizens with whom their officers have had contact. And they would treat officers with the same procedural justice that they demand of officers in their encounters with citizens, thereby nurturing officers' trust in the organization and their sense of obligation to obey its rules.

Procedural Justice and Management Accountability

In most if not all large police departments, the organizational infrastructure is not conducive to the procedural justice model. Even in an era that stresses managerial accountability, the procedural justice with which officers act is typically not measured in police agencies, nor is it an outcome for which police managers are held accountable.

The New York City Police Department's "Compstat" management accountability mechanism has been widely emulated. One of its primary virtues, we believe, is its potential to fix police attention not only on the means—arrests, tickets, and so forth—but on the ends of policing: crime reduction, disorder control, the enhancement of quality of life, and community satisfaction. Accountability mechanisms should stress outcomes, and not simple counts of outputs. If unit commanders are to be held accountable for outcomes, and for mounting good-faith efforts to affect those outcomes in desirable ways, then outputs are important mainly as the manifestations or by-products of effective tactics.

A drawback of Compstat is that the measurement of outcomes is normally confined to crime, and it thus omits important outcomes that ought to be the objects of police attention. Mark Moore describes a range of outcomes, or performance dimensions, that reflect the value of policing, including:

- Reduce criminal victimization;
- Call offenders to account;
- Reduce fear and enhance personal security;
- Guarantee safety in public spaces;
- Use financial resources fairly, efficiently, and effectively;
- Use force and authority fairly, efficiently, and effectively;
- Satisfy customer demands and achieve legitimacy with those policed. (Moore 2002, 131–33)

With reference to case studies of six police departments that were, in the 1990s, implementing community policing, Moore found that only one department accorded high overall importance to performance measurement. More to the object of our concern here, Moore found that three of the six agencies used citizen complaints as a measure of performance with respect to the use of authority, and two used repeated citizen surveys to measure citizen satisfaction. The agencies that tapped these sources of information for performance measures were among the agencies originally selected for study because they "were judged to be making unusually rapid progress toward community policing" (Moore 2002, 159), so they are hardly representative.

We should add that the general community surveys that are administered on an annual or biannual basis by some departments are of limited utility for management accountability. Measures of performance that are derived no more often than once every year (or two) are unlikely to either guide police managers or form the basis for holding them individually accountable (Behn 2008). And general, communitywide perceptions of police performance—for example, whether police are in general polite or fair—may not reflect officers' actual performance in police-citizen encounters. We should also add that the procedural propriety of police actions is not measured validly with citizen complaints, which are rarely filed even when citizens are dissatisfied with police service, and which are not infrequently based on misunderstandings of police procedure or on (intentional or unintentional) misrepresentations of police action.

For the purposes of the research summarized here, we therefore undertook to measure citizens' subjective experience, and especially their perceptions of procedural justice, through surveys of people who had recently interacted with police. In each of the two study departments, in Schenectady and Syracuse, New York, semi-monthly samples were drawn from police records from mid-July 2011 through mid-January 2013. Respondents were interviewed by phone within one to five weeks of their contact with police. Following the accumulation of survey data to form a baseline, survey results on citizens' satisfaction and judgments about procedural justice in the contact were summarized and reported to command staffs on a monthly basis through the departments' respective Compstat meetings. Across the eighteen months of surveying, we completed 3,603 interviews, or approximately 100 per month in each city. In this way the project provided for measures of police performance with respect to procedural justice with sufficient periodicity that the information was potentially useful in managing performance. We also interviewed "key informants" in each city, that is, community leaders attentive to police services and knowledgeable about community attitudes, as a potentially larger and more representative slice of public opinion about the police.

Theories of organization form two divergent sets of expectations for how police managers would use the new measures of performance. The management guru Peter Drucker is reputed to have said that "what gets measured gets managed." Thus we might suppose that with monthly feedback about officers' performance in procedural justice terms, managers would pay more attention to how, and not merely whether, their subordinates used their authority and interacted with citizens. As managers—platoon commanders—pay more attention to these dimensions of police work, we might suppose that field supervisors would likewise pay more attention to it. They might remind patrol officers at roll calls about the virtues of procedural justice: its effects on citizen compliance with police, citizen cooperation with law enforcement, compliance with the law, and the public image of the department—its stock of legitimacy. The department might mount in-service training on the rationale for procedural justice and the actions that comprise it.

It was not our place as researchers to tell managers how to manage; as we told them at the outset, we were there to learn from them.

The second set of expectations for how police managers would manage procedural justice is derived from an institutional perspective on organizations, which we describe in greater depth in chapter 2. From this perspective, we might expect to see the management of what is measured only in a market-driven organization whose productive operations apply a well-known technology with well-established connections to productive output, and we would instead expect to see little such effective management in an institutionalized organization, whose technical "core" is only loosely coupled with many organizational structures. In many respects, as we will explain, police departments resemble institutionalized organizations.

We met with the command staffs of the departments each month to report on survey results, and those meetings also afforded us an opportunity to hear from police managers about their efforts to manage performance. In addition, we interviewed patrol officers and field supervisors at two points in time, about halfway through the eighteen-month survey of citizens, and after the conclusion of surveying, in order to learn more about what, from their perspective, the department was doing to manage this dimension of their performance, and also to learn their reactions to this emphasis on the quality of police-citizen interactions.

Finally, because the Schenectady Police Department had for a number of years provided for audio and video recordings of its officers' activities, we drew a sample of encounters about which citizens had been surveyed and conducted structured observation to independently code features of those police-citizen interactions. For this purpose we formulated an observation protocol that built on the platform of more than forty years of systematic social observation of police in the field. Because we were able to link survey data on citizens' subjective experience to trained observers' independent coding of the behavior of officers and citizens toward one another, encounter by encounter, we can for the first time analyze citizens' subjective experience in terms of independent measures of police behavior. With the observational data we formed a measure of officers' procedural justice and a separate measure of officers' procedural *injustice*. Thus we can better assess the value of citizen surveys for measuring (and managing) the overt procedural justice with which officers treat citizens.

COMING ATTRACTIONS

Readers need not wait to learn what we found in this research, inasmuch as we briefly summarize it here. We found that what gets measured does not always get successfully managed. With the introduction of monthly measures of the quality of citizens' subjective experience in their contacts with police reported through Compstat meetings, we detected no substantively significant changes overall in either city. Police performance in these terms was fairly high at the outset in both cities, leaving only a little room for improvement. We nevertheless found that efforts to manage the measured outcomes took various forms in each police department, which we arrayed on a management continuum. Among patrol officers and field supervisors, we found a mixed reception to the administrative push for better "customer service": some officers were quite receptive; some exhibited a tempered receptivity; others were quite skeptical.

We can make sense of these findings about management and performance by applying an institutional perspective. Management accountability is only "loosely coupled" to management and to street-level practices. The officers in whose behavior implementation of the procedural justice model rests are not all equally receptive to making customer service a priority, and the implementation of any administrative mandate is mediated by officers' interpretations of its meaning. Officers must make sense of administrative demands, and they vary in the sense that they make of it.

But the story does not end there. In our analysis of police-citizen encounters for which observations were conducted, we found that citizens' subjective experience is very weakly related to officers' procedural justice and only moderately related to officers' procedural injustice. *Whether* officers used their authority—by using physical force or conducting searches—proved to be much more important than *how* officers used their authority—their procedural (in)justice—in shaping citizens' assessments of procedural justice. To a significant extent, it appears that the weak relationship stems from citizens' overestimation of police procedural justice: citizen ratings of procedural justice were fairly high even when observed procedural justice was fairly low. These findings challenge the supposition that legitimacy is "created" through police-citizen interactions, and also call into question the extent to which survey data on citizens' perceptions reflect officers' performance. Nor did we find change overall in observed procedural justice by officers in Schenectady, which was moderately high in the first place, and no change in procedural injustice, which was uniformly low. However, in one platoon, whose commander and first-line supervisors were among the more supportive of a customer-service orientation, we detected a modest increase in officers' procedural justice.

These findings raise doubts about the efficacy of the procedural justice model as an approach to police reform. Although it is based on voluminous research concerning public perceptions of police, it is based on assumptions about the strength of the connections: between those perceptions and police actions in police-citizen contacts, and between the adoption of a process-based model of policing and officers' practices on the street.

With that as an overview, we proceed to detail our empirical study. In chapter 3 we summarize what we know about public trust and confidence in police and the forces that influence trust, and present survey-based measures of public trust in the two cities. Chapter 4 presents a detailed quantitative analysis of citizens' subjective experiences, while chapter 5 summarizes the sources of citizen dissatisfaction in survey respondents' own words. Chapter 6 presents the findings about officers' behaviors, and especially those that comprise procedural justice, as well as procedural injustice. In chapter 7 readers will find an analysis of citizens' subjective experience in terms of officers' behavior. Chapter 8 summarizes the measurement of procedural justice performance and its incorporation into Compstat, the forms that the management of customer service took, evidence on the effects of management. Chapter 9 describes the varied interpretations of "customer service" that officers applied, and how they made sense of the administrative emphasis on the quality of their treatment of citizens. Chapter 10 summarizes what we found, overall, and discusses the implications of our findings for understanding police legitimacy and procedural justice, for police departments' efforts to build legitimacy, and for future research. We believe that our findings about management, management accountability, and procedural justice can be understood by considering them from an institutional perspective, to which we turn next in chapter 2.

2

Police Departments as Institutionalized Organizations

Police departments can be described from many perspectives, but one useful perspective is an institutional one. Institutional theory has been widely used in the study of private- and public-sector organizations generally, and it has been applied previously to police departments. We sketch that perspective here. We did not set out to test propositions drawn from institutional theory, nor do we purport to offer tests of that theory in the chapters that follow. But we believe that institutional theory can in large measure account for our findings, and we adopted this perspective because we think that it is very useful in understanding the dynamics of police administration in general and the management of procedural justice in particular.[1] Thus we explain what it means for an organization to be institutionalized, and we describe at some length relevant parts of the institutional environment of police departments in the United States. Then we turn to the study departments, and describe them in terms of their institutional environments.

PERSPECTIVES ON POLICE ORGANIZATIONS

The technology of policing—that is, how the work gets done—is an intensive one, with choices about how to proceed made in any one case as events unfold. Policing thus requires the exercise of discretion, and that discretion is exercised in its most palpable forms on the street and by the lowest-ranking members of police organizations. The task environment of policing is heterogeneous, ambiguous, and turbulent, with countless contingencies that bear on officers' choices, factors to be weighed even though their meaning and implications are not clear, and subject to a great deal of uncertainty surrounding the consequences of alternative courses of police action (Thompson 1967). What police officers should do in most of the situations that they handle on a day-to-day basis cannot be specified in policy and procedure manuals. "You can't go by the book," as police are wont to say.

The task environment and the technology of police work have far-reaching implications for how police work can be managed. Police departments are what James Q. Wilson (1989) describes as "coping organizations"—those organizations whose managers cannot easily observe their subordinates' operations or assess the value of those operations for achieving desired social outcomes. The managers of such organizations are not powerless, but they are sharply constrained in their capacity to direct what the organization does and how it is done. Police officers work for the most part outside of direct supervision, they perform work that is rife with situational contingencies, and information about what they do and the circumstances under which they do it is normally recorded by the officers themselves. The consequences or effects of what police do are subject to a host of influences other than police action, so managers cannot infer from observed or documented consequences what officers actually did; even scientifically structured evaluations of police intervention cannot provide definitive evidence about the effectiveness of what police do, and scientific evaluations are seldom performed.

Police departments are also what Michael Lipsky (1980) calls "street-level bureaucracies," whose front-line workers exercise wide discretion in their interactions with the agency's clients. Street-level bureaucracies are "people-processing" organizations (Prottas 1978). Teachers, social workers, police officers, and others are all street-level bureaucrats, and they must cope with some common conditions of work: chronically inadequate resources, including time and information; vague, ambiguous, and sometimes conflicting organizational goals; and an inability to control the pace or outcomes of their work. Consequently, according to Lipsky, street-level bureaucrats develop patterns of practice that are in some respects dysfunctional for the organization's clients but enable the workers to cope: they husband resources; they routinize their processing of cases; they reconceptualize their jobs in order to reduce the discrepancy between the ideal and the achievable; and they reconceptualize their clientele. These systemic forces have impacts that are largely beyond the capacity of managers to control.

Michael Brown (1981) argues that the police bureaucracy exerts control over only the more mundane aspects of police work, such as the timeliness and neatness of officers' reports, and that the substantive exercise of police discretion is controlled—insofar as it is controlled at all—by the peer group, or the police culture. We often think of the police culture as a set of outlooks that are widely shared among police officers: strong loyalty to co-workers, an "us vs. them" mentality; suspiciousness and cynicism; an occupational focus on crime control and law enforcement, and a correspondingly derisive regard for order maintenance and service functions; and a willingness to bend or break rules governing the use of force or search and seizure. Moreover, the police culture has long been recognized as an impediment to bureaucratic control, and the paramount value of loyalty manifests itself in a norm of mutual cover-ups of bureaucratic (and legal) transgressions. Elizabeth Reuss-Ianni (1983) describes street cop culture and its codes, including "don't give up another cop," as antithetical to management cop culture.

If this was ever an accurate characterization of an entire occupational group, it is no longer (Herbert 1998; Paoline 2004; Paoline, Myers, and Worden 2000; Paoline and Terrill 2014), but police culture remains an important consideration. Brown's portrayal of police culture is simpler and it may be timeless. He asserts that the police culture is comprised of two core values: loyalty and individualism. As other accounts of police culture hold, loyalty to co-workers—backing them up in the face of the threats to their safety, and honoring their accomplishments in the context of a police bureaucracy that is "punishment-centered"—is an occupationally universal value, owing mainly to the danger in the occupational environment. Individualism allows officers to practice their own styles and apply their own priorities, and to do so without second-guessing. Individualism allows for heterogeneity among officers in their conceptions of the police role, in their degree of cynicism, in their respect for restrictions on their authority, and in their "operational styles" (Brown 1981). Research has repeatedly found such heterogeneity, rather than a monolithic police culture. So it is that Brown's description of police culture can be reconciled with the research that has found not a single occupational culture but rather multiple subcultures. This more delimited and accurate rendition of police culture has important implications for how tenuously bureaucratic controls are connected to the discretionary choices that together comprise the delivery of police services. The culture legitimizes street-level individuality in doing police work, and the nature of the work makes it very difficult to apply bureaucratic controls.

Front-line supervisors can affect some types of officers' behavior, but not all supervisors are created equal, and the impact of supervision on behavior will be attenuated or amplified by individual supervisors' own orientations and styles (Engel 2001, 2002). William Ker Muir Jr. (1977) explains how supervisors can be instrumental in their subordinates' professional growth and moral renewal *if* they are actively engaged in developing their subordinates' skills and judgment. But such forms of supervision have not been normal in law enforcement (Brown 1981; Engel 2001, 2002; Van Maanen 1983); the potential impact of supervision probably remains unfulfilled in many cases. Immediate supervisors are caught in the middle, between management and the street, and, as Brown observed, "the pressures for loyalty and solidarity are refracted throughout the police bureaucracy" (1981, 90), with norms that prohibit second-guessing and micro-management. Many supervisors keep their priorities limited and expectations low (Van Maanen 1983), and they may not even be comprehended by their subordinates (Engel and Worden 2003).

Furthermore, many efforts to change the way that street-level policing is per-formed are subject to a process of interpretation by the officers whose behavior is the target of the change, a process known in the study of organizations as "sen-semaking." Officers' interpretations will not always conform with those of police executives. Some police subcultures will be receptive to a reform proposed by management, such as community policing, and others will tend to resist, based on the compatibility of the reform (as officers make sense of it) with officers' own occupational values and attitudes.

AN INSTITUTIONAL PERSPECTIVE

Every organization is subject to the environments in which it operates, includ-ing a technical environment and an institutional environment. Technical environ-ments are those in which the goods or services produced by an organization are exchanged, as in private markets, and that reward the effective and efficient pro-duction of those goods or services. Institutional environments, by contrast, con-tain requirements or expectations for the structure of an organization and reward the adoption of required or favored structures, not effective or efficient production as such.

Some types of organizations, such as manufacturing firms, operate in a well-developed technical environment, where production processes are well understood and a market establishes the value of the products, and a weak institutional envi-ronment. Other types of organizations operate in a weakly developed technical environment and a strong institutional environment. For these organizations, the technical environment provides a limited understanding of cause-and-effect rela-tionships in the production technology, such that it may be hard to assess the tech-nical performance of an organization or even to say what effective and efficient production is. But the institutional environment contains well-developed expecta-tions or requirements for how the organization should be structured. These ex-pectations are institutional "myths," or "idealized cultural accounts" of how an or-ganization should operate (Hallett 2010). Structures are adopted and maintained, not because they have a well-established and well-understood utility in effective and efficient production, but rather because they are expected or demanded by external stakeholders, or "sovereigns," as markers of proper and/or professional operations. Thus, even if they do not serve to make the organization more effective or otherwise perform better, the structures serve to confer legitimacy: "a general-ized perception or assumption that the actions of an entity are desirable, proper, or appropriate within some socially constructed system of norms, values, beliefs, and definitions" (Suchman 1995, 574).

Institutional pressures take several forms, and they may tend to yield a high degree of structural homogeneity among the organizations in an organizational "field" (DiMaggio and Powell 1983). Some such pressures are "coercive," such as statutory, regulatory, or judicial requirements or mandates, or widely shared cultural expectations. Other pressures arise from the structures and practices of other organizations in the same field that are perceived to be successful; the presumed virtues of those structures or practices make them appear worthy of emulating. Still other pressures stem from professional or occupational norms or standards. These various forces in an organizational field tend to produce institutional "isomorphism" of corresponding kinds—coercive, mimetic, and normative, respectively—such that organizations in a field tend to be structurally similar to one another. Conformity to these various demands and expectations is the price of legitimacy for organizations whose institutional environments are strong. Legitimation is achieved by an organization not through its technical performance but by meeting these environmental demands, that is, adopting structures and practices that institutional myths prescribe.

Police departments are particularly susceptible to forces in their institutional environments. By virtue of the nature of the work that they perform, police departments have:

· vague, ambiguous, conflicting goals;
· uncertain technologies for turning raw materials—people and their problems—into valued outputs;
· great difficulty in monitoring the work of turning raw materials into outputs; and
· great difficulty in evaluating the effects of the work that is done.

As many have observed, technical performance by police organizations encompasses many dimensions. Moore (2002) identifies several dimensions of performance as part of the mission of police, including reducing crime and criminal victimization; holding offenders to account; reducing fear and enhancing a sense of security; regulating public spaces and traffic safety; and providing emergency medical and social services. In addition, the economy with which police operate, in terms of the expenditure of money and/or authority, is a basis for assessing police performance, so the efficient use of public resources and the fair and judicious use of police authority may be considered. Not all of these facets of the police mission are compatible with one another, as improving performance in one area (e.g., respecting civil liberties) may come at the expense of performance in another (e.g., crime control), and people inside and outside of the organization may not agree on the relative importance of those areas. Little information is available about the technical performance of the police, and to a large degree judgments about technical performance require inferences about causal relationships among police inputs, outputs, and outcomes that are embedded in larger systems of social and economic forces; even when police strategies or programs are subjected to scientific evaluations, inferences about the impacts of police interventions are subject to some doubt. These challenges weaken the technical environment of policing.

The institutional environment of policing is fairly well developed, however. Among the structures that police might adopt in order to conform to broad cultural expectations are "appropriate titles, uniforms, badges, and insignia indicating rank, department and assignment" (Crank and Langworthy 1992, 342–43). Indeed, even the Weberian bureaucracy in U.S. policing, dating from the Progressive era, is an organizational form that was adopted and maintained because it is expected by external stakeholders, as well as by many inside of policing, despite its questionable compatibility with the technical demands of police work (Brown 1981); the task environment and technology of policing is more compatible with a much less bureaucratic form of organization. But institutional forces compel police organizations to maintain a bureaucratic form—some would say a "presentational strategy" or façade (Manning 1977)—that includes thick books of policies and procedures and a quasi-military chain-of-command, which (at least partially) satisfies the public expectation of control over the exercise of police authority. The appropriateness of a bureaucratic form for police departments is largely taken for granted. In a police department that is institutionalized, then, structural features—the division of labor, the allocation of resources, and recruitment, selection, training, supervision and management practices—may be continued or changed based, not on their demonstrable technical utility, but rather on widespread suppositions about their value.

The range of actors whom we would consider sovereigns in police departments' institutional environment encompasses what Moore describes as the "authorizing environment," including "all those political actors or agents who have the *formal* power to review police department operations, or the *informal* power to influence those who do" (2002, 84). They include elected and appointed officials—mayors and city councilors, city managers, comptrollers, civil service commissions—as well as the representatives of interest groups and "watchdog" organizations (e.g., the American Civil Liberties Union), police unions, and the media. They also include other law enforcement organizations at higher levels of government, professional organizations (e.g., the International Association of Chiefs of Police) and accrediting bodies (such as the Commission on Accreditation for Law Enforcement Agencies), as well as actors with regulatory authority, e.g., the courts, and the Civil Rights Division of the Department of Justice. In the United States, most but not all of these sovereigns are local. These external stakeholders, whose support is required for the organization's survival and prosperity, are as hard-pressed as anyone is to ascertain what the organization does and the contribution that it makes to social outcomes. They tend to fall back on suppositions about how an organization should be structured, even if the structural prescriptions have not been tested and validated. The suppositions represent "ordinary knowledge" (Lindblom and

Cohen 1979). To the degree that external stakeholders rely on such suppositions, the organization's legitimacy is determined, not by how well the work is actually performed, but by how closely the organization conforms to the expectations of its institutional environment.

The expectations of these various sovereigns need not and often do not agree with one another, and any one sovereign's expectations need not be internally consistent, making the institutional environment complex. Demands for community policing, for example, are not entirely compatible with demands for public accountability: pushing discretion down as much as possible to field supervisors and beat officers, and thereby unleashing the creativity of officers in addressing the many and varied problems that communities confront, is a prominent feature of community policing, but expanding officers' discretion is not entirely compatible with demands for public accountability and administrative rule-making, which tend to emphasize constraints on police discretion. An institutional environment of such complexity and, potentially, contradiction, has implications that we consider below.

We would add that to recognize the strength of the institutional environment of policing is not to hold that the technical environment is irrelevant or that police executives deliberately adopt structures merely for symbolic purposes. The adoption of structures that serve institutional purposes may also serve more conventional technical-rational purposes in an organization, and even if the structures serve only more symbolic purposes, for reasons that we discuss below, it does not follow that their adoption was an act of administrative duplicity.

Institutional myths may be incompatible with the requirements of the organization's tasks (as they are perceived by operators such as teachers or police officers), or with one another, creating the potential for structural conflict. One way that such conflict can be averted is through the "loose coupling" of structures with technical activities, which allows the continued performance of technical tasks without hindrance by structures that satisfy sovereigns' expectations but are not compatible with the work. Such buffering need not be by executive design. When the structures that police departments adopt are incompatible with one another, with previously existing structures that remain in use, or with the technical demands of the work itself, something has to give. Often, the "technical core"—in policing, that would be the street-level work of patrol officers or detectives—is, in effect, buffered from the structures with which the work is not compatible. We do not doubt that when police executives adopt new structures such as community policing or Compstat, they do so in good faith and for the intended instrumental benefits that they promise in accomplishing the work of the organization. Structural forces are more powerful than the wills and good intentions of police executives, however, and as the complexity of the organization's structure mirrors that of the institutional environment, with features that are incompatible with one another and with the technical core, loose coupling (or decoupling) can result. Technical performance that is loosely coupled (or decoupled) from structural reforms may not be readily detected, for the same conditions that make it difficult for sovereigns to judge technical performance make it difficult for managers to detect such loose coupling. Thus institutionalization stems from the nature of the work, not from managerial ineptitude or resistance (though some managers are inept and others have their own agendas).

In an organization whose goals are vague and ambiguous, whose operators work largely independently, and whose technical activities bear an uncertain relationship to organizational outcomes, structures are subject to interpretation—a process of "sensemaking" (Weick 1995; also see Bechky 2011; Hallett and Ventresca 2006; Sharma and Good 2013). Schools fit this description, as do police departments. Efforts to change such organizations require winning the "hearts and minds" of operators. The adoption of structures that are incompatible with work requirements may breed cynicism toward managers who are seen to engage in political posturing.

We pause here to note that legitimacy in the context of institutional theory certainly bears a resemblance to the constellation of outlooks that social psychologists have labeled legitimacy, but there are important differences. Institutional theory treats legitimacy as a property of organizations. Organizations can establish and maintain their legitimacy. Organizational legitimacy can be challenged or threatened. And organizations can lose legitimacy. An organization's legitimacy turns on perceptions and judgments by actors—sovereigns—in its environment, but its relationship to public attitudes is less proximate. We will return to these connections in the next chapter.

Research on policing provides a number of illustrations of institutionalization in addition to those mentioned above, and we briefly describe a few of these here, reserving more extended descriptions of others for discussion in conjunction with the institutional environment of U.S. policing a bit later. Consider, for one example, the Junction City Police Department (a pseudonym). When the department adopted a specialized gang unit, it was not because the department's chief perceived street gangs as a threat to the safety of Junction City (Katz 2001). It was a consequence of external pressure brought by segments of the community that saw gangs as a community problem warranting the formation of a specialized unit, and in spite of the chief's conviction that gangs were not a problem. The newly created gang unit, comprised of a sergeant and four investigators, represented a feature of the department's structure whose existence was owed not to the technical requirements of policing, but rather to the demands of powerful external constituencies for an organizational response of the expected form. The operation of the unit, in the absence of a serious gang problem toward which to direct their efforts, consisted first of public presentations and subsequently of forming partnerships with other, well-established units—such as homicide— thus gaining unit legitimacy through its association with reputable partners.

Another example involves training in drunk-driving enforcement (Mastrofski and Ritti 1996). Among six police agencies—two each of city police departments, township police departments, and state police troops—three exhibited a strong connection between training in enforcement against driving under the influence (DUI) and officers' actual enforcement practices, while three others did not. In the former, DUI enforcement activity was actively encouraged and rewarded; the training was tightly coupled to practice. In the latter, however, police management was not supportive of DUI enforcement; in two of those agencies, managers perceived that high levels of DUI enforcement conflicted with other organizational goals. DUI training served a purpose, but it was an institutional one, uncoupled from the work of enforcement. Consider one agency:

> Township 2 has a well-developed institutional presentation of DUI enforcement, in which training is an important element. The local MADD chapter provided some incentive for addressing the DUI issue. . . . None of these, however—banquets, awards, donations of breath-testing equipment, and public education campaigns— were tied to the actual work of making DUI arrests. DUI training was also part of the highly developed professional reputation cultivated by the leaders, based (for example) on being well-equipped, well-dressed, and client-oriented. (Mastrofski and Ritti 1996, 316)

Specialized training, which certainly can serve instrumental purposes when the subject of the training is reinforced by other organizational practices, can instead serve institutional purposes. The same might be said, more speculatively in the absence of empirical research, about other police training curricula. Stephen Mastrofski and R. Richard Ritti allow as how "a police brutality scandal . . . generates pressures for reform, which leads to an extensive training program on race relations, less-than-lethal methods, and 'verbal judo'" (1996, 292).

One final example, for now, is a pro-arrest policy for spouse assault. In the 1980s and 1990s, many police agencies adopted policies that mandate or encourage arrests for some types of domestic violence. Many factors contributed to the adoption of such policies: a grass-roots battered women's movement pressed for legislative changes that would facilitate or compel law enforcement to invoke the law against offenders (Ferraro 1989); the threat of litigation against police departments; recommendations by the Attorney General's Task Force on Family Violence; and the findings of the Minneapolis domestic violence experiment, which concluded that repeat violence was less likely when police made arrests (Sherman and Cohn 1989). Pro-arrest policies have increased the incidence of arrests in cases of spousal assault, though compliance by officers is only partial (Cross and Newbold 2010; Eitle 2005; Ferraro 1989; Hirschel et al. 2007; Jones and Belknap 1999). Evidence from replications of the Minneapolis experiment have cast doubts on the conclusions that were drawn from that study, but it is doubtful that many departments have abandoned pro-arrest policies, which are still expected by sovereigns.

THE INSTITUTIONAL ENVIRONMENT OF POLICING

Police departments across the United States have been subject to a number of environmental forces for change in the past twenty to thirty years, but as Mastrofski and James Willis (2010, 57) observe, "the core police patrol technology has remained essentially unchanged for decades." Notwithstanding the panoply of accoutrements that adorn an officer's belt and, increasingly, his/her patrol car, police work is now and has always been a human service occupation that is performed through direct interaction with people, and that relies mainly on verbal communication. Coercive authority is the occupational prerogative that makes a police force a unique domestic organization, but most of the functions that police perform, most of the time, turn on how they talk with and to people. These basic features of police work have not changed with the introduction of the radio, the vehicle, computers, or cell phones.

The stability of the basics of police work stands in contrast with changes in the institutional environment. Local officials and other constituencies, state officials, and federal officials have all exerted pressures on police departments. Some of the pressures conflict with one another. These environmental forces have led police officials to adopt structural forms that are widely considered desirable, even in the absence of clear connections to valued outputs or outcomes, but that may be and often are only loosely coupled with street-level practice. We would direct attention to three such forms that the institutional environment of U.S. policing has, in general, promoted: community policing; mechanisms of public accountability; and mechanisms of management accountability.

Community Policing

With roots in team policing and foot patrol, community policing had by the 1980s emerged as a new strategy of policing. It includes establishing a new kind of relationship between police and communities and new practices in addressing the public's safety concerns. Police form partnerships with neighborhood groups and community agencies, seek and accept community input and influence on police priorities so that police address the concerns of the community, and foster more cooperative relationships between officers and community members. Officers make the acquaintance of community members and learn about neighborhood norms and concerns, and police address community problems through the practice of problem-oriented policing. Thus community policing calls for far-reaching structural and operational changes in police departments (Sparrow et al. 1990): establishing structures that facilitate community input and influence; forming partnerships with community agencies (e.g., sanitation, public works) through which community problems can be addressed; flattening the police hierarchy and decentralizing authority; providing for stable beat assignments for officers in order to inculcate attachments to and knowledge of communities; training officers in new practices; supervising and evaluating officers in new ways. Community policing is no programmatic "add-on" to existing organizational structures.

Community policing has enormous appeal to local constituencies, invoking images of "the friendly night watchman" who walks a beat and of a "'community' in the sense of groups of like-minded individuals, living in urban areas, who share a common heritage, have similar values and norms, and share a common perception of social order" (Crank, 1994: 335–336). The adoption and implementation of community policing was given a major federal boost in 1994 with the enactment of the Violent Crime Control and Law Enforcement Act, Title I of which provided for grants to state and local police agencies that subsidized the hiring of new officers, so long as the grantee agencies adopted some version of community policing. So it was that multiple forces in the environment of police agencies led (or pushed) them in the direction of this strategic innovation.

Research on the implementation of community policing, however, has generally found organizational innovations of a more limited, programmatic nature. A national survey conducted by the Police Foundation in 1993 found that only one-third of the respondents agreed that structural change was necessary for community policing, and almost 40 percent did *not* agree that "community policing requires major changes of organizational policies, goals, or mission statements" (Wycoff 1994, 32). Jeffrey A. Roth et al. (2004) report on a succession of agency surveys, in 1995, 1998, and 2000, in which they asked agencies about each of ten organizational practices that are associated with the implementation of community policing, such as establishing neighborhood patrol boundaries, alternative response methods to free up time for proactive work, and revising employee evaluations. In 2000, their survey showed that the percentages of even large agencies that indicated that they had adopted these practices ranged from about 40 to 80. A previous survey and site visits led them to observe that "funding conditioned expressly on community policing implementation, coupled with substantial peer pressure to embrace this model of policing, has also led a substantial number of law enforcement agencies to stretch the definition of community policing—to include under its umbrella traditional quick-fix enforcement actions, draconian zero tolerance policies, long established crime prevention programs, and citizen advisory councils that are clearly *only* advisory" (Roth 2000, 237).

Other research has recounted resistance to community policing among rank-and-file police, whose hearts and minds have been difficult to win over to a new definition of the police role, new ways to relate to the community, and new practices. Some officers who are more service-minded, and who may have been practicing a community-oriented style on their own, are quite receptive to the implementation of community policing. Eugene A. Paoline III (2004) describes "peacekeepers," for example, as having (relatively) positive attitudes toward the community and a role orientation that emphasizes order maintenance. But Paoline also finds a group he labels "traditionalists," whose outlooks resemble those of the conventionally described police culture: they prize crime-fighting and denigrate order maintenance, they endorse aggressive policing tactics and resent legal restrictions, and they are skeptical about citizen cooperation. More generally, we can surmise that officers are likely to embrace the practice of community policing to the degree to which it is consistent with their occupational outlooks, and consequently the implementation of community policing will face resistance in many though not all quarters (see Skogan 2008; Wood et al. 2004).

Problem-oriented policing (POP) is a key element of community policing, which focuses attention on constellations of related incidents—"problems"—and the conditions that contribute to them, on the plausible assumption that if one or more of the conditions can be changed, the problem may be ameliorated or even solved entirely. POP is contrasted with incident-driven policing, which provides only for handling incidents one by one, as police typically do when they respond to 911 and other calls for service. POP requires not only a recognition that incidents are related to one another, but also analysis of conditions that contribute to the problem and that are within the power of police (and/or their partners) to alter. Moreover, POP is thought to be most effective when the search for responses that might alter the identified conditions is not limited to the enforcement of the penal law. Whether the scope of the targeted problem is wide or narrow, POP calls for a reorientation from incidents or cases—an orientation to which police become accustomed by their experience—to problems, and also from provable, concrete facts and evidence to more abstract patterns based on data that are not always accurate or complete.

Experience with POP teaches us that its practice is not easily achieved (see Capowich et al. 1994; Cordner and Biebel 2005; Police Executive Research Forum 2000; Sampson and Scott 2000). The popular SARA model of the POP process—Scanning, Analysis, Response, and Assessment—makes analysis central to the practice of POP (Eck and Spelman 1987; see also Tilley 2003); analysis, as the SARA model highlights, is the bridge from problem identification to the formulation of possible solutions. The problem-analysis triangle is a tool in whose use many officers have been trained, and it highlights the role of analysis in problem-solving. The problem-analysis triangle encourages those doing problem analysis to consider three components that all problems have in common: an offender, a victim, and a location. Each of these may afford some leverage on the problem, though police attention has traditionally focused on the offender. Situational crime prevention, by contrast, focuses on features of the location, changes in which may reduce the opportunities for offending. Similarly, changes in the behavior of would-be victims may reduce the opportunities for offending. Studies of POP have found that police officers tend to focus on narrowly defined problems; skip over or give short shrift to the analysis that supports problem-solving; and rely on conventional, enforcement-based responses. Instead of POP, then, research has found more narrowly conceived "problem-solving" (Clarke 1998).

Even when community policing is implemented as a strategic reform, as it was in Chicago as much as (and probably more than) it was in any other city, it is fragile. There, after a decade of community policing and in the wake of a media-generated "crime scare" that coincided with the selection of a new superintendent of police, the new administration prioritized tough enforcement.

> The new chief . . . reorganized and refocused the department on guns, gangs, and homicides. Soon commitment to the department's community policing program withered. Most districts lost their community-policing managers, lieutenants who were instead put in charge of flying squads. All of the department's slack resources were rounded up to staff them. Police hoping to get ahead organizationally gravitated toward crackdown units, for they are the focus of the top brass. Headquarters accountability reviews, which used to include community-policing activities and goals, were scaled back dramatically to make time for discussion of homicide patterns. Activities that better fit a recentralized management structure driven by recorded crime have become what matters. The only thing that protects the shell of the program that remains is that it was politically infeasible to shut it down, so deeply are the beat-oriented parts of community policing woven into the political and organizational life of the city's neighborhoods. There it lurks, waiting perhaps to be resurrected when a crisis of legitimacy again haunts the police, and they have to rediscover community policing in order to rebuild again their credibility with the community. (Skogan 2008, 33)

There is much to commend community policing as a police strategy, but the adoption and implementation of community policing has confronted the challenge of coupling its organizational structures to street-level practice.

Public Accountability

Police brutality and other forms of police misconduct have been recurring issues at both the local and national levels for decades, and over the past forty years the country has seen the proliferation of one presumptive remedy: citizen oversight. This typically takes the form of what are widely known as civilian review boards, which are authorized to oversee the processing of citizens' allegations of police misconduct. Citizen oversight might provide for the involvement of civilians, rather than sworn officers, in the receipt of complaints, in monitoring or assessing police investigations of alleged misconduct, or even in conducting their own "external" investigations pursuant to citizen complaints. The establishment of citizen oversight in the 1980s and 1990s has been characterized as a "national movement" (Walker 2001). City after city adopted some version of citizen oversight, usually in the aftermath of a widely publicized incident of what was perceived as police brutality, and in response to local demands. The popularity of citizen oversight appears to rest on a deep-seated distrust of the willingness of the police to police themselves, that is, to conduct thorough investigations of complaints against fellow officers, or even to faithfully accept complaints when citizens seek to file them. Police departments did not, in general, welcome the establishment of citizen oversight. The push for citizen oversight is a force in the institutional environment to which departments have had to adapt.

However, there is no evidence that citizen oversight alters patterns of police behavior or performance. Indeed, there is no evidence that citizen oversight has impacts even on more proximate outcomes: the rate at which the allegations in citizen complaints are substantiated or "sustained" by investigation; or complainants' satisfaction with the complaint review process (DeAngelis 2009; Perez 1994; Sviridoff and McElroy 1989; Walker 2001; also see Livingston 2004; National Research Council 2004). There is, however, good reason to believe (and some evidence) that, at the margin, citizen oversight elevates the confidence of the public (if not of individual complainants) in the integrity of the complaint review process (Kerstetter and Rasinski 1994; Skolnick and Fyfe 1993; Worden and Becker 2015). Citizen oversight thus serves the purpose of promoting police legitimacy, but it appears to be decoupled from the technical core of policing.

Citizen oversight of police is not the only structural demand in the institutional environment that relates to public accountability. In the past twenty years, the Civil Rights Division of the Department of Justice (DOJ) has used authority with which it was endowed by the 1994 Crime Act to investigate allegations of a "pattern or practice" of civil rights violations by local police departments. DOJ can pursue (or threaten) litigation, one frequent outcome of which has been a settlement in the form of either a consent decree or a memorandum of agreement that stipulates the adoption of a series of organizational reforms (Harmon 2009; Walker 2003). Beginning with the Pittsburgh police in 1997, DOJ has investigated and reached agreements with numerous agencies, including the Cincinnati Police Department, the Los Angeles Police Department, and the New Jersey State Police. Court-appointed monitors oversee the implementation of the reforms, and the decree is lifted only when the agreed-upon reforms are implemented to the court's satisfaction. Even when the investigation does not lead to an agreement, DOJ may issue a "technical assistance letter" that includes a series of recommendations for organizational change. The reforms that DOJ mandates through consent decrees (or recommends in letters) tend to emphasize the establishment or strengthening of citizen oversight, the implementation of early intervention systems, and policy development. These mandates purportedly are based on "best practices," but in fact they are based on the kinds of suppositions that we described above, lacking empirical validation of their effectiveness. We have already considered citizen oversight.

Early intervention (EI) systems (also known as early warning systems) synthesize and use management information about police outputs that are "risk-related" (Bobb and staff 2009) to identify "problem officers," whose performance displays symptoms of misconduct, and to intervene as early in the emerging pattern as possible with training or counseling, thereby preventing further misconduct. Given the well-documented concentration of citizen complaints and use-of-force incidents among a small fraction of a police force, EI systems rest on a compelling logic. Several studies of EI systems have produced results that suggest that they reduce the incidence of complaints and the use of force, but the designs of these studies were weak, with either no control group or a nonequivalent control group; one recent study, with a much stronger design, found that one agency's EI system was ineffective in reducing complaints, the use of force, or secondary arrests, but had the unintended consequence of inhibiting officers' initiative (Worden et al. 2013; also see Lersch et al. 2006). An assessment of Pittsburgh's EI system, implemented as part of the consent decree there, found that even officers who had not been subject to EI system intervention reported feeling such inhibitions, and supervisors complained about the demands for paperwork that left them with less time to supervise officers directly, in the field (Davis et al. 2005). Thus, as promising as the concept may be, the jury is still out on the utility of EI systems as they are currently designed and operated. Furthermore, EI systems are not infrequently only loosely coupled with practice, as some recent investigative journalism has found (Kelly 2016).

DOJ lawyers have also required or recommended the formulation or further development of policy and procedure, especially concerning the use of force by police. Such administrative rule-making can be effective under some circumstances in regulating police behavior (Prottas 1978; Walker 1993; Worden 1995). James Fyfe (1979) demonstrated, for example, that the administrative rules established by the New York City Police Department to govern the use of deadly force were effective in reducing police-involved shootings; Fyfe's research (1979, 1988) also makes it clear, however, that the effectiveness of the rules turned on their enforcement, which was effected by a firearms-discharge review process, and which was feasible because, for the most part, the use of deadly force by police is difficult to conceal. For another example, as noted above, policies mandating or encouraging officers to make arrests when they have probable cause in cases of spousal assault have increased the incidence of such arrests. The documentation that comes with officers' compliance with these rules facilitates their enforcement by supervisors, but even so, given officers' near monopoly on information about cases in which arrests are *not* made, compliance is only partial at best, (Cross and Newbold 2010;

Ferraro 1989). Generally, we might hypothesize that the lower the visibility of the discretionary action that is the subject of administrative rules, the less able the department is to enforce the rule and the lower the rate of officers' compliance will be. Little of the discretionary behavior in which officers engage is readily visible to supervisors and managers (Goldstein 1960), and Michael Brown (1981) concluded that bureaucratic controls did not by and large extend to the substantive exercise of police discretion.

A national survey of law enforcement agencies revealed a dizzying array of permutations with respect to the placement of particular forms of force relative to others on a use-of-force continuum, and no one policy emerged as "best" in an intensive examination of the use of force in eight police departments, with neither bivariate nor multivariate analysis detecting "consistent policy effects" (Terrill, Paoline, and Ingram 2012, 198–99). However, in an analysis of three of the eight departments, whose policies varied in their restrictiveness, Terrill and Paoline (2016) find that officers in the department (Charlotte-Mecklenburg) with the most restrictive policy used less force than those in the departments (Albuquerque and Colorado Springs) with less restrictive policies. We think it quite likely that the impact of use-of-force policies will be contingent on the will of administrators and supervisors to enforce the policies. Terrill and Paoline note that "perhaps Charlotte-Mecklenburg supervisors were more active with respect to emphasizing use of force policy, thereby giving policy on paper more 'substance' so to speak. Alternatively, perhaps Colorado Springs and Albuquerque supervisors were more lax in terms of policy guidance (e.g. 'rubber stamping' force reports)" (2016: 19). In other words, policies designed to guide and constrain officers' discretion in the use of less-lethal force can be coupled with practice, so long as police managers and supervisors enforce their department's policy; lax supervision and management concerning the use of force is liable to leave policy loosely coupled with officers' practices. One success story of change in this regard appears to be Cincinnati, whose officers' rates of using force declined following reforms to which the police department agreed in a settlement with DOJ in 2002 (Schatmeier 2013; Chanin 2015); we consider the experience of Cincinnati further in chapter 10.

Demands for public accountability in the institutional environment of policing have promoted the adoption of particular organizational structures—citizen oversight, early intervention systems, and administrative rules governing the use of force—that have little or no demonstrated efficacy in regulating officers' behavior, and are in many or most instances only loosely coupled to street-level performance. But their adoption by police departments is taken as a signal of good practice, and the Department of Justice has been one external stakeholder demanding the adoption of these structures, with the threat of litigation. Use-of-force policies may hold more promise, with tighter coupling possible so long as managers and supervisors implement the policies.

Management Accountability

Compstat is an administrative innovation introduced as part of the "reengineering" of the New York City Police Department wrought by Commissioner William Bratton in the mid-1990s (Bratton 1998, esp. chap. 14). Seeking to make the commanders of NYPD's seventy-five precincts the engines of crime-reduction initiatives, Commissioner Bratton gave precinct commanders more authority to develop operational plans and to allocate their resources accordingly, holding them accountable through Compstat for using their authority to achieve crime-reduction results. Compstat originated in meetings with borough and precinct commanders at which their performance could be assessed, justified, and critiqued, with information on that performance available to all present; the information about crime, initially available in a book of weekly crime totals, became increasingly detailed and rich, so that what started as "crime meetings" evolved into "computer-statistics" meetings.

NYPD's Compstat was—correctly or not—credited with the dramatic decline in New York City's crime rate through the latter half of the 1990s, and consequently it has been widely emulated by police agencies across the United States and the world. In 1996, Compstat was recognized with an "Innovations in American Government" award by the Ford Foundation and Harvard's Kennedy School of Government. By 2000, one third of the 515 American police agencies with 100 or more sworn personnel had adopted a Compstat-like program, and an additional one quarter were planning such a program (Weisburd et al. 2003). Compstat has also been adopted by other types of public agencies, and by city mayors and even state governors. Compstat *can* be an organizational mechanism that serves, first, to direct attention to important police outcomes—crime, disorder, fear of crime, quality of life, citizen satisfaction—and, second, to stimulate the formulation and implementation of tactical and strategic operations directed toward those outcomes (Moore 2002). Like POP, Compstat is data-driven and outcome-oriented. Using timely, accurate data is one of its principles, and the selection of effective tactics on the basis of those data is another. "Relentless follow-up and assessment" is also based on data about police action and outcomes. Compstat requires the development of an analytic capacity, and when it operates properly, it also serves to exploit the potential of crime and intelligence analysis more completely, for it is a mechanism that can stimulate the translation of analytic products into crime-reduction operations.

But the replication of NYPD's Compstat in other agencies has not always adhered to the same principles, and it has not proved to be effective in prompting precinct commanders or their subordinates to engage in innovative problem-solving; it has not proved effective even in holding commanders accountable for outcomes (Behn 2008; Silverman 2006; Weisburd et al. 2003; Willis et al. 2003, 2007). Compstat in NYPD would not have been so effective as an accountability tool were it

not for the larger reengineering of the department, including "structural, operational, and strategic reconfigurations" (Silverman 2006, 273). One of the keys was
the recognition that precinct commanders could be held accountable for reducing crime only if they were granted greater latitude to formulate crime-reduction
initiatives and to allocate resources accordingly. Grafting Compstat onto a police
department's preexisting organizational arrangements is unlikely to produce similarly salutary effects; Compstat would then be liable to be no more than loosely
coupled with either management or tactical operations. The adoption and continued operation of Compstat could serve the organization's interests, enhancing its
legitimacy, but without stimulating the kinds of operations that have been credited
with New York's crime decline.

That is exactly what was found in a study of three police departments in which
the adoption of Compstat amounted to "mimetic isomorphism," which is to say
that they simply copied "other organizations that have received recognition and
support for appearing effective" (Willis et al. 2007, 152). Compstat was loosely
coupled to operations: in none of the departments did accountability extend down
past the precinct or district commanders, with no "efforts to get the rank-and-file
to respond to the direction of middle managers," and consequently Compstat "did
not strengthen control over lower-ranking officers who continued to exercise the
same high level of discretion long recognized as a characteristic of police work"
(165–66). Commanders succeeded in the context of the Compstat meetings by being prepared with facts and figures to respond to the chief's questions, and not by
devising and implementing effective crime-reduction strategies. More generally, it
appears that Compstat reforms tended to strengthen the existing top-down chain
of command, rather than stimulating innovative problem-solving—"changing everything so that everything can remain the same" (Weisburd et al. 2006).

Complexity and Conflict

The institutional environment is complex, and its demands on police departments
are not all mutually compatible. Pushing discretion down as much as possible to
precinct commanders or, even further, to field supervisors and beat officers, and
thereby unleashing the creativity of officers in addressing the many and varied
problems that communities confront, is a prominent feature of community policing. But expanding officers' discretion is not entirely compatible with demands
for public accountability and administrative rule-making, which tend to emphasize constraints on police discretion. And as Wesley Skogan's (2008) observations
about numbers-driven policing in Chicago illustrate, community policing and
management accountability can be difficult to reconcile, especially since so much
of what community policing involves and seeks to accomplish is not readily subject
to quantitative measurement. This kind of complexity in the institutional environment of policing helps to explain how it is that day-to-day police work might be

decoupled from or loosely coupled with the structures that agencies adopt: when the structures that police departments adopt conflict with one another or with the nature of the work, something has to give. When something gives, however, it need not give way entirely: we need not and should not suppose that technical-rational considerations are absent or that organizational structures—even those adopted to satisfy demands of the institutional environment—have no impact on technical performance. But insofar as street-level practices are loosely coupled to organizational structures, the impacts of the structures on practices are attenuated.

Procedural Justice and Police Legitimacy

As police executives have acknowledged the significance of legitimacy, and the role of procedural justice in improving legitimacy, they have responded to an emerging force in their institutional environment. Summarizing research on policing, the National Research Council drew attention to these issues in its volume titled *Fairness and Effectiveness in Policing* (2004), an entire chapter of which was devoted to police legitimacy. DOJ has supported the development of training in procedural justice through the Office of Community Oriented Policing Services (COPS), and it has supported research on procedural justice and legitimacy (including the inquiry on which we report here) through the National Institute of Justice. The International Association of Chiefs of Police (IACP) has held sessions on procedural justice and legitimacy at its annual conference. The Police Executive Research Forum, a well-known not-for-profit membership organization of police officials, recently published two reports on legitimacy and procedural justice (Fischer 2014a, 2014b). As we noted in chapter 1, the DOJ-funded National Initiative for Building Community Trust and Justice is designed to serve as a demonstration project, piloting in six police departments structures that promise to enhance public trust in local police. The President's Task Force on 21st Century Policing highlighted measures to enhance procedural justice, and, with it, police legitimacy, in its recommendations and implementation guide.

Legitimacy and procedural justice have not supplanted the other forces in the institutional environment, however, and the procedural justice model is not entirely compatible with them. The procedural justice model will not be compatible with Compstat-like mechanisms unless procedural justice can be regularly quantified as a performance measure with sufficient validity and reliability for it to be incorporated into a management-accountability system. Procedural justice may be celebrated, in ceremonial fashion, as an important consideration in the practice of policing, but it is liable to assume the position of an only symbolic feature of police administration and not a set of principles that are infused into the technical core of police departments and manifested in officers' day-to-day interactions with citizens. The implementation of the procedural justice model may also confront some of the same obstacles that so challenged the implementation of community policing: winning the hearts and minds of officers and field supervisors. It is subject to the same process of street-level interpretation, or sensemaking, as community policing, and it is likely to be accepted by some officers and resisted by others. Street-level procedural justice probably cannot be achieved through the formulation and promulgation of administrative rules, since the procedural justice that officers demonstrate in their behavior is of decidedly low visibility, and rules governing procedurally just action would be difficult to enforce. Procedural justice is arguably more a matter of "workmanship" than "legality" (Bittner 1983), and putting standards of workmanship into place confronts legal, bureaucratic, union, and other practical issues.

THE INSTITUTIONAL ENVIRONMENTS OF POLICING IN SCHENECTADY AND SYRACUSE

We have sketched the institutional perspective on organizations, and selected features of the institutional environment of U.S. policing, in order to better understand the findings of our research on Schenectady and Syracuse, whose police departments accommodated survey-based measures of procedural justice into their management-accountability systems. We turn now to a description of these departments as settings for this research, attending particularly to the rationale for conducting the research in these two departments, and to the elements of their institutional environments that are important for understanding the contexts in which research results were generated.

The Schenectady and Syracuse Police Departments are mid-sized agencies, and in this respect they resemble many other departments; among the respondents to the 2007 Law Enforcement Management and Administrative Statistics (LEMAS) survey, one can find nearly 500 agencies with 100 to 500 sworn, full-time employees, but only 89 agencies with more than 500 sworn personnel, about half of which have more than 1,000 sworn. No sample of two agencies could possibly be representative of American municipal police departments, but insofar as the external validity of empirical findings about the dynamics of organization and management is circumscribed by the size of the studied departments, Schenectady and Syracuse are propitious sites for research. Moreover, an examination of two departments rather than one allows us to ascertain the extent to which the findings are idiosyncratic to a single department.

The two cities are similar in a number of respects. They are both rustbelt cities that are coping with demographic and economic shifts that have strained governmental capacities with greater demands for services and an eroding tax base. The populations are comparable in their racial and ethnic composition. Both cities have fairly high rates of violent crime, especially for cities of their size.

The two departments also share a number of similarities. Their sworn ranks are disproportionately white, relative to the cities' populations, with limited representation of women. However, both departments had, at the beginning and through most of the project, a black chief executive; Syracuse had a female deputy chief. These facts may have a bearing on perceptions of the departments' legitimacy.

We had a relationship with each department before we approached either chief about his department's participation in the project. In Syracuse, we had worked since late 2004 as the research partner to a criminal justice task force that included the police department. We had worked as a research partner to the Schenectady Police Department since 2004. Both departments afforded the proximity that was required for ongoing data collection and appearance at Compstat meetings. Both chiefs were, as we anticipated, receptive to the project, based on their avowed interest in ensuring high-quality police service to the citizenry. Finally, the two departments had contrasting public images. Schenectady's had a poor image acquired through years of extraordinary turmoil and scandal. Syracuse's had what we take to be a fairly typical image, free of the taint of extraordinary mishaps. Accordingly, we presumed that there would be a degree of contrast with respect to levels of respect and trust among those they serve.

Schenectady

According to 2010 Census figures, the city of Schenectady has 66,135 residents and is comprised of ten distinct neighborhoods across its ten square miles. Nearly one-quarter (24.4 percent) of the population was under the age of 18; 61 percent of it was white, 20 percent, African American, 10.5 percent, Hispanic or Latino, and 3.6 percent, Asian. The proportion of Schenectady's population living in poverty (22.5 percent) was half again that of the nation (15 percent). The city's violent crime rate exceeds the average of the largest U.S. cities: in 2010, Schenectady's violent crime rate of 1117.7 per 100,000 population was 183 percent higher than that of cities of comparable size (394.6) and 57 percent higher than that of the largest U.S. cities. The rates are as striking with respect to homicide. In 2010, the homicide rate in Schenectady was 13.2, which was more than three times greater than in cities of comparable size (3.9), and 47 percent higher than that of the largest cities.

The Schenectady Police Department had a sworn strength of 160 and an actual strength of 158 in 2007, 114 of whom were uniformed and regularly assigned to patrol duties.[2] Most (94.3 percent) of the sworn personnel were white, 3.8 percent were black, and 1.9 percent were Hispanic; 5.1 percent were female. Schenectady's chief of police is appointed by the mayor but enjoys civil service status and protection. The chief who in 2010 agreed to participate in this project was first appointed in 2008 and retired at the beginning of 2013. The assistant chief of the Field Services Bureau oversees uniformed patrol, which is organized into three platoons, each commanded by a lieutenant, with officers deployed across eight patrol zones.

Like many U.S. police departments, Schenectady had established a community policing unit, to which 24 of its 158 officers were assigned, though it had no formal, written community-policing plan. The unit was part of the Field Services Bureau. Training in community policing was provided to all officers through either recruit or in-service training. The department encourages officers to conduct SARA-guided problem-solving projects, but it does not include officers' work on those projects in personnel evaluations.

Citizen oversight exists in Schenectady, though it is not prominent. In 2002, after two years of deliberations, the Civilian Police Review Board (CPRB) replaced the Police Objective Review Commission. Modeled on the citizen-oversight mechanism in neighboring Albany, the CPRB is comprised of eleven members appointed by the mayor to serve two-year terms. The CPRB reviews the investigations of citizen complaints by police internal affairs investigators, and in cases involving allegations of excessive force or (other) civil rights violations, the board may hire an independent investigator to review the police investigation. The board may return a complaint to internal affairs for further investigation or reevaluation, and when it is satisfied with the investigation, it renders findings of approved, disapproved, or unable to be determined.

The department initiated Compstat in late 2010, following nearly a year of deliberation about its design and preparation. Thus Compstat had been operational for just a year at the outset of this project. Schenectady's Compstat provides for monthly meetings, at each of which units of both the Field Services Bureau (patrol and traffic) and the Investigative Services Bureau (detectives) are subject to review. The three platoon commanders report individually on platoon performance, so each platoon is examined separately. Statistics on crime and enforcement, citywide and at the platoon level, are displayed as appropriate. We further describe Schenectady's Compstat in chapter 8, but suffice it to say here that although it unmistakably makes each platoon commander individually responsible for his or her platoon's performance, it is not—and was not intended to be—punitive. Whereas management accountability requires the application of formal or informal sanctions when performance falls short of expectations, Schenectady's Compstat does not provide for it. More generally, the operation of Compstat in Schenectady bears a strong resemblance to that of Compstat in the three departments described by Willis et al. 2007.

The Schenectady Police Department has a long and troubled history of unfavorable portrayal in the media and scandals involving the misbehavior of its members. In 2001, after years of complaints by citizens about the use of excessive force and mounting pressure by civil rights activists to address the problem, the department became the subject of a probe by the DOJ Civil Rights Division. The

New York Times recounted some of the incidents that were symptomatic of the problem, one of which was this:

> Suspecting that David Sampson was up to no good but having no proof, the two white police officers chose instead to take him for a ride that summer's evening in 1999. A long, long ride. They drove in silence, ignoring the young black man's questions as their patrol car crossed the city limits and continued 11 miles deep into the countryside's enveloping dusk. "I kept asking them 'Where am I going?' over and over, 15, 16 times," Mr. Sampson, 29, said recently. "I was really scared." They came to a stop on a gravel road. While his partner stayed behind the wheel, Officer Richard Barnett later recalled, he removed their passenger's boots, tossed them into the surrounding trees and told Mr. Sampson "to get out and have a nice walk back to Schenectady." Then the car, emblazoned with the name of the Schenectady Police Department, sped into the darkness, its back seat emptied. This is Schenectady, where the police do things differently. Officer Barnett later said under oath that it was "common practice for a lot of midnight shifts taking intoxicated people out of the city." It was called "relocation," he said, and had been the source of great amusement among officers. (Barry 2001)

"Relocation" was later characterized as an official unwritten policy to DOJ investigators. The officers involved in the Sampson incident became the subjects of an FBI investigation, but not because of their practice of relocation; one of them admitted in a plea agreement that "he and his partner once paid an informer with crack that they had just extorted from a drug dealer" (Barry 2001). Other officers were also prosecuted on similar allegations; one of them had tipped off an informer to police surveillance.

In March 2003, DOJ issued a "technical assistance" letter (Cutlar 2003). Based on its review of the department's written policies and procedures, interviews with officers at various levels of the department's hierarchy, and ride-alongs with officers, DOJ identified a number of deficiencies and made a number of recommendations. Those recommendations for the most part followed the template described above: further development of policies governing the use of force; strengthening the procedures for complaint intake and investigation (since Schenectady already had a citizen oversight body); and establishing an early warning system, including the information infrastructure that such a system requires (including use-of-force reporting). More specifically, and for example, DOJ recommended that "the SPD adopt a progression of force model that describes the available force options on a continuum . . . that relates the appropriate officer response to the specific actions of a suspect." For another example, DOJ recommended that "every officer in the department be required to accept a written complaint presented by a citizen," and that written policy should specify the types of complaints that can be investigated by the subject officer's unit and those that are investigated by internal affairs. DOJ also recommended the formulation of a "comprehensive risk management plan," including specific supervisory responsibilities, in addition to an early warning system.

The turnaround was slow, and the local media continued to report with some regularity on officers' driving while intoxicated, engaging in domestic assaults, "cooping" (sleeping on duty), and worse. A veteran detective of the department pled guilty to possessing drugs and tampering with evidence from the vice squad locker, and as part of a plea agreement, he was sentenced to four years in state prison and one year of probation. Following an investigation of the vice squad, a number of vice detectives were reassigned or retired and the assistant chief over the unit was ultimately reassigned. "For the Schenectady Police Department, a department with a well-documented history of controversy and scandal, this latest news seemed to most of us almost unfathomable," the mayor told a press conference (Schenectady 2007). In a later article articulating allegations of an officer collecting overtime pay while inside an apartment complex instead of on patrol, Schenectady City Councilman Gary McCarthy said: "It's human nature to make mistakes, but this just seems so institutionalized" (Nelson 2009). In 2009, a former Schenectady chief and his wife were arrested and pleaded guilty to possession of a controlled substance and their role in a drug ring. It was found that the ex-chief, his wife, and his stepson were part of a group of "some two dozen people who funneled large quantities of cocaine and heroin from Long Island and Manhattan onto the streets of Schenectady" (Nelson 2010).

Due to the widespread disrepute of the department and its members, the mayor of Schenectady is reported to have considered in 2009 multiple options for the future of City's policing; these options included, but were not limited to, martial law, disbanding the police department, contracting out to the New York State Police or county sheriff's, or using the National Guard. The mayor did not in fact take any of the aforementioned routes; instead he was able to start removing problem officers and enacted a zero-tolerance policy for the officers. A retired superintendent of the New York State Police was appointed commissioner in 2007, with greater authority than the chief had to fix discipline. By August of 2010 the City had removed eight officers from its force that year.

If residents of Schenectady still hear of their city's police officers being apprehended or investigated for driving while intoxicated, assault, or domestic issues, they also hear of them having to face consequences and being held accountable for their actions. In late 2012, DOJ ended its investigation, declaring that the department was not in violation of federal law, and citing its adoption of some of DOJ's 2003 recommendations (Nelson 2013). We may reasonably consider that chapter of the department's history to be closed, but memories of it may linger, potentially tarnishing the image of the department as a whole among the city's residents and throughout the entire region.

It might not be an exaggeration to say that in 2009, the Schenectady Police Department suffered a crisis of legitimacy, with the city's mayor publicly contemplating dismantling it. Even allowing for the possibility that the mayor's public posture was struck as a move calculated to gain some leverage in collective bargaining negotiations, it is probably a measure of how far the department's stock with its sovereigns had fallen that the mayor would openly speculate, for public consumption, about the wisdom of abolishing the police department.

Syracuse

The city of Syracuse covers 25 square miles and had a population of approximately 145,170 in 2010. According to the Census, nearly one-quarter (23.3 percent) of the population was under the age of 18; 56 percent of it was white, 29.5 percent, African American, 8.3 percent Hispanic or Latino, and 5.5 percent, Asian. The proportion of the city's population living in poverty (33.6 percent) was more than double that of the nation (15 percent).

Syracuse is not a big city, but it has big-city violence. Despite some decreases in the past several years, violent crime in Syracuse remains well above not only the average for cities its size (100,000 to 249,999) but even above the average for the largest U.S. cities. In 2011, the violent crime rate (per 100,000 population) in Syracuse was 892.9, 79 percent higher than the rate for cities of comparable size (498.5), and 27 percent higher than that of the largest U.S. cities. The rate of aggravated assaults that same year (576 per 100,000) was 94 percent higher than the rate in similarly sized cities, and 54 percent higher than that of the largest U.S. cities.

In 2007, the Syracuse Police Department had a sworn strength of 498 and an actual strength of 485, of whom 203 were uniformed and regularly assigned duties that included responsibility for responding to calls, with 16 assigned to community policing. Most (91.8 percent) of the sworn personnel were white, 7 percent were black, and 1 percent were Hispanic; 11.8 percent were female. The chief of police is appointed by and serves at the pleasure of the mayor. The chief who agreed to participate in this project was first appointed by a newly elected mayor in late 2009, and continues to serve at the time of this writing. The deputy chief of the Uniform Bureau oversees patrol, which is organized into three platoons, each commanded by a captain.

The community policing unit was part of the Community Services Bureau, which was commanded by a deputy chief. The department had a formal, written community-policing plan, though it did not encourage officers to conduct SARA-guided problem-solving projects. Training in community policing was provided to all new officers through recruit training.

Syracuse has a Citizen Review Board, which was originally established in 1993, and which is authorized to "hear, investigate and review" complaints of police misconduct.[3] The CRB has a full-time, paid administrator. The Internal Affairs (IA) Division of the police department conducts "initial investigations" (Cintron 2003, 21), which are forwarded to the CRB for review. However, if the complainant so requests, the CRB is authorized to hold a full fact-finding hearing, which is conducted by a CRB panel of three members. The CRB was the subject of some controversy during the project, which we discuss below.

The department initiated Compstat (but spelled "Comstat") in 1999.[4] Compstat had reportedly evolved over time, but had always been convened on a regular, biweekly basis. Compstat provides for presentations by platoon commanders and other unit commanders, as well as by a representative from the crime analysis unit. We further describe Syracuse's Compstat in chapter 8, but suffice to say here that, like Schenectady's, its operation resembles that of the departments studied by Willis et al. (2007).

By way of contrast with Schenectady's recent history at the outset of this project, the Syracuse Police Department appears to be fairly typical, insofar as the department received a share of bad press locally but nothing extraordinary. For example, in 2005 the then-chief resigned following his arrest for driving while intoxicated; the print media followed the troubles of one Syracuse officer who was involved in (and arrested for) giving cigarettes, marijuana, and alcohol to minors, drug trafficking out of his home, and sexually abusing two young boys. More commonly, the coverage of the Syracuse police focused on use of force that was alleged to be excessive.

During the project and while the police services survey was in progress, the Syracuse police were subject to further negative print media attention. One high-visibility source of bad press was a dispute between the department and the Onondaga County district attorney. A sexual abuse case against a well-known Syracuse University basketball coach received local and national media attention, and a conflict between the district attorney's office and the police department played out in the media, with the district attorney issuing a subpoena requiring the police to turn over the records of their investigation. The district attorney continued to publicly air his disagreements with the leadership of the department in what one local media outlet described as an "extraordinary public war of words with . . . [the chief] for more than a year" (O'Brien and O'Hara 2013).

Tensions between the mayor's office and the department arose when the mayor refused to sign a commendation for an officer in 2010 because he was previously found to have used excessive force against a suspect in a drug and assault case. The mayor said that she has been working to clean out a minority of police officers whose behavior had been inappropriate: "[W]e are actively changing the culture and the behavior," she said (O'Brien 2010b). As a response, the police union and its members boycotted the city's annual awards ceremony in June and held their own in August.

The Citizen Review Board (CRB) was disbanded by the mayor and recreated. In February 2011, the mayor fired the CRB administrator because she "failed to do her job" (Knauss 2012). The CRB is an eleven-member panel, eight members of which are appointed by the Common Council and three by the mayor. The mayor appointed her three new members in January 2012 and the new administrator was announced in April that year. Although the chief of police supports the CRB, the police union sees it as "unnecessary" (Reiner 2012). The union particularly objected to the CRB's subpoena power, which requires a police officer to appear in front of the board's panel, but does not force the officer to speak. The union president said that the CRB did not have the proper training to investigate a police officer; the officers had twenty weeks' worth of training, he observed, and they (the CRB members) would not do twenty hours' worth (Reiner, 2012).

In addition to citizens' complaints about unfair treatment that filter into the media, officers' complaints about unfair treatment have also received coverage. In March 2010, a female officer was awarded $400,000 in a sexual discrimination suit. She was reportedly the third officer in a ten-month period to receive a large award for sexual discrimination (O'Brien 2010a). Then, in February 2012, three black officers sued the department for racial discrimination, stating that they had been passed over for promotions and discriminated against by the police force and their own union because of their race (Eisenstadt 2012).

Contrasts

Some negative media attention is inevitable for a city police department, and we know of no well-established metric of bad press. Both of the study departments received some unfavorable attention in local media. But Schenectady's police had been the subject of extraordinary attention, not only in the form of uncomplimentary media coverage, but also in the form of a DOJ civil rights investigation, and even public speculation by the city's mayor about the wisdom of disbanding the department. Whether the unfavorable distinction that Schenectady police earned translated into a lower level of public trust is intuitively likely, though it is an empirical question. We supposed that if one of the two departments stood to enhance its legitimacy more through improvements in the procedural justice of police-citizen encounters, it was Schenectady's. But the two agencies were similar in many respects, and as the project began in 2011, the worst of Schenectady's scandals were behind it. We would do well to bear Schenectady's recent history in mind, but we can nevertheless think of the study of either department as a replication of the study of the other.

SUMMARY

When police departments are viewed as institutionalized organizations, we can better understand how it is that reforms, such as community policing or the procedural justice model, tend to come undone. Vats of ink have been spilt on the difficulties in organizational change, and police departments are no exceptions to the rule that organizations tend to resist change. Change in the form of the procedural justice model can be done in all executive sincerity and with the best of intentions through, say, pronouncements about the importance of legitimacy and how police treat citizens, changing procedures,[5] or even rolling out a training curriculum, but we should be skeptical that these reforms will produce systematic changes in the department's technical core, in police-citizen interactions at the street level. Structures that are designed to be tightly coupled with day-to-day practice may, upon inspection, be no more than loosely coupled (or decoupled) from practice. To administrative exhortation we may anticipate rank-and-file resistance, the likes of which we will describe in more detail in chapter 9. If there are domains of police work that are susceptible to control through administrative rule-making, procedural justice is probably not one of them. Police departments cannot mandate procedurally just treatment, and even if they tried to do so, the mandate would be virtually unenforceable. Departments can prohibit some forms of procedural injustice, such as discourtesy, as many already do, though these prohibitions are (or have been) difficult to enforce. And in any event, police managers will need to make judgments about the extent to which they want to and should micro-manage their subordinates' behavior. Training can be (and in some instances, has been) delivered, but the lessons of training must be reconcilable with the (interpreted) requirements of the streets, and reinforced by supervisors, or its effects are likely to decay; that is, then, training must be tightly coupled with the day-to-day reality of officers' experience, and if it is not, it will prove ineffective.

With this institutional perspective as background, we proceed now to the findings of our empirical research in and with these departments. In chapter 3 we examine public trust and confidence in the police and police legitimacy, and then in chapters 4 and 5, citizens' subjective experience with police, and especially citizens' judgments about procedural justice.

3

Police Legitimacy

Police legitimacy—that is, public trust in and a felt obligation to obey the police—forms the fulcrum of the procedural justice model of policing. Such outlooks are intrinsically important, of course, and they are important also because research suggests that they lead to other valued outcomes: compliance with the law, providing information to police, working with them on community problems, and accepting police directions and decisions in police-citizen encounters. Tom Tyler's model of process-based regulation (Tyler 1988, 1990, 2003, 2004; Tyler, Goff, and MacCoun, 2015) holds that trust is influenced by the procedural justice with which authorities are perceived to wield their powers, and so it would appear to be susceptible to enhancement through improvements in the procedural justice with which police act.

In this chapter, we explain our use of terms and concepts, lest we confuse the meaning of legitimacy as a construct of institutional theory with that of the constructs in social psychological theory. We first consider trust and obligation in the context of public attitudes toward the police more generally, including their historical trends and the forces that influence those attitudes. Public attitudes toward the police are subject to some broad social factors that have shaped attitudes toward government and other social institutions, as well as factors more peculiar to policing. We discuss those here so that we can better understand the role that citizens' own experiences with the police play in contributing to (or detracting from) their trust and confidence in police. Citizens' direct contacts with the police are not the only influence on trust; moreover, citizens' interpretations of their contacts with the police are themselves subject to the influence of prior attitudes and contextual factors. We also assess citizens' satisfaction with the police as a special case of "customer" satisfaction. We consider the respects in which citizens resemble customers, and those in which the analogy to customers breaks down, and briefly discuss selected findings from research on customer satisfaction that may serve to place citizens' satisfaction with the police in perspective. Then we consider how levels of public trust may be related to the legitimacy of police departments, as an organizational property, and discuss challenges to police legitimacy in the form of diminished trust and also, more overtly, protests and riots.

We then present survey results that bear on public trust and obligation in Schenectady and Syracuse, which serves two purposes. First, an analysis of the levels of public trust of the study departments enables us to consider them in the larger context of their public images. Second, by establishing the measurement properties of the trust and obligation constructs that can be derived from the survey data, we will be better able in the next chapter to determine the extent to which the subjective experiences of people in Schenectady and Syracuse exhibit the same kinds of associations with trust and obligation as those commonly reported in previous research.

PUBLIC TRUST AND OBLIGATION

From the perspective of social psychology, at least two strands of legitimacy have been identified; we will call them trust and obligation. With respect to the police in particular, the Committee to Review Research of the National Research Council (2004, 291) explained that by "legitimacy we mean the judgments that ordinary citizens make about the rightfulness of police conduct and the organizations that employ and supervise them." However, Tyler has emphasized the obligation to obey an authority as a hallmark of its legitimacy. For his seminal study of Chicago, Tyler conceived legitimacy as not only "support for legal authorities" but also a "perceived obligation to obey," and the latter aspect—obligation—is prominently featured: "When people feel that an authority is legitimate, they authorize that authority to determine what their behavior will be within a given set of situations" (Tyler 2004, 87).

However, empirical research that has examined the dimensionality of these legitimacy constructs has shown that indicators of trust in or support for police are manifestations of a latent construct that is distinct from that of obligation. In an analysis of the construct validity of process-based measures, Reisig, Bratton, and Gertz 2007 concluded that trust and obligation are distinct constructs only moderately related to one another. Similarly, Jacinta Gau (2011) found a two-dimensional structure underlying these indicators. Moreover, Reisig et al. (2007, 1022–23) found that trust affected both cooperation and compliance, while obligation affected neither cooperation nor compliance. Hence, we treat trust and obligation as two distinct social psychological dimensions.

Tyler's model of process-based regulation is the predominant social psychological theory of legitimacy. In this model, procedural justice is the central antecedent of legitimacy: "legitimacy develops from and is maintained by the fair exercise of authority on the part of the police when they deal with the public—that is, through the provision of procedural justice" (Tyler, Goff, and MacCoun 2015; also see Tyler 1988, 1990, 2003, 2004; Tyler and Fagan 2008; Tyler and Huo 2002). Procedural justice is not about *whether* but rather *how* authority is exercised. As Schulhofer, Tyler, and Huq 2011 indicates, police need not choose between being tough and being fair; they can be both tough and fair.

Although Tyler's model has been the conceptual touchstone for social psychological research on police legitimacy, it would be an exaggeration to say that a consensus has emerged on the definition of legitimacy. Justice Tankebe (2013; 2014) insists that legitimacy should not be conflated with either trust or obligation; police legitimacy, he argues, has four dimensions: lawfulness; procedural fairness; distributive fairness; and effectiveness. James Hawdon (2008) maintains that legitimacy is different from trust. And Ben Bradford and Jonathan Jackson (2009) note that though there may be important differences among trust, confidence, support, satisfaction, and legitimacy, much of the research on public attitudes toward the police is predicated on an assumption that people tend to subscribe to a single outlook about the police that shapes their judgments about various aspects of the police. We acknowledge these cautions without accepting their implications. In view of these competing views of legitimacy, and the potential for confusing it with organizational legitimacy, we focus as appropriate on trust and obligation.

Public Trust of Police in Context

Our understanding of trust and confidence in the police is enriched by placing it in the larger context of facts about public attitudes. First, the public's trust in "government," which has been tracked for many years in the American National Election Studies (ANES), declined from 76 percent in 1964 to 25 percent in 1980, and since then has exceeded 50 percent only once, in 2002.[1] The ANES trust in government index, which combines responses to four survey items that all concern the federal government, fell from its peak of 61 in 1966 to 27 in 1980, and through 2008 never again reached 50, fluctuating mainly in the 20s and 30s.[2] This decline in trust in the government to some extent paralleled a broader decline in trust and confidence in social institutions, such as the press, medicine, and education (Smith 2008).

Second, in general, the public now has more confidence in state and local governments (Gerstenson and Plane 2007; Orren 1997), and more confidence in some institutions than it has in others. In June 2014, 53 percent of the respondents to a Gallup poll had a "great deal" or "quite a lot" of confidence in the police, which was a level of confidence lower than that of only the military and small business. Other institutions did not stack up so well in the public's eyes. Only 34 percent expressed a comparable level of confidence in medicine, 26 percent in public schools, 23 percent in the criminal justice system, and less than 10 percent in Congress. Between 1993 and 2014, confidence in the police fluctuated between 52 and 64 percent. Over the same time period, confidence in the public schools dropped from 39 percent to 32, while confidence in the Supreme Court dropped from 44 percent to 34 (with an intervening rise to 50 percent between 1997 and 2002). Confidence in the criminal justice system improved over that same span, from 17 percent in 1993 to 23, peaking at 34 percent in 2004, but it was uniformly lower than that in the police.[3]

Even in the immediate aftermath of the series of deadly force incidents in 2014–15, a Gallup poll in June 2015 found that 52 percent of Americans had a "great deal" or "quite a lot" of confidence in the police (Jones 2015), and though that figure was the lowest since 1993, the police still enjoyed more of the public's trust and confidence than all but two of the social institutions about which Gallup inquires. Public ratings of the honesty and ethics of police likewise dropped in 2014, but by the end of 2015 they had rebounded (Saad 2015). We have previously seen such dips in confidence following high-profile incidents, with rebounds thereafter (Weitzer 2002).

Analyses of the decline in trust in government have identified several sources. Gary Orren (1997) notes the backdrop of "traditional skepticism" of governmental power among Americans, and the long-term trend in the United States and elsewhere in the first world toward "post-material values" that foster "authority-challenging attitudes," such as self-expression and self-realization. Shorter-term changes in trust stem from: assessments of government performance against public expectations; disagreement with the direction of government policy; negative assessments of the honesty and integrity of public officials; and denunciations of government by public officials and the media. Trust and confidence in police has not declined so much as that in government generally, but it has not improved as much as police performance and fairness has arguably improved, which Lawrence W. Sherman (2002) attributes to broad cultural shifts in public expectations. We might suppose that trust and confidence in the police would turn especially on the perceived integrity of the police, and not very much on (actual) performance, since the public's perceptions of and concern about crime are not closely linked to actual crime levels.

Much of the research on the public's attitudes toward the police has addressed, not trust or confidence as such, but rather "satisfaction" with police. The referent in survey items varies—for example, it might be either police services in your neighborhood or the police department in your city—but the satisfaction about which respondents are queried is in many instances not specific to a particular, concrete experience with the police but rather more global and abstract. Even people who have not had (ever or recently) contact with the police typically have an opinion about the police. We suspect that citizens' global satisfaction with their local police is strongly associated with their trust and confidence in their local police, and if that is so, we can learn something about trust from previous research on satisfaction with the police.

The racial disparity in Americans' attitudes toward the police has been as durable as it is remarkable. Blacks have less favorable attitudes than whites do, and Hispanics' attitudes also tend to be less positive than those of whites. This gap is nearly uniform in its direction, if not its magnitude, across time and space in the United States (for a rare exception to the more general rule, see Frank et al. 1996). Much of the research on attitudes toward the police has dwelled at least to some degree on the origins, meaning, and implications of this disparity.

It appears that attitudes toward the police are shaped to some degree by the severity or perceived severity of social and physical disorders in urban neighborhoods, for which (we might infer) the public holds the police responsible (Reisig and Parks 2000; Sampson and Bartusch 1998). Thus attitudes are more positive where (and by those whom) such incivilities—for example, vandalism, noise, open-air drug markets, abandoned cars—are perceived to be less serious problems. Variation in these quality-of-life conditions may account for at least some of the racial disparity in attitudes toward the police.

Attitudes toward the police also correlate with citizens' subjective experiences with the police in individual contacts, both voluntary contacts—when citizens report crimes or request assistance—and involuntary contacts—when they are stopped by the police. The correlation reflects reciprocal causal effects: satisfaction with the individual contact affects more global satisfaction with the police, but more global attitudes toward the police also shape the perceived quality of police performance in individual police-citizen encounters (Brandl et al. 1994; Rosenbaum et al. 2005; Tyler 1987, 1990). Most of the research that reports on this correlation is cross-sectional, and so it is unable to tease the reciprocal effects apart; multiwave panel surveys are necessary, providing for interviewing the same respondents at two (or more) points in time. Global satisfaction—satisfaction with the police overall—is measured at both times, and in a second survey wave, subjective experience is assessed retrospectively, such that the effects of prior (first-wave, or T_1) attitudes on subjective experience can be estimated, and the effects of subjective experience on later (second-wave, or T_2) attitudes can be separately estimated, controlling for the effects of T_1 attitudes on T_2 attitudes. See figure 1.

Such panel studies find that a substantial fraction of the association between the perceived quality of citizens' experiences with the police and their more general attitudes toward the police reflect the effect of the latter on the former: citizens' subjective experiences are shaped by their prior attitudes much more than their experiences shape their subsequent attitudes. Global attitudes tend to be stable, and any one contact has a limited effect on citizens' broader views of police. But global attitudes have strong effects on citizens' interpretations of their experiences.

Wave 1 survey   Wave 2 Survey

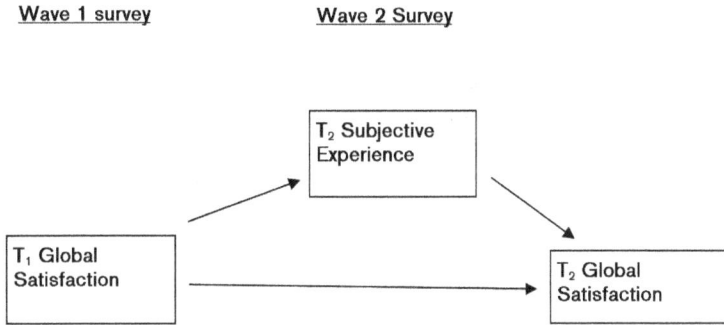

FIGURE 1. Panel Survey Logic.

The effects of global attitudes on subjective experience may be greater for blacks than for whites. Jon Hurwitz and Mark Peffley (2005) surveyed samples of blacks and whites about their beliefs about the fairness of the justice system, and also elicited respondents' judgments about the propriety of police enforcement actions in each of two scenarios in which the race of the citizen was experimentally manipulated. They found considerable support for their "perceived discrimination hypothesis":

> Given the history of racial bias in the system, African Americans should be more vigilant to signs of discrimination in encounters between police and black civilians. Brutality and profiling are so familiar to many African Americans that they constitute chronically accessible "scripts" that are frequently primed and likely to guide interpretations of ambiguous events. . . . Thus, blacks as a group are likely to view confrontations between police and black civilians as yet another instance of police discrimination. (Hurwitz and Peffley 2005, 767)

The effects of global attitudes on citizens' interpretations of the scenarios were greater among blacks than among whites.

One recent study (Braga et al. 2014), which also employed experimentally manipulated scenarios, further suggests that citizens' assessments of police conduct are affected by broader matters of context, such as the climate of police-community relations: whether "the police department had been cited for its strong community policing work, had received extensive negative media coverage for poor community relations and civil rights violations."

Moreover, the effects of subjective experiences on more global attitudes toward the police are asymmetrical: unfavorable experiences have a more detrimental effect on attitudes toward the police than favorable experiences have a beneficial effect. Skogan (2006) goes so far as to assert that police are in a no-win situation, finding that positive experiences do not move the attitudinal needle, whereas negative experiences detract from global satisfaction. He locates this asymmetry in a broader set of findings in psychological research that reveals

> a strong "negativity bias" that shapes the interpretation that people give to their day-to-day experiences. . . . The lessons of bad things are learned more quickly, and forgotten more slowly, than the lessons of positive experiences. When people are faced with a mix of positive and negative experiences, the negative ones predominate in shaping both attitudes and behavior. They pay more careful attention to negative experiences, and think about them and recall them later in more elaborate and fine-grained fashion. (Skogan 2006, 106)

These relationships may also help to account for the disparities in the attitudes of whites and blacks.

Skogan's findings about the effects of subjectively positive experiences with the police are as dispiriting as they are consistent with the psychological research to which he alludes, though one need not conclude that positive experience has no effect on more global attitudes toward the police in order to see merit in the proposition about negativity bias. The panel studies cited above found that positive experience has a beneficial effect of modest magnitude and negative experience has a detrimental effect of greater magnitude. These results have been consistent, though they do not demonstrate that the estimated effects of subjective experience are rooted in the overt actions of police.

However, all of these findings are difficult to reconcile with the fairly high levels of satisfaction with and trust in the police. Given the asymmetrical effects of experience, and given that about one-fifth of the American adult population has a contact each year with the police (mostly through traffic stops), we might deduce that satisfaction and trust would spiral down over time with the predominantly negative effects of experience. Yet that is not what we have seen over time. Clearly, other forces are at work in shaping attitudes toward the police, forces of a longitudinal nature that previous research has missed. Perhaps the effects of experience decay over time.

Research on the etiology of attitudes toward the police is thin. We can safely assume that the typical adult is not a blank slate on which direct experiences with legal actors leave their mark, but to say that prior attitudes influence an individual's judgments about direct experiences is to beg the question: whence do prior attitudes come? We would do well to consider the "primacy principle" of political socialization (Searing et al. 1976), comprised of three assumptions: that political orientations are learned in childhood; that childhood learning shapes later modifications of political attitudes; and that the scale of any such modifications tends to be small. Insofar as the police are one of the most visible manifestations of government, we should take seriously the idea that attitudes toward the police are shaped in important ways through childhood socialization.[4] Parents and other adult guardians would presumably play a large role in childhood legal socialization, as they do in political socialization more generally (see, e.g., Jennings and Niemi 1968, 1975; Jennings, Stoker, and Bowers 2009). Parents can overtly influence their children's outlooks through direct communication that establishes and reinforces ways of interpreting and understanding the world, and they can unobtrusively model beliefs and attitudes for their children. But studies of the influence of parents in legal socialization are few in number, and those that exist appeared only recently.

Amie Schuck (2013) found that youths in 5th or 6th grade (i.e., aged 11 or 12) hold positive attitudes toward the police, though even at this early age, the attitudes of African American youths are less positive than those of white or Latino youths. Further, she found that youths' attitudes tend to become more negative from age 12 until the age of 17, and that the downward trend holds regardless of adolescents' race, sex, or socioeconomic status; as Schuck observes, "this pattern strongly resembles the archetype theorized for adolescents' perceptions of figures of authority, including parents and teachers, as well as, the pattern described by Fagan and Tyler . . . for adolescents' perceptions of legitimacy of the law and legal authorities" (2013, 597). Jeffrey Fagan and Tom Tyler argue that "there is a developmental process of *legal* socialization, and that this process unfolds during childhood and adolescence as part of a vector of developmental capital that promotes compliance with the law and cooperation with legal actors." Summarizing early studies of childhood legal socialization, they observe that "early orientations toward law and government were found to be affective in nature, and characterized by idealized and overly benevolent views about authority. These early views shaped the later views of adolescents, views that were both more cognitive and less idealized in form. In other words, each stage of the socialization process influenced later, more complex, views" (Fagan and Tyler 2005, 218).

The findings of two recent studies testify to the influence of parents on their children's outlooks. Analyzing the attitudes of nearly 1,000 adjudicated delinquents aged 14 to 17, for each of whom "collateral" interviews were also conducted with a parent, and controlling for a wide range of potentially confounding influences, Wolfe, McLean, and Pratt 2016 found that "parental attitudes regarding the legitimacy of legal authorities influence those same attitudes in their children." Analyzing the attitudes of 315 first-time juvenile offenders aged 13 to 17 and their mothers or female guardians, Cavanagh and Cauffman 2015 similarly found that the mothers' attitudes toward the justice system influenced their sons'. That both studies detected such effects in samples of youth restricted to adjudicated delinquents, all of whom had passed the point at which Schuck found youths' attitudes becoming more negative, suggests that their estimates of parental effects are probably quite conservative.

In a third study, a survey of 9th grade students in schools in Queensland, Australia, in which respondents completed items about their attitudes toward the police and one on their parents' attitudes toward the police, Elise Sargeant and Christine Bond found that even controlling for police-initiated contacts, prior delinquency, and peer delinquency, perceived parental attitudes are associated with youths' attitudes. (Sargeant and Bond 2015). They point out that "theory suggests that attitudes attributed to others may be more important than actual attitudes," and conclude (albeit speculatively) that "if young people learn attitudes to police from their parents, it may be that negative attitudes to police can then lead to negative police contacts."

Parental influence on their children's attitudes toward the police may be exerted through other mechanisms of childhood and adolescent socialization. Research has shown that parents' monitoring and discipline shapes their children's level of self-control (e.g., Hay, 1981; Pratt, Turner, and Piquero, 2004). Self-control, in turn, is associated with justice system attitudes (Reisig, Wolfe, and Holtfreter 2011; Nivette, Eisner, Malti, and Ribeaud 2014). Thus parenting has both direct and indirect effects on youth attitudes toward the police.[5]

Most research on the attitudes of juveniles has not controlled for the socializing influences of parents, however, and so it risks overestimating the effects of contacts with the police. Piquero et al. 2005 analyzed youthful offenders' trajectories of legitimacy and legal cynicism over an eighteen-month period. The trajectories proved to be largely stable, but they exhibited different levels, and from associations between the levels of these attitudes and subjects' baseline assessments of the procedural justice of police and courts, Alex Piquero and his colleagues inferred that "situational experiences with criminal justice personnel influence more general attitudes about the law and legal system" (296). But they also acknowledge that the stability in the differences "suggests that inter-individual differences among study participants in their cynicism about the legal system likely were established before their first assessment in this study, perhaps as young as fifteen years of age" (287), and the same could be said about their judgments about legitimacy. Megan Augustyn (2015) examined the same sample over a longer time period, finding a decline in offenders' procedural justice judgments, much as Amie Schuck (2013) did, and also that later judgments were influenced by prior judgments. She also found that, curiously, arrests *improved* offenders' perceptions of procedural justice, and that the positive effect of an arrest increased as offenders aged. In contrast, Amy Nivette et al. (2014) found that, among a general sample of youth, police contacts increased legal cynicism, controlling for prior cynicism (which accounted for half of the explained variance). They further found that self-reported delinquency in the preceding year was a strong predictor of legal cynicism, which they took to suggest that negative (or cynical) attitudes may serve a neutralization function, justifying juveniles' own delinquency. They opine that "following a negative police contact, we venture that cynicism operates as a cognitive distortion that denies the shameful aspects of sanctioning and instead places blame on the law itself" (287).

Furthermore, much of the research on juveniles' attitudes, like that on adults' attitudes, is cross-sectional, and so the effects of prior attitudes cannot be estimated or controlled. Fagan and Tyler (2005), for example, estimated the effects of procedural justice—the quality of interactions with police, school disciplinary personnel, and private security—on legitimacy, legal cynicism, and moral disengagement among 215 youths aged 10–16, who were interviewed once each. They controlled for a number of personality and contextual factors, but they could not control for prior attitudes. They must therefore assume that procedural justice affects—but is not affected by—legitimacy, and thus they almost certainly overestimate the effect of procedural justice. Other cross-sectional research, however, has found that the effects of youths' experience are mediated by community ties and delinquent subcultures (Brick et al. 2009; Leiber et al. 1998)

The lessons that we take from the research on youths' attitudes toward the police are that trust in the police and other legal institutions, like political attitudes more generally, are to a large degree formed early in life, and while they are not immutable, early attitudes influence later attitude formation. They shape the experiences to which adolescents and young adults are exposed, and they form the lens through which those experiences are interpreted. Adult attitudes toward the police are not simple functions of the treatment that they receive from the police.

We would also note that much of the previous research on procedural justice and legitimacy concerns abstract characterizations of the procedural justice with which police perform and not judgments about how police acted in specific police-citizen encounters. This research has consistently found that people who believe that police act in procedurally just ways tend also to trust the police, and vice versa. That these more abstract judgments about the procedural justice of policing are related to equally abstract outlooks about trust and confidence in police does not necessarily tell us much about how police actually perform, but they do tell us about how people think about the police.

"Customer Satisfaction" in Policing

Police administrators sometimes invoke a customer analogy in order to promote a more service-oriented mentality and style of policing. Thinking of the people with whom police interact as customers would presumably lead to a heightened attentiveness to what it is that citizens want from the police and greater appreciation of the importance of interpersonal relations. A more customer-friendly approach by police would entail the very actions that comprise procedural justice: asking for and listening to citizens' accounts of the situations in which police and citizens meet one another; courteous treatment; explaining what police are doing and on what basis. Research suggests that these features of the process are important to the people who interact with police. The customer analogy has limits, however, and ambiguities in the boundaries of the analogy allow or invite differing interpretations by officers.

A true customer, in a private market transaction, is someone who chooses to seek out a product or service, finds a provider for that product or service and ascertains the price, and enters into a transaction that involves the exchange of the agreed price for the product or service. The exchange is voluntary on the part of both parties, and the price that the customer is willing to pay for the product or service reflects the minimum value that she attaches to the product or service. Her satisfaction with the product or service will turn on a later judgment about the extent to which it met her expectations of it, relative to the price that she paid for it. Chances are that the benefit of the product or service will be limited to her alone (or her household) and not extend to others who are not party to the transaction.

A citizen who calls police to report a stolen bicycle or a loud party, say, resembles such a customer in some respects. He seeks a service—official recognition and recording of a crime of which he is the victim, or third-party intervention to resolve a situation that he defines as a disturbance. His contact with the police is at his initiative and is largely voluntary; he could instead choose to forego any assistance in recovering the bicycle or making an insurance claim, or to tolerate the disturbance that the party represents to him until it ends without intervention.

This transaction, however, is nonvoluntary insofar as the citizen has no options in a police market; in most instances, he must contact his municipal or town police force if he is to receive police service from any agency. Furthermore, he does not pay a discrete price for the service on the occasion on which it is provided; the community has paid for the service, and so beyond any taxes that he might pay (which he is compelled to pay whether he uses the service or not), the service is free to him.

Indeed, any individual member of the community is a customer who pays for the presence and availability of police even if she never requests assistance from the police with respect to a particular situation. These are collective and not individual services; whatever benefits flow from the police services for which she pays in this way are also enjoyed by other members of the community at the same time, and not limited to her or her household. In addition, the payment for these services is nonvoluntary in a different sense: taxes paid to finance police operations are coerced payments.

Mark Moore (2002) points out that police availability to answer emergency calls might come at the expense of quality service to individuals; the time that an officer devotes to high-quality service to one complainant can compromise her capacity to respond promptly to a more urgent situation. More generally, police cannot give "customers" what they want when it exceeds the resource capacity or legal authority of the police to do so.

Of course, the police also interact with citizens whose contacts with police are not voluntary; suspected offenders have "obligation encounters" with police (Moore 2002). In what sense is a service delivered to people who are taken into police custody for booking, drivers to whom traffic citations are issued, or pedestrians who are stopped on suspicion for questioning? To what kind or level of service are they entitled, given that they may have crossed a legal and/or moral line? At a minimum they are entitled to a level of service mandated by the Constitution: their rights—to be secure in their persons and property against unreasonable intrusions, to be subject to no more than the amount of force necessary to overcome any resistance that they may offer, and against self-incrimination—set a floor on the level of service to be delivered. We might expect a still higher level of service than that, in the form of respectful treatment, because not only of its intrinsic value but also of its hypothesized instrumental value in achieving compliance, and minimizing injuries (to citizens and officers). But the term "customer" is surely stretched in application to these recipients of police service; "client" might be more appropriate.

Like the recipients of many human services, many of the people who interact with police, including even some of those who request police assistance, do not know or recognize what they need and should want. Some of them are incapable of making informed judgments because they are impaired by mental disability or intoxication. Even if they suffer from neither mental illness nor mind-altering substances, they may be ill-equipped to make assessments of the quality of the service options, though that is true of many consumer choices. The single mother of a rebellious teenager who, at her wits end, calls the police may not know what the police should or can do for her. If we suppose that the customer is always right, then, we will be misled by the customer service analogy.

Thus the customer service analogy breaks down in several respects: the recipients of police services—let us call them, generally, clients—are not voluntary in the sense of having a meaningful range of choice in service providers; some encounters are distinctly involuntary; some clients may be incapable of making informed judgments; and clients may lack essential information in assessing the quality of the services they receive. We might add that, unlike private-sector firms, police do not welcome repeat customers; however, police would welcome public "loyalty" insofar as that means public support and cooperation.

Research on customer satisfaction reinforces these observations and offers some additional perspective on citizen satisfaction with police. First, customers tend to be more satisfied with "products" than they are with services (Fornell et al. 1996). Services are "co-produced" by both the provider and the recipient, allowing the provider less control over the process, and services rely more on the human resources of the provider organization, such that they are less susceptible to standardization (Anderson, Fornell, and Rust 1997; Johnson and Fornell 1991; Nilsson et al. 2001). Services are more intangible than products, making it "difficult for customers to understand service quality" (Nilsson et al., 2001, 12). This is all surely equally true for police organizations.

Second, employee management has a direct effect on business results (Nilsson et al. 2001)—organizational effectiveness, the use of resources, profits, and revenue growth—as well as indirect effects, through organizational orientations to both customers and processes. Furthermore, customer loyalty to a service provider tends to be earned through high-quality performance, while customer loyalty to a product tends to be "bought" through product discounting, which is not generally feasible with service provision (Edvardsson et al. 2000). These patterns may not hold equally well in public agencies.

Third, customers' expectations of a product or service shape their evaluations of it (Anderson and Fornell 2000; Fornell et al. 1996; Szymanski and Hernard 2001) when they compare their experience with what they expected. Customers have weak or no expectations of a new product with which customers have no experience, meaning that product performance drives satisfaction, but "as customer experience with the product grows and past performance information becomes available, more product-specific expectations develop" (Johnson and Fornell 1991, 275). Hardly anyone has an interaction with the police—even their first personal contact—without having formed expectations—positive or negative—about the police through the socialization process.

Fourth, and relatedly, customers' opportunity for choice can be expected to influence customer satisfaction, since customers who are dissatisfied with one firm's product will turn to those of other firms: "in a competitive environment, people generally do not continue to purchase products toward which they are ambivalent or hold negative evaluations" (Johnson and Fornell 1991, 278). As noted above, clients' range of choice in receiving police services is very restricted.

Some police officers have misgivings about—or reject—a customer-service orientation in policing, reasoning that the people with whom they interact in their day-to-day work are not customers as such. They might well sense the limits of the customer analogy.

PUBLIC TRUST AND ORGANIZATIONAL LEGITIMACY

The social psychological dimension of trust (but not obligation) bears a fairly strong resemblance to the legitimacy construct that appears in institutional theory. Even so, the two theories diverge somewhat in their conceptions of legitimacy. For social psychological theory, legitimacy—trust—is a property of individuals and it is continuous or at least ordinal: differences in degree matter, both for the level of support that the organization enjoys and for the likelihood of individual compliance with the police and the law. For institutional theory, legitimacy is by and large a dichotomous or perhaps trichotomous variable: organizations that are legitimate survive, those that lose legitimacy cease to exist, and organizations whose legitimacy is challenged or threatened can be expected to take steps to regain legitimacy.

Two very important differences between institutional theory and social psychological theory lie in who makes these judgments, or perhaps more accurately, whose judgments matter for the organization, and the basis on which those judgments rest. In social psychological theory, the relevant judgments are those of "ordinary citizens," who evaluate the fairness with which policing is performed. In institutional theory, the pertinent judgments are made by sovereigns such as legislators, professional bodies, and courts—that is, audiences with some standing to make or influence authoritative decisions that have clear implications for the organization. But institutional theory holds that these judgments are based not on technical performance, which is difficult for any audience to judge, but on the police department's conformity to expectations for structural forms. Social psychological theory attributes far greater significance to judgments about the routine exercise of police authority, that is, the technical performance of the organization.

Notwithstanding the trichotomous character of legitimacy in institutional theory, finer differences of degree can be discerned. First, one strategy for maintaining legitimacy is to "stockpile" goodwill (Suchman 1995), so it would seem that an organization can accumulate more or less legitimacy. Second, legitimacy can be challenged by less powerful constituencies, and so, as W. Richard Scott observes, "'legitimate' structures may, at the same time, be contested structures" (2014, 73), arguably resting on a lesser foundation of trust.

For all but social survey purposes, citizens' trust in police is not aggregated by computing means or percentages; it is filtered through the judgments of sovereigns. So an agency might thrive despite suffering the distrust of a significant minority of its population. In the absence of polling, it is difficult to say what level of trust an agency enjoys. Citizens' trust, in this political context, is a weighted mean (perhaps a weighted mode)—weighted by political standing and other resources, and not to achieve sample representativeness of the population. Even so, notwithstanding such political weighting, public trust can drop to a level that stimulates a crisis of legitimacy for an agency. John Crank and Robert Langworthy (1992) write about what happens then: a ceremonial replacement of the chief and perhaps some other symbolic, structural reforms (reforms, we would add, that are likely to be only loosely if at all coupled to street policing). The Baltimore Police Department in the wake of the Freddie Gray incident may be a case in point, since its commissioner was fired amid violent protests that erupted following Gray's death. The crisis was averted and legitimacy restored, at least at a level that suffices. In the twenty-first century, there are other options for restoring legitimacy: accepting mandated reforms in a consent decree, or asking the COPS Office to undertake the collaborative reform initiative in your department.

Agencies whose legitimacy is not threatened may be able to build up levels of trust beyond that necessary for survival; stockpiling good will is a legitimation strategy (Suchman 1995). A symbolic display may be a way to gain some additional trust, even when an agency has enough to get by without it. So while organizational legitimacy is dichotomous or trichotomous, aggregate public trust is continuous, and public trust can sink to levels at which organizational legitimacy may be threatened.

Challenges to Legitimacy

Challenges to a police department's legitimacy can surely be mounted most effectively by its sovereigns—say, the city's mayor, the courts, or DOJ litigators—but they can also be initiated by a mobilized public. The protests surrounding shootings by police and other deaths while in police custody in 2014 and 2015 illustrate such threats to police legitimacy, and so does the civil unrest and rioting in the 1960s. Protests over police use of deadly force, or other police practices, can be characterized as a challenge or threat to an agency's legitimacy in that they are claims that the department's operations are not "proper, or appropriate within some socially constructed system of norms, values, beliefs, and definitions" (Suchman 1995, 574). Certainly large-scale demonstrations, and those that are repeated over days or weeks, attract attention to a set of grievances and mobilize support for addressing those grievances. While they may not jeopardize the survival of a police organization, they may be able to generate pressure that is sufficient to prompt organizational change, at least change of a symbolic nature. But in order to do so, the support of sovereigns for change must at some point be enlisted.

It would be easy—but mistaken—to see the riots that rocked Ferguson, Missouri, Baltimore, and other cities in 2014–15 as reflections of the depth of distrust of police, just as it would have been a mistake to interpret the 1967 riots in Detroit, Newark, and elsewhere as a products only of grievances against the police. The Kerner Commission surmised that the riots of 1967 were rooted in a number of intersecting conditions:

- *Pervasive discrimination and segregation in employment,* education, and housing, which have resulted in the continuing exclusion of great numbers of Negroes from the benefits of economic progress;
- *Black in-migration and white exodus,* which have produced the massive and growing concentrations of impoverished Negroes in our major cities, creating a growing crisis of deteriorating facilities and services and unmet human needs;
- *The black ghettos,* where segregation and poverty converge on the young to destroy opportunity and enforce failure. Crime, drug addiction, dependency

on welfare, and bitterness and resentment against society in general and white society in particular are the result.

Police practices were among the grievances held at the highest level of intensity, along with unemployment and inadequate housing, but inadequate education, poor recreational opportunities, and others were enumerated by the commission. Commentary on the 2014 rioting in Ferguson offered similar diagnoses (Sneed 2014).

Academic research on race riots has confirmed that the conditions that underlie such violent protest extend well beyond police practices, even as policing may contribute to those conditions, and an incident involving the police may be the final (if not the only) precipitating event. Empirical support has been found for the role of social marginality or disadvantage in racial violence, and also for the impact of "closed and unresponsive political systems" that provide no channels through which grievances can be addressed (Lieske 1978, 1329). Other research has pointed toward "hypersegregation of Blacks in urban settings" that breaks down, with increasing interracial contact and competition (Olzak et al. 1996).

Insofar as police practices comprise a patch in a much larger quilt of social, economic, and political conditions that give rise to racial unrest, reforming police practices is by itself no solution. Confronted by a galaxy of problems that are in many ways intractable, local and even state and national sovereigns might be expected to direct attention to police reform as a feasible response. Those reforms need not, however, be compatible with the technical demands of police work or with other existing organizational structures.

TRUST AND OBLIGATION IN SCHENECTADY AND SYRACUSE

Previous research has identified several categories of outlooks that may relate to the social psychological construct of legitimacy, and which may be strongly intercorrelated: trust; confidence; and identification. In addition, these attitudes are thought to be strongly associated with citizens' support for police, belief in empowering police, and citizens' sense of obligation to obey. Both the police services survey and the key informant survey included items on trust, identification, and empowerment, and the police services survey also included items on obligation. We summarize our analyses of these survey responses here, and we also construct indices of trust and obligation based on the police services survey data for analysis in a later chapter.[6] We reserve an examination of survey results over time until chapter 8. First, however, we describe the police services and key informant surveys; some readers may wish to skip over this treatment of research methods and go directly to the findings in the section on trust and confidence.

Survey Methodologies
The Police Services Survey

The police services survey was designed primarily to capture citizens' subjective experience with police, that is, the quality of police service from citizens' perspectives, but it also extended to citizens' more general judgments about and attitudes toward the police. We sampled police records of various kinds to represent, as much as possible, the entire population of police contacts with citizens. Thus the design provided for sampling records of calls for service, stops, and arrests. After a pilot test of the survey in July 2011, we commenced it on August 1, beginning with samples of incidents that occurred in the latter half of July (July 16–31). We continued to draw new samples semi-monthly over thirty-six waves of surveying, or eighteen months. We treated the first 7–10 waves as a baseline, and thereupon began providing monthly summaries of the previous month's performance to each department's command staff in the context of the department's Compstat meeting. The survey also served as an outcome measure, of course, as one month's performance measures were the previous month's outcomes.

Three Types of Contacts.   Half or more police-citizen contacts in cities arise from calls for service (Parks et al. 1999; also see Eith and Durose 2011). They are in important respects voluntary contacts, initiated by citizens, who request some form of assistance.[7] The nature of the problems or issues about which citizens seek assistance is quite heterogeneous, however, and the assistance that citizens request takes many different forms; sometimes citizens want or demand services that police cannot provide. But citizens who dial 911 or other police numbers bear as close a resemblance to "customers" as any with whom police deal.

Traffic stops, and other field stops, have been and continue to be the subject of much controversy. Police claim that high levels of such police proactivity have crime-control benefits, and research tends to bear those claims out (Boydstun 1975; Sampson and Cohen 1988; Whitaker et al. 1985; Wilson and Boland 1978; also see Cohen and Ludwig 2003; McGarrell et al. 2001; Sherman and Rogan 1995; Rosenfeld et al. 2014). But critics point to frequent violations of constitutional limits on police authority, and racially disparate impacts, as reasons to more closely regulate police-initiated contacts. Stops are also a heterogeneous category of events, including routine stops of traffic law violators, pretext stops of traffic law violators motivated by crime-control objectives, and investigatory stops of pedestrians, which are often based only on reasonable suspicion. Stops are not, of course, sought by citizens, and they are thus thought to raise more doubts among citizens about the propriety of police intervention (Reiss 1971).

Both calls for service and stops are defined by how they begin. Either type of contact may end in a variety of ways. Calls for service can prompt a wide range of police responses, at the discretion of officers, varying simultaneously along dimensions of control and support. The dispositions may or may not accord with citizen preferences, and they may or may not resolve the situations satisfactorily. Citizens may or may not consider the outcomes favorable. Stops also can involve any of a variety of police actions and eventuate in any of a variety of dispositions, though arguably a narrower range of dispositions than calls for service. Traffic law violators may be lectured, admonished, and/or ticketed. Motorists' vehicles may be searched, with or without the consent of the motorist. Warrant checks may be conducted. Questions may be asked, citizens frisked. Most stops that do not culminate in a ticket will end with the citizen being released in the field. Some, however, will be arrested and taken into custody.

Arrests might stem from either calls for service or stops. They are a type of contact defined by how the contact ends rather than how it begins. The outcome for the citizen is unambiguously unfavorable, and unfavorable to a degree that far exceeds that of a ticket; the citizen is often booked and at least briefly incarcerated, and may be held pending arraignment. The arrest could be based on another citizen's complaint, on an officer's own observations, or both. Many arrests, as Egon Bittner (1974) surmised, are made in order merely to handle the situation, and not primarily because the law has been violated. Arrestees are people who, for whatever reason, did not benefit from the tendency of the police to underenforce the law (Wilson 1968), which is often a discretionary choice. Previous research, with very few exceptions, has not examined the judgments of arrestees about their treatment by police.

The sample of contacts in each site represented all of these contacts, but we oversampled those in which procedural justice is presumptively more challenging: stops and arrests. In this way we were more likely to achieve subsamples of a size that would support separate analysis. Results were weighted as necessary in order to represent the entire population of contacts (i.e., calls were weighted more heavily for such analysis).

Survey Content. We formed a survey instrument based on previously fielded surveys, such that all of the items had been pretested, in effect, and many of the items have a lineage that includes many surveys over decades. Some items, for example, were drawn from the surveys that Wesley Skogan administered in Chicago in the 1990s, and they had also been used in surveys by the Police Foundation in the 1980s. Many other items, tapping elements of procedural justice or legitimacy, were drawn from survey research conducted by Tom Tyler and others. Still other items were drawn from the Police-Public Contact Survey (PPCS), developed and administered by the Bureau of Justice Statistics in the 1990s. Respondents were informed that their names had been drawn from police records, and that we were interested in their contact with the police on a specified date, but were not told that we had information on the nature of that contact. Like the PPCS, our survey instrument allowed respondents to tell us how their encounter with police began, with a series of questions tailored to the nature of the contact: a motor vehicle stop; a pedestrian stop; a call to report a crime; a call for some other kind of assistance; or being contacted by police in some other way (e.g., when someone else calls police). The instrument also allowed respondents to self-report arrests.[8] Most of the interview concerned the sampled contact, but prior to that series of questions, respondents were asked a set of items about the legitimacy of their city's police more generally. Some items were unique to particular types of contacts, for example, only those who had called for assistance or to report a crime were asked whether the police had solved the citizen's problem, and queries about experiences with searches were posed only to those who were stopped by police. Demographic information was also collected.

Samples.   Our design provided for sampling contacts from police records of calls for service, stops, and arrests in each department, and conducting interviews by phone with the citizens named in those records. Samples were drawn semimonthly from records of contacts that occurred between July 15, 2011, and January 15, 2013. Calls for service records were extracted from each department's computer-aided dispatch (CAD) system. Arrest records were extracted from each department's record management system, and included custodial arrests as well as cases in which suspected offenders were either issued appearance tickets or released on their own recognizance. Records of stops differed across the departments: Syracuse has for many years provided for a citizen contact form on which officers record all stops that do not result in arrest; these records include stops in which a traffic ticket is issued. Schenectady, however, does not have a comparable record of stops, but rather separate records of traffic tickets and "field interview cards." Field interview cards may be completed pursuant to any contact with a citizen, whether it is police-initiated or not, but most field interview cards are based on police-initiated contacts. In Schenectady we sampled only field interview cards, since sampling traffic tickets was not at that time feasible. Thus the samples of stops in the two cities are different, in that routine traffic stops are included only in Syracuse.

In general, the interviewed sample resembles the eligible population in each site fairly closely (details are provided in the methodological appendix). Since the samples are stratified, with different probabilities of sample selection across the different subpopulations, and since the response rates varied across subpopulations, we weight the cases for most analyses of the survey data in order to represent the entire contact population in each site. We apply weights that reproduce the original population proportion that each subpopulation represents, though these weights are very nearly the same as those that are based only on the probabilities of sample selection (with correlations over 0.90).

Key Informant Survey

We administered a three-wave key informant panel survey with two objectives: to provide a description of the legitimacy that community members attribute to the study police departments, and then to compare responses over time to assess whether departments' efforts to cultivate improved police-citizen relations by actively assessing satisfaction had an impact on the public's views about police legitimacy. While the police services survey included items about police legitimacy, it was limited to people who had contact with the police, and the key informant survey complements the police services survey by providing information on the perspectives of the community more generally.

In general, key informants are persons whose organizational roles imply they have special knowledge about the population being studied. For our purposes, we operationalized key informants as current leaders of a neighborhood association in Schenectady or Syracuse. To identify neighborhood associations and their respective leaders in each city, we relied on contact lists provided to us by representatives of the police departments. Both police departments maintain up-to-date lists of associations and contact information for leaders, which include, in many cases, email addresses.

In Wave 1, surveys were distributed to key informants by a private e-mail weblink and paper copies were mailed, with a prepaid postage return envelope, to respondents for whom we had no e-mail address. We asked respondents in Wave 1 for whom we had no e-mail address to provide us with one for follow-up surveying; all respondents complied. Therefore, in subsequent waves we relied exclusively on the e-mailed weblink.

Nine in ten of Syracuse informants had lived in the city for six or more years (75 percent for eleven or more), and the majority (83.4 percent) had lived in their current neighborhood for six years or more. All Syracuse respondents reported they had been active members of their neighborhood association for more than one year, with the greatest proportion (45 percent) reporting three to five years of active involvement, and one-third reporting involvement for six or more years. The majority (68.2 percent) reported holding a leadership position for three years or more.

Consistent with Syracuse, nine in ten Schenectady informants (92.8 percent) reported that they had lived in the City for six years or more, and the majority (85.7 percent) had lived in their current neighborhood for six or more years. All Schenectady respondents reported being active in their neighborhood association for more than a year with the majority (64.2) reporting six or more years of active membership, with the greatest proportion (57.1 percent) reporting eleven or more years of active membership.

Trust and Confidence

Legitimate authorities can be trusted to do the right thing, and to make proper decisions. The surveys provide for several measures of trust and confidence in the form of statements with which survey respondents could agree or disagree:

- I have confidence that the S____ PD can do its job well.
- I trust the leaders of the SPD to make decisions that are good for everyone in the city.
- The police can be trusted to make decisions that are right for the people in my neighborhood.
- There are many things about the SPD and its policies that need to be changed.

In general, two-thirds to three-quarters of the people with whom police had contact during the eighteen months of the survey expressed trust and confidence in the police, though the proportions were somewhat higher in Syracuse—particularly the proportions expressing strongly favorable views. By comparison, the proportions of key informants expressing trust in the police were somewhat higher in Syracuse and lower in Schenectady, but the samples are small and not too much should be made of the differences across the surveys. But among both sets of respondents, the Syracuse police appear to enjoy a more favorable public image, which is consistent with the recent histories of the departments and hence consistent with our expectations. The exception to the generality about trust lies in citizens' assessments of the need for change: 62 to 69 percent of the police services survey respondents in both sites said that there were "many things" about the police department and its policies that needed to be changed, with still higher proportions among key informants.

Identification

People identify with and feel connected to authorities that they consider legitimate, and from their association with legitimate authorities people derive a measure of status (see Tyler and Fagan 2008). Identification is measured through statements with which respondents could agree or disagree:

- I am proud of the work of the S_____ police.
- You can usually understand why the police who work in my neighborhood are acting as they are in a particular situation.
- If you talked to most of the police officers who work in my neighborhood, you would find that they have similar views to my own on many issues (police services survey only).
- Most of the police officers who work in my neighborhood have similar views to my own on many issues (key informant survey only).

With responses that were largely congruent with those on the trust items, 62 to 75 percent of the people with whom police had contact identified at least somewhat with the police, with similar to somewhat larger proportions among key informants.

Empowerment

People are willing to grant a lot of latitude to authorities they consider legitimate, thereby empowering the authority (Sunshine and Tyler 2003). We measure empowerment with these survey items:

- The police should have the right to stop and question people on the street.
- There need to be clear limits on what the police are allowed to do in fighting crime (police services survey only).
- The police should have the power to do whatever they think is needed to fight crime (police services survey only).
- Leaders of the SPD believe that police should work with citizens to try to solve problems (key informant survey only).

People appear to be somewhat conflicted, as more than 80 percent espouse the need for clear limits on crime-fighting by police, while more than half say that police should have wide latitude in fighting crime.

Key informants were also asked for their views on a few other items:

- The SPD take a tough stance on improper police behavior.
- The SPD has effective procedures for preventing improper police behavior.
- Leaders of the SPD believe that the police should be accountable to the communities they serve.
- The SPD considers community satisfaction an organizational priority.

Responses to these statements also reflected perceptions that were predominantly favorable to the police, expressing faith in the orientation of the police and police leadership toward the community, and in its commitment to police rectitude. Half to two-thirds of key informants agreed with these statements. But insofar as the responses differ across the cities, the differences on these items are in favor of Schenectady police.

Obligation

Obligation is the belief that an authority should be obeyed; the greater the legitimacy, the greater the obligation to obey. Police services survey respondents were asked to agree or disagree with these statements:

- Communities work best when people follow the directives of the police.
- There are times when it is okay to ignore what the police tell you to do.

- You should do what the police tell you to do even when you don't like the way they treat you.
- You should accept the decisions made by police even if you think they are wrong.

Generally, three-quarters or more of the people who had a police contact believed that people should obey police commands. About two-thirds believed that such obedience was called for even when police do not treat them properly. Nearly half believe that people should obey police even when they think that police are wrong. Patterns of responses were very similar across the two sites.

Attitudinal Dimensions

As we discussed earlier in this chapter, previous social psychological research on legitimacy exhibits no clear consensus on the measurement of legitimacy or its presumed component dimensions, but it appears prudent for both theoretical and empirical reasons to treat obligation as a distinct construct, separate from trust and confidence in police. In their analysis of the construct validity of process-based measures, Michael Reisig et al. (2007) concluded that trust and obligation are distinct constructs only moderately related to one another, and Jacinta Gau's (2011) findings led to the same conclusion.

Our analysis of the fourteen items posed on the police services survey and summarized above suggests that the trust and identification items reflect a single attitudinal dimension, which we will simply call trust. (In this respect our findings are consistent with those of Tyler and Fagan 2008.) Factor analyses of the fourteen items and of subsets thereof repeatedly yield a factor on which the seven trust and identification items load strongly, and the average inter-item correlation among these seven items is 0.51.[9] The obligation items also formed a distinct dimension, as in previous research. The empowerment items, however, loaded on a separate factor, and these items do not comprise a reliable scale, with an average inter-item correlation of only 0.25. Thus we formed two indices, one of trust and the other of obligation.

The trust index is a simple additive scale based on the seven trust and identification items, each of which was centered at zero (don't know responses and refusals) and provided two values above and below zero for strong and moderate (dis)agreement, respectively (and reverse coded as necessary). This additive index is virtually identical statistically to the factor scale that is formed by weighting the items in proportion with the factor coefficients. The trust index ranges potentially from -14 to 14, with an alpha of 0.88. The distribution of cases across categories of trust for each site is shown in Figure 2, along with the means for each subpopulation.

If we translate the trust index into a 4-point scale resembling those formed in previous research (with high distrust assigned a 1 and high trust assigned a 4), the means of 2.8 and 3.0 (in Schenectady and Syracuse, respectively) are similar to the

FIGURE 2. Trust Index.

Syracuse

Calls for service: 4.43
Stops: 2.22
Arrests: -1.55

Schenectady

Calls for service: 3.34
Arrests: -0.71
FIs: -0.98

■ High distrust   ■ Moderate distrust   ■ Moderate trust   ■ High trust

levels of legitimacy reported by Tyler (2005) and Tyler et al. (2010). Inflated (by 25 percent) to render the index comparable to five-point scales formed in previous research, the means of 3.5 and 3.8 are similar to the levels of legitimacy reported by Tyler and Fagan (2008), Murphy and Cherney (2012), and Murphy et al. (2008).

The obligation index is also an additive scale, based on three (of the four) obligation items, each of which was centered at zero (and reverse coded as needed).[10] The obligation index ranges from - 6 to 6, with an alpha of 0.64. The distribution for each site, and the mean for each subpopulation, is shown in figure 3. Overall, the means are 1.77 and 1.67 for Schenectady and Syracuse, respectively. The obligation index scores are not different across the sites, on average.

The disparity in the public images of the departments, which we described in chapter 2, is not clearly detectable in the distributions and central tendencies of the trust index in the two sites. The mean scores are different—higher in Syracuse than in Schenectady—and the difference is statistically significant. Three-quarters of the Syracuse respondents, compared with about two-thirds of the Schenectady respondents, have index scores in the higher ranges of values. But the difference is not wide, especially in view of the circumstances that detracted from the legitimacy of the Schenectady police. Two-thirds of the people who had contact with the Schenectady police expressed, on balance, trust rather than distrust. Two-thirds or more of the key informants in Schenectady likewise expressed trust in the department and its leaders.

The expected difference in trust levels across the two cities is further contradicted by a comparison of trust levels in individual contact populations, which are not all of the same magnitude or even direction: among people who called for service, trust is higher in Syracuse, but among people who were arrested, trust is lower in Syracuse. The sample of people who were stopped in Syracuse exhibit higher levels of trust, but the two samples are not directly comparable, since the stops in Schenectady do not represent as well as those in Syracuse the people subject to routine traffic stops.

Thus we do not see in these data on public trust and confidence a clear indication of the crisis of legitimacy that Schenectady police suffered. Sovereigns in Schenectady could plainly see in the misadventures of individual officers symptoms of mismanagement, which (we infer) led them to challenge the department's legitimacy. The judgments of the broader public, however, were seemingly less affected by the unflattering reports of officers' misconduct. Compared with the judgments of those who encountered the Syracuse police, the legitimacy of which was not at issue, the judgments of those who encountered the Schenectady police were only slightly less positive. We lack data on public trust and confidence over time, and so we cannot establish that public attitudes were stable. But these findings are consistent with the proposition that a police department's legitimacy turns principally on the judgments of sovereigns such as legislators, elected executives,

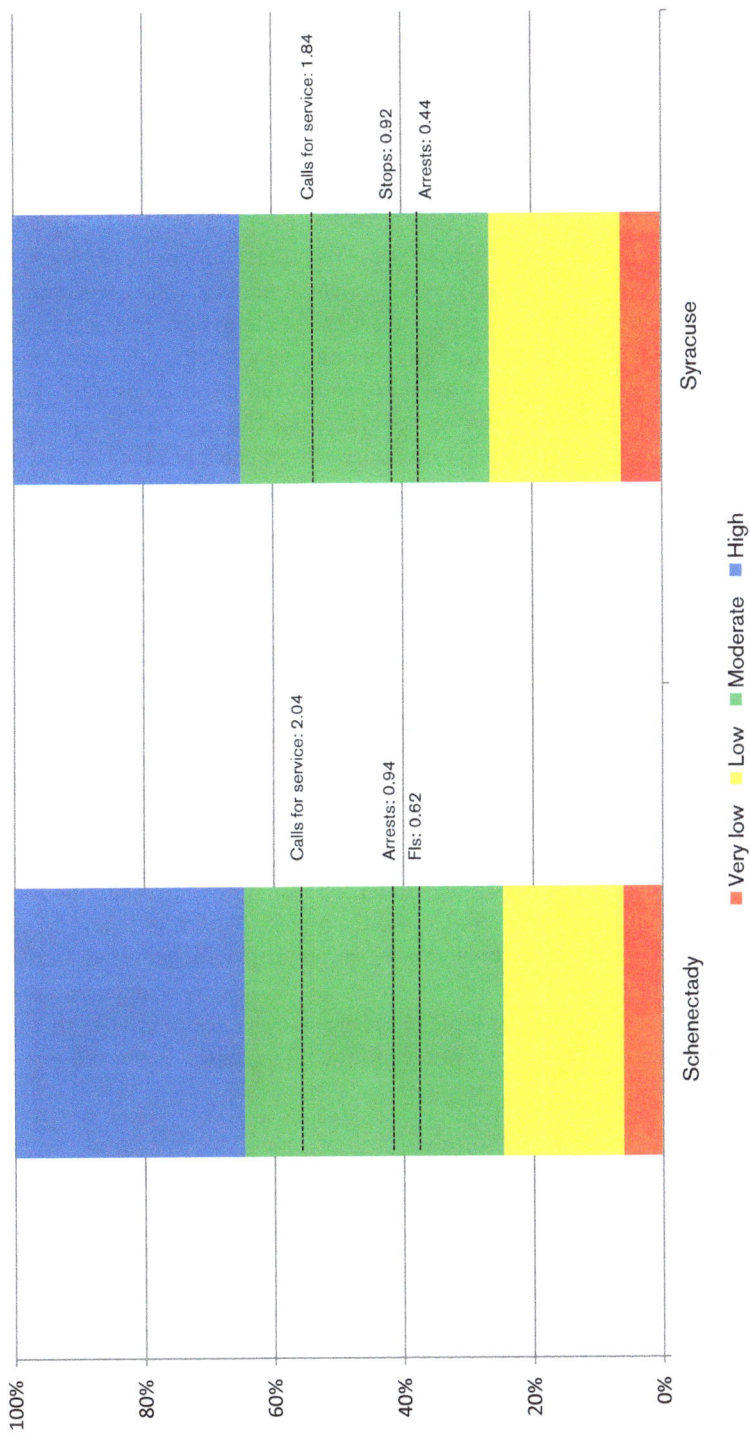

FIGURE 3. Obligation Index.

courts, and other parties—such as the Civil Rights Division of the Department of Justice—to make or influence authoritative decisions about the organization.

SUMMARY

We briefly reviewed extant research on police legitimacy and, more generally, citizens' attitudes toward the police. Previous research findings testify to the myriad influences on citizens' outlooks, which are subject to long-term forces (e.g., postmaterial values) and to factors that are more narrowly circumscribed temporally and spatially, such as the perceived level of social and physical disorder in one's neighborhood and the reputation of the local police (for good or ill), but among which the performance of the police in police-citizen encounters is but one. Citizens' attitudes are rather tenuously connected to their direct, personal experiences with the police.

Using survey items identical to those used in previous survey research, we find in Schenectady and Syracuse patterns of trust and obligation that resemble those reported in previous research. First, citizens overall reported fairly high levels of trust and confidence in their police departments, with two-thirds to three-quarters in agreement with statements that police can be trusted to make good decisions, that they have confidence in the police, and that they are proud of their police. Second, seven survey items were strongly intercorrelated and form a scale of trust and confidence that is reliable. As in previous research, obligation forms a distinct construct, and while it is related to trust, the obligation items appear to tap a separate attitudinal dimension. Finally, the two sources of data on citizens' perceptions were only weakly consistent with our initial supposition that Syracuse police enjoyed greater public trust and confidence at the project's outset, and the differences were not nearly so stark as might have been expected, given Schenectady's crisis of legitimacy in the decade preceding our surveying. Public trust, it appears, was less susceptible to the reported misdeeds of Schenectady police than were the judgments of sovereigns, suggesting that organizational legitimacy turns more on the latter than the former.

4

Procedural Justice in Citizens' Subjective Experiences

One premise of this research was that the quality of service that citizens receive in their encounters with the police is a dimension of police performance to which police managers should pay attention. We undertook to measure this dimension of performance by asking citizens who had contact with the police about their experience, and to make the results regularly available to managers in Schenectady and Syracuse. In this chapter, we describe those measures and the subjective experience that they documented in police-citizen encounters. In addition to summarizing the contours of citizens' subjective experience in each of the cities in terms of citizen satisfaction and the discrete components of procedural justice, we also form a composite measure of procedural justice on which further analysis will focus in a later chapter.

Citizens' subjective experiences with the police have been conceptualized and measured in previous research in two principal ways. One approach has been concerned with citizens' satisfaction with their contact, which has been operationalized in terms of satisfaction with "the police" (Brandl et al. 1994), with "how the police responded" (Skogan 2005), with "the officer's overall performance" (Wells 2007), with the citizen's treatment by police (Reisig and Parks 2000), and with how the situation was handled by police (Reisig and Parks 2000).

The second approach has dwelled on procedural justice. Procedural justice has to do with how authority is exercised and how people experience it. It is not unique to law enforcement and police-citizen encounters; many people use the same criteria in judging the character of their interactions with authorities of many kinds, such as the interactions that people have with their supervisors at work. These criteria include:

- *Voice:* people want and are more satisfied when they are given an opportunity to tell their side of a story, explain their situation, and communicate their views.
- *Quality of interpersonal treatment:* people want to be treated with dignity and respect.
- *Trustworthy motives:* people are more satisfied when they believe that authorities care about their well-being and are considering their needs and concerns, and they draw inferences about that when authorities explain their decisions and justify and account for their actions.
- *Neutrality:* people believe that decisions are made fairly when they see evidence of evenhandedness and the consideration of objective facts.

These two approaches are not mutually exclusive; indeed, insofar as subjective experience has been treated as an object of explanation, it has been mainly through an examination of the extent to which satisfaction with the contact is shaped by the elements of procedural justice (Skogan 2005; Wells 2007). Most of this research has been cross-sectional, and so it has seldom accounted for the effects of citizens' prior attitudes toward the police on their subjective experiences. As we pointed out in chapter 3, when the effects of prior attitudes have been analyzed in panel surveys, we have found that subjective experience is strongly influenced by those prior attitudes. Citizens who have favorable attitudes toward the police are, ceteris paribus, more satisfied with their subsequent interactions with the police, and citizens whose attitudes toward the police are unfavorable tend to be less satisfied. This could be a function of selective perception, as citizens tend to interpret what police do in terms of what citizens expect (Brandl et al. 1994). It could be a function of how citizens with different attitudes behave in their contacts with police and how police respond to that behavior (Tyler and Fagan 2008). Both of these dynamics could operate at the same time. Finally, we note that none of the previous research has empirically estimated the extent to which citizens' perceptions are shaped by what police actually do as opposed to other factors that police do not control, including the attitudes and expectations that citizens bring to the encounter.

In this chapter we examine citizens' subjective experiences with the Schenectady and Syracuse police: citizens' satisfaction with how police treated them and how police handled their problem; citizens' judgments about the procedural justice of the police in their contact, and citizens' judgments about the outcomes of their contacts. We also formulate and test a preliminary model of citizens' subjective experience.

SATISFACTION

Citizens' satisfaction is in some respects a bottom line, in police as in other organizations. Private sector businesses are concerned with *customer* satisfaction, which has implications for customer loyalty and long-term profitability. Public sector organizations do not compete in markets, and they are sometimes accused of becoming complacent as a consequence, but "reinvented" agencies have exhibited a concern with customer service that rivals that of private firms. Police organizations have direct contact not only with "customers," that is, people who request services and to whom they are delivered, but also involuntary "clients" to whom police authority is applied. The experiences of the latter are nevertheless important, in respects that parallel customer loyalty, insofar as their experiences may affect their cooperation and compliance with the police, and also in that their experiences are shared with others whose views of the police are influenced by the vicarious experience.

We measured citizens' satisfaction with respect to how citizens were treated by police and, for people who called for service, satisfaction with how their problem was handled. Figure 4 summarizes citizens' satisfaction with how they were treated by the Schenectady and Syracuse police; in the bar labeled for each city, the bar's segments represent the proportion of contacts for which citizens reported the various levels of satisfaction: very satisfied, somewhat satisfied, somewhat dissatisfied, and very dissatisfied.[1] About three-quarters were very or somewhat satisfied with how they were treated (78.9 percent of those with an opinion in Schenectady, and 77.1 percent of those with an opinion in Syracuse); slightly more than one-fifth were very or somewhat dissatisfied. Most people had an opinion about how police treated them, and most of those were at one pole or the other: very—and not merely somewhat—satisfied or dissatisfied.

While the levels of satisfaction in these two cities are quite comparable to one another, we would naturally wonder whether they are comparable to those found in other places for other police departments. Results from other surveys in other jurisdictions suggest that they are. Citizen satisfaction with Chicago police was somewhat lower, as 72.8 percent of respondents in that city were satisfied. Satisfaction levels in the three municipalities surveyed in 2010 for the National Police Research Platform were somewhat higher than those in Schenectady and Syracuse (81.5 percent satisfied), and satisfaction with New York City police about the same (74.4 percent satisfied), though the differences are quite small relative to sampling error.[2]

We also measured citizens' satisfaction with how police handled their problems, though only among those who called for police assistance. A bit more than two-thirds (nearly three-quarters of those with an opinion) were very or somewhat satisfied with how their problem was handled; about one-quarter or fewer were very or somewhat dissatisfied. Again, satisfaction levels across the two sites were much the same: 70.3 percent very or somewhat satisfied in Schenectady, and 68.5 percent satisfied in Syracuse.

Most people, then, were satisfied with the service that they received, though room for improvement can be seen. These percentages are based on 182,034

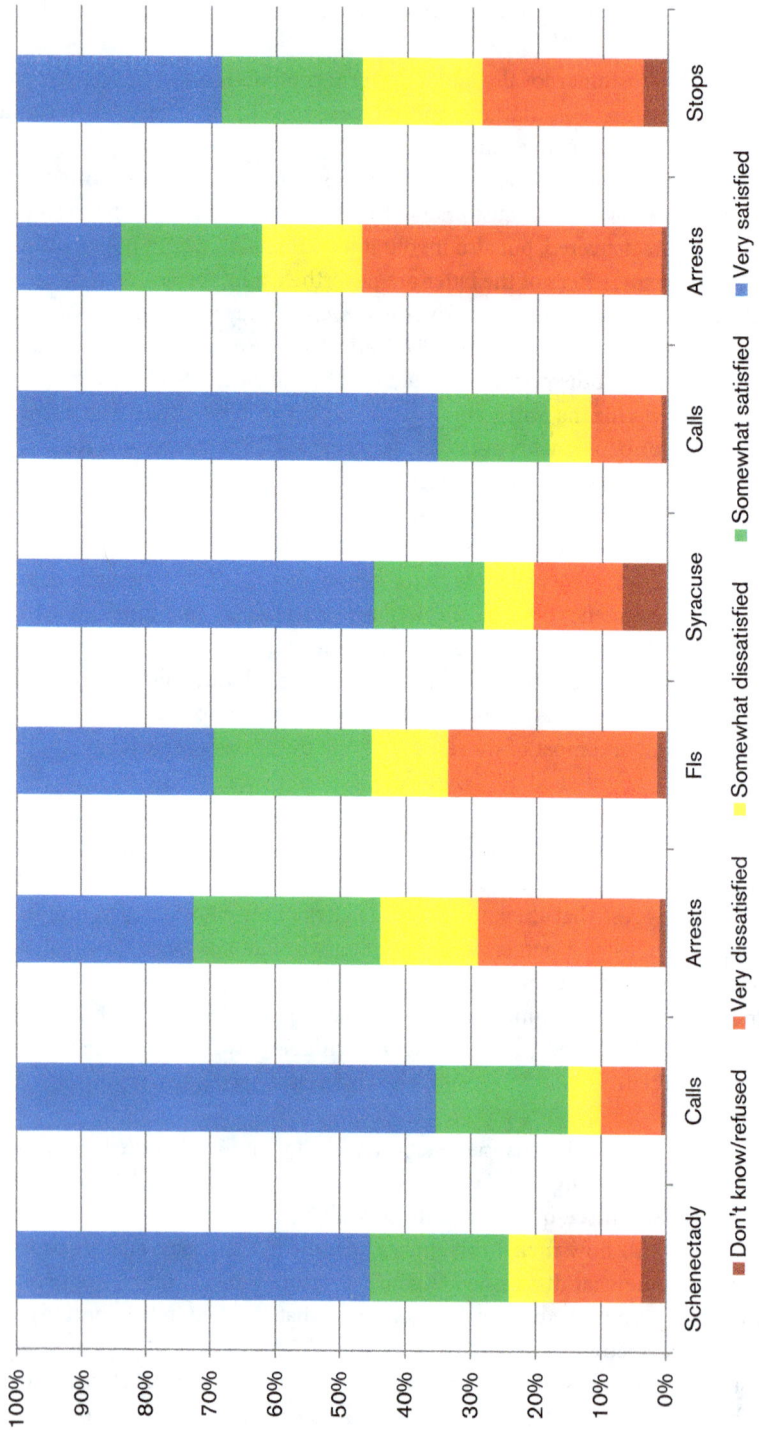

FIGURE 4. Satisfaction with Treatment by Police.

eligible cases: 43,752 in Schenectady and 138,282 in Syracuse. Thus across these eighteen months of surveying, an estimated 8,925 people came away from their contact with Schenectady police dissatisfied with how they were treated, and an estimated 29,316 people were dissatisfied with their treatment by Syracuse police. Of the 33,880 who called for police assistance in Schenectady, an estimated 8,639 were dissatisfied with how their problems were handled; 29,258 of 117,031 who called for service in Syracuse were likewise dissatisfied with the handling of their problems. When we consider the ways that these unsatisfactory experiences could ripple through the population, by way of the relatives, neighbors, and friends of those who have direct contact with the police, the significance of these experiences is multiplied.

Correlates of Satisfaction

Previous research suggests that citizens are more prone to accept police intervention, and to be satisfied with their encounters with police when they or other citizens initiate the contact, compared with occasions on which police initiate the contact on their authority. The latter tend to cast citizens in the role of suspected offenders, their participation in the interaction is not voluntary, and it is the officer who is responsible for their involvement. In the former, even citizens who are—or become—suspected offenders can attribute police intervention to another citizen, whose request serves to legitimize police involvement. We would therefore expect to find lower levels of citizen satisfaction in police-initiated encounters, and that is exactly what we do find in both sites. About half of those whose contacts were initiated by police were satisfied (slightly more than half in Schenectady and less than half in Syracuse); about 80 percent of those whose contacts were citizen-initiated were satisfied. As we found with respect to their treatment by police, citizens tended toward one pole or the other in their judgments about how police handled their problems; about three-quarters of those who were satisfied were very satisfied, and two-thirds of those who were dissatisfied were very dissatisfied.

It surely comes as no surprise that people who were arrested were the least satisfied. Outcomes are not determinative of subjective experience, as we further discuss below, but they are not unimportant. It might come as a surprise, however, that more than one-third of the arrestees (and nearly half in Schenectady) were very or at least somewhat satisfied with their treatment by police, in spite of what is obviously an unfavorable outcome for them; refer to figure 4, in which the bars to the right of each city's overall bar displays the proportions of each subpopulation that were satisfied with their treatment by police. More than half of those who were stopped by police were satisfied with their treatment (with somewhat lower levels of satisfaction among those whose contacts culminated in a ticket, not shown in the figure).

PROCEDURAL JUSTICE

We posed to survey respondents a number of items that have been used in previous surveys to measure judgments about the procedural justice with which people were treated:

- The police treated me with dignity and respect.
- The police considered my views.
- The police tried hard to do the right thing.
- The police made their decision based on facts.
- The police respected my rights.
- The police paid attention to what I had to say.
- The police explained their actions.
- The police were very/somewhat [un]fair.
- The police were very/somewhat [im]polite.

In general, 70 to 80 percent of the citizens report very or somewhat favorable experiences on each component of procedural justice, and the proportions are remarkably similar across the two sites, seldom with differences greater than 2 percentage points. Whether the judgment was favorable or unfavorable, respondents tended toward the extreme response categories—namely with strong agreement or disagreement.[3] For example, among the citizens who had contact with Schenectady police, 82 percent said that police treated them with dignity and respect, and most of those gave police the most favorable rating (i.e., "strongly" agree); among their counterparts in Syracuse, 81 percent reported that police treated them with dignity and respect. About 70 percent in each city said that police considered their views, an indicator of "voice." About three-quarters said that police tried hard to do the right thing, and made their decision based on facts—reflections of the perceived quality of decision-making.

It is also clear that, in Schenectady and Syracuse as in the sites of previous survey research, these aspects of how police are perceived to exercise their authority are strongly associated with citizens' satisfaction with their encounters with the police. In cases where citizens believed that police had acted with procedural fairness, all but small fractions (i.e., 10–15 percent), with few exceptions, were satisfied with how they were treated and how their problems were handled. But when citizens believe that police did not act with procedural fairness, they tend not to be satisfied with either how police treated them or with how police handled their problem, with satisfaction levels ranging from 10 to 30 percent (again, with a few exceptions). We would add that these factors together may account for a large fraction—but not all—of the differences in satisfaction among the contact populations we surveyed—those who call for service, those who are arrested, and those who are stopped. There is good reason to believe that these cross-sectional associations are to a degree spurious, however, insofar as they are produced by the common influence of prior attitudes toward the police, for which we cannot control.

Some previous accounts of procedural justice have distinguished the quality of authorities' decision-making from the quality of their treatment of those on whom they act, while other accounts have drawn distinctions among four dimensions of procedural justice: voice; quality of interpersonal treatment; trustworthy motives; and neutrality. Be all that as it may, empirical analyses of survey items that tap these features of subjective experience tend to find that these various items are so strongly intercorrelated that these conceptually distinguishable dimensions cannot be discriminated from one another in citizens' perceptions, such that the survey responses form just a single scale of procedural justice. That is what we find in the survey data collected in Schenectady and Syracuse: citizens who rated the police favorably on one aspect also tended to rate police favorably on others. This unidimensional structure holds among respondents in each city and in both combined.[4] Either citizens do not differentiate among these dimensions very well, or these different facets of police performance are strongly associated in officers' overt behavior. Thus we form a single index of procedural justice for further analysis that more economically summarizes citizens' subjective experiences; adding the numerical values assigned to the items' response categories,[5] the index ranges from -16 to 16. Figure 5, below, shows a simplified form of the index for tabular presentation, with four categories of equal range. The figure also depicts the mean scale scores for each contact population: calls for service; arrests; and stops or field interviews.

This summary index of procedural justice varies in expected ways across types of contacts. Among the people who called for service, most reported favorable experiences. In Schenectady, the mean score on the procedural justice index (9.9) was in the range that we have characterized as most favorable, and in Syracuse the mean fell just short of the lower bound of that range. The fraction who reported procedurally unfair treatment by police is rather modest, about 14–16 percent in all. We should add, however, that the absolute numbers are fairly large. Based on our sample, and subject to a margin of sampling error, we would estimate that across the eighteen months of the survey, 4,811 people who called for service in Schenectady and 19,544 who called for service in Syracuse assessed their experience with the police as procedurally unfair. More specifically, we would project—again, subject to a margin of sampling error—that among people who called for service in these cities, 24,457 encountered police whom they considered very or somewhat impolite, 32,809 encountered police who did not pay attention to what they had to say, and 40,979 came away from their interactions thinking that police did not consider their views.

People who were arrested had less favorable subjective experiences, as we might expect. The means on the procedural justice index were near the midpoint of

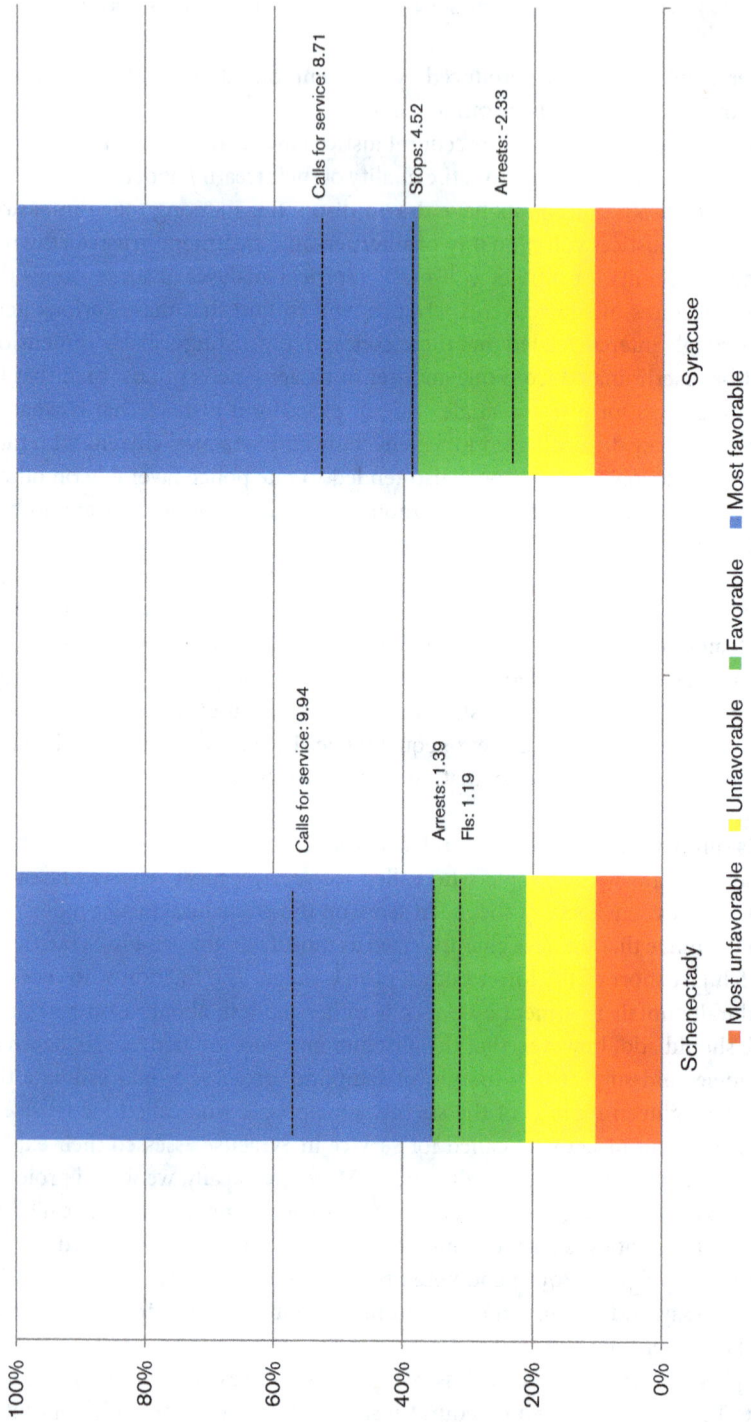

FIGURE 5. Procedural Justice Index.

zero—just above the midpoint in Schenectady, and somewhat below the midpoint in Syracuse. Among those arrested by Schenectady police, 44 percent thought that their treatment was procedurally unfair; in Syracuse, 59 percent of the arrestees rated their treatment as unfair, on balance. Extrapolating to the arrestee populations, we would estimate that 2,988 of the 6,745 people arrested by Schenectady police and 5,197 of 8,779 people arrested by Syracuse police judged their experience with police to have been procedurally unjust. Similar projections for those who were stopped are 1,676 of the 3,127 people stopped in Schenectady and 4,166 of the 12,472 people stopped in Syracuse.

A comparison of these levels of procedural justice to those reported in previous research on police-citizen contacts is complicated by differences in sampling, and particularly the representation of arrestees in this sample. But overall it appears that citizens' subjective experiences in Schenectady and Syracuse are neither distinctly better nor worse than those in other cities that have been the sites of previous research (e.g., Rosenbaum et al. 2011; Skogan 2005, 2006).

SUBJECTIVE OUTCOMES

Citizens' experiences are also colored by their judgments about the outcomes that they receive, even if they are not entirely determined by outcomes. Outcomes take different forms, and the relevant outcomes turn to a large degree on the role that citizens play. Suspected offenders may be taken into custody, issued a ticket, or released without any legal action. Citizens who request police assistance may have their problem resolved entirely by police at the scene, may be referred elsewhere for assistance, or find their situation unaltered by police intervention. Moreover, the quality of any of these outcomes is subject to citizens' interpretations. People who request police assistance will make a judgment about whether police solved their problems. People who are arrested or ticketed will make a judgment about whether that outcome, which is in an objective sense clearly unfavorable for them, was one that they deserved.

People who called for service were, other things being equal, more satisfied with police when they judged that police were able to solve their problems, or at least made an effort to help; two-thirds said that police took care of their problem, while slightly more than three-quarters found police to be very or somewhat helpful. In general, experiences are also shaped by distributive justice—with whether people believe that the outcome was fair or deserved. Overall, nearly two-thirds of the citizens believed that they received the outcome that they deserved. While people who were arrested tended to be less satisfied, more than one-third (35.7 percent) acknowledged that they deserved the unfavorable outcome that they received.

SUBJECTIVE EXPERIENCE ACROSS DEMOGRAPHIC
SUBGROUPS

Subjective experience varies somewhat across demographic subgroups of citizens, that is, by citizens' sex, race and ethnicity, age, educational background, and employment status. The differences that emerge in each site tend to mirror the findings of previous research, and most of the differences are of fairly modest magnitude. Men and women on average report similarly favorable experiences. Citizens' education is related to subjective experience, inasmuch as the college-educated are more positive about their experiences, compared with either of two groups with less education: high school or less; and some college. People who are employed tend to be more positive about their contacts with the police than those who are not employed. Subjective experience is better with age: in general, the older the citizen, the more positive the experience with police. With respect to education, employment, and age, differences on the procedural justice index are greater than those in satisfaction levels.

Whites report more positive experiences than blacks do, though two-thirds or more of both whites and blacks are (very or somewhat) satisfied with their contact, and both groups have mean scores on the procedural justice index that are in the favorable range. Greater disparities can be seen at the extremes, with three-fifths of whites and fewer than half of blacks *very* satisfied with their treatment by police. Hispanics report less favorable experiences that whites do, and in Schenectady, their judgments about procedural justice are even less favorable than those of blacks.

Any of these simple bivariate relationships could be confounded by the other characteristics discussed here or by other factors, such as the nature of the contact with police. Insofar as men, racial and ethnic minorities, the less educated, or the unemployed are overrepresented among those police stop, for example, we would expect differences stemming from these characteristics to be overstated in a bivariate analysis. So no firm conclusions about cause-and-effect relationships are warranted from such bivariate results.

SPATIAL AND TEMPORAL PATTERNS OF SUBJECTIVE
EXPERIENCE

So that we might better understand the patterns of citizens' subjective experiences, we also dissect them in terms of the features of the encounters that we can identify in police records: the patrol beats in which the encounters occurred; the nature of the problems for which citizens called for assistance; the times of day during which the encounters transpired; and citizens' judgments about police response time.

Patrol Beats

We might expect to find variation across patrol beats in citizens' subjective experiences with police due to differences in the character of the problems and the backgrounds of the people, as well as perhaps differences across the officers assigned to those beats. In addition, since attitudes toward the police vary by neighborhood context, and particularly with the social and economic disadvantage of neighborhoods—for example, the levels of poverty and social disorganization (Sampson and Bartusch 1998)—variation across beats could stem at least in part from features of the areas. We measured the concentrated disadvantage of police beats in Schenectady and Syracuse, interpolating as needed from Census tracts to beats, based on a factor derived from the percentage of the population that is black; percentage of children under eighteen living in a female-headed household; percentage of the population between five and seventeen years of age; percentage of households on public assistance; and percentage of the labor force unemployed.

Beat-specific estimates of the percentage satisfied are subject to sampling errors of 8 to 10 percent, in most instances; the procedural justice index scores have a margin of error of 1 to 2 or so. Some of the differences that can be detected among the beats in either city are likely real differences and not sampling artifacts, but in the main, the variations that we find across beats are not large relative to the sampling fluctuation. Procedural justice, at this beat level, correlates moderately with concentrated disadvantage, with coefficients of -0.56 in Schenectady and -0.50 in Syracuse. Satisfaction levels are for the most part more weakly associated with neighborhood disadvantage, with correlations around -0.25 in Syracuse and -0.46 and -0.71 for treatment and problem handling, respectively, in Schenectady.

Calls for Service

We would expect to find variation across types of calls, since different types of calls are more or less susceptible to resolution by police, and more or less contentious or interpersonally charged. For these analytic purposes, we have classified calls based on the code entered into the CAD system by dispatchers, and into generic categories first developed in 1982.[6] These category-specific estimates of satisfaction are subject to sampling errors of 5 to 12 percent, in most instances. Some of the differences that emerge—for example, between traffic problems (such as crashes or disabled vehicles), on one hand, and interpersonal conflicts (disputes) or suspicious circumstances (persons or vehicles) on the other hand—are likely real differences and not sampling artifacts. We can say with a fair degree of statistical confidence that citizens whose calls concern interpersonal conflicts or suspicious circumstances have the least favorable experiences, and those whose calls concern violent crimes or nuisances (e.g., noise or other disturbances; animal problems) are less satisfied than many. That statistical confidence must be tempered by the fact that the codes entered by dispatchers contain some error; a substantial fraction are probably misclassified, through no fault of dispatchers, but rather due to the limitations and inaccuracy of the information available to them (Klinger and Bridges 1997).

Time of Day

We would expect to find variation across time of day, due to differences in the nature of the problems that police confront and the people with whom officers interact at different times of the day, and also perhaps due to differences in the composition of the police and in supervisory practices on different platoons. Thus we define times of the day to correspond to the platoons' working hours, though we caution that these results are based only on a time-of-day breakdown, and not on the assignments of the individual officers involved in the encounters. (Officers assigned to one platoon, say the day platoon, might at times work a shift on another platoon on an overtime basis.)

In general, citizens whose contacts with police transpired during the hours of the first platoon—the "graveyard" shift—reported the least favorable experiences. On daytime platoons, for example, the mean procedural justice index score was nearly or higher than 8.5, while the mean index scores on other platoons were at or under 8, and even as low as 5.59 on the midnight platoon in Syracuse. When we include statistical controls for the type of contact, beat, and call type, however, the differences across times of the day are reduced to negligible magnitude. We infer that differences in performance across the hours of the day are mainly a function of the kinds of problems that police handle and the people with whom they interact.

Response Time

The findings of previous research testify to the role of police response time, relative to citizens' expectations of response time, in shaping citizens' subjective experience. Citizens' expectations are malleable to a degree, so long as call-takers advise them about likely delays and when the arrival of an officer can be anticipated; but such practices by telecommunications personnel are not ubiquitous, and citizens form their own expectations. We asked survey respondents whether police arrived faster than they expected, slower, or as fast as they expected, and their assessments of response time bear the expected relationships to subjective experience. When subjective experience is disaggregated in these terms, we find some wide disparities. Among those who judged the police response to have been faster than expected, 90 percent or more were satisfied with how police treated them, and 85–90 percent were satisfied with how police handled their problems; procedural justice index scores among this group were 11.5–12.5. Citizens who thought that the police response was as fast as expected were somewhat less favorable, but not greatly so.

But among people who assessed the police response as slower than they expected, two-thirds to three-quarters were satisfied with their treatment, a bit more than half were satisfied with how their problems were handled, and procedural justice index scores were under 7 in Schenectady and under 5 in Syracuse.

These associations could be produced in several different ways. It might be that the celerity of the police response colors a citizen's entire experience. It might be that officers who respond more quickly also tend to be more efficacious and procedurally just. Or it might be that citizens who are treated well and whose problems are addressed successfully by police tend to evaluate response time more favorably in retrospect. It might even be that citizens' prior attitudes affect both their assessment of response time and other elements of subjective experience. Not all of these accounts are equally plausible, but neither are they all mutually exclusive.

THE USE OF POLICE AUTHORITY

Procedural justice concerns how and not whether police authority is exercised, but certainly it is plausible that citizens' subjective experiences are shaped by officers' decisions to apply their occupational prerogatives. One form of authority is that to search or frisk. Of the (weighted) sample of those who were reportedly stopped, 72 percent were stopped in a car and 28 percent on foot. Based on citizens' reports through the survey, nearly half (46.8 percent) of those who were stopped were searched or frisked; one-quarter had their vehicle searched. Officers reportedly asked for permission to search or frisk the person in one-fifth of the cases, and asked for permission to search the vehicle in 12 percent. Citizens reportedly consented to a search of their person—whether or not police requested it—in 23 percent, and they consented to a vehicle search in 11 percent. Across both sites, four-fifths of the searches were in connection with arrests, but we have no way to tell from the survey whether the search/frisk preceded or followed the arrest.

Citizens' subjective experience is associated with the exercise of officers' authority to search or frisk: in both sites, satisfaction and subjective procedural justice is greater in police-initiated contacts overall than in the subset in which citizens were searched or frisked. About half of those whose contact was initiated by police were satisfied with how police treated them, and in both cities, their mean procedural justice index score was positive, in the moderately favorable range. Of those who were searched or frisked, less than one-half (as few as one-third in Syracuse) were satisfied with their treatment, and their procedural justice index scores were below zero, in the moderately unfavorable range. Comparable judgments are found among those whose vehicles were searched. Only about one-third (36.4 percent) of the citizens who were searched or frisked considered the search legitimate; nearly one-quarter of the citizens whose vehicles were searched considered the vehicle search legitimate. Not surprisingly, subjective experience was substantially more favorable when citizens were subjected to a search that they considered legitimate.

Arrests vary with respect to:

- the seriousness of the charge(s)—felony, misdemeanor, violation, infraction;
- the basis for the arrest, such as a complaint, a crime in progress, or a warrant; and
- the immediate disposition of the arrest, particularly whether the arrestee is held or released.

Arrests also vary with respect to the legitimacy of the arrest in citizens' eyes. In both Schenectady and Syracuse, subjective experience was most favorable when the charges were the least serious (less than a violation in the New York State penal code), but otherwise the seriousness of the charges was unrelated to citizens' subjective experience. Subjective experience was most favorable when arrests were based on warrants, whose execution is not (normally) a matter over which the officer exercises discretion, and least favorable when arrests were based on crimes in progress. Arrestees are, not surprisingly, more satisfied when they are released rather than incarcerated, though the immediate disposition of the arrest is also associated with procedural justice, index scores of which were much higher among those who received appearance tickets and released than among those who were held in custody. Finally, subjective experience is more favorable when the citizen regards the arrest as legitimate.

A PRELIMINARY MODEL OF SUBJECTIVE EXPERIENCE

The simple bivariate associations reported above are of course potentially confounded by the effects of the other factors on subjective experience, and so we conducted multivariate regression analyses of satisfaction, procedural justice, and subjective outcomes based largely on the model depicted in figure 6. Citizens' satisfaction is posited to be a function of subjective procedural justice, subjective outcomes, citizens' backgrounds (sex, race, ethnicity, age, education, and employment), and the situational context, including the beat in which the encounter transpired, the platoon on which the encounter transpired, the response time relative to citizens' expectations, the call type, and (as applicable) the arrest basis and arrest disposition, the charge seriousness, and a search/frisk of the citizen and/ or search of the citizen's vehicle. Procedural justice and subjective outcomes are a function of citizens' backgrounds and the situational context. We allow as how procedural justice and subjective outcomes could have reciprocal effects, but we believe that it is likely that procedural justice has a greater effect on subjective outcomes than vice versa, and so our equation for subjective outcomes includes procedural justice. We consider this analysis to be preliminary in the sense that it

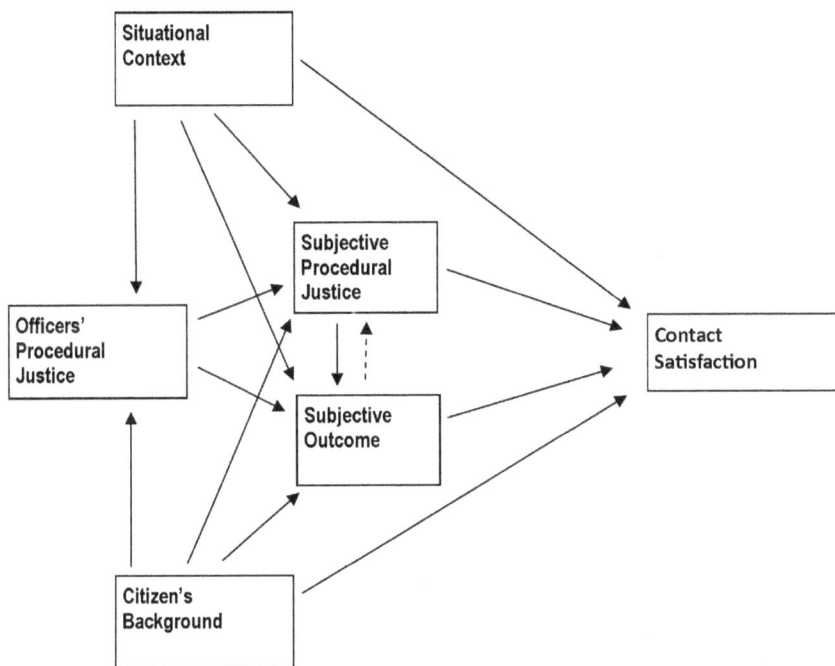

FIGURE 6. A Model of Citizens' Subjective Experience.

includes only the constructs that we can measure with survey data and information in police records; it omits the procedural justice of officers' actions, which we
will add in chapter 7. We note that since we do not have data on citizens' attitudes
toward the police prior to their contact with the police, prior attitudes are omitted
from this model, and this omission is likely to produce inflated estimates of the
effects of procedural justice and subjective outcomes.

Table 1 includes the regression coefficients estimated for this preliminary model
of subjective experience. The baseline contact is an encounter initiated by neither
the police nor the citizen—that is, by a third party. The principal findings from this
set of analyses is the extent to which the elements of subjective experience are in-
terrelated, and the fairly weak explanatory power of either citizens' backgrounds or
the situational context of the contact. Satisfaction is driven mainly by procedural
justice and subjective outcomes. Together these variables account for 74 percent of
the variation in citizens' satisfaction with their treatment by police, and 71 percent
of the variation in citizens' satisfaction with how their problem was handled. Very
little explanatory power is added by citizens' background characteristics or even
characteristics of the situation. A few categories of calls have higher or lower levels
of satisfaction (relative to the omitted category of nuisances), and satisfaction bears

TABLE 1 Regression Analyses of Subjective Experience

	Satisfaction: Treatment	Satisfaction: Handling	Procedural Justice	Outcome Deserved
Constant	2.37*	2.19*	−0.89	−0.05
Call for service	0.17*	—	5.08*	−0.14
Arrest	−0.04	—	−1.48	−0.00
Police-initiated	−0.07	—	2.34*	0.06
Citizen male	−0.02	−0.02	0.81*	−0.01
Citizen black	0.00	0.00	−0.70*	−0.07
Citizen Hispanic	0.01	0.06	0.54	0.08
Citizen's age	0.00	0.00*	0.04*	−0.00**
Citizen's education	0.00	0.02	0.15	−0.06*
Citizen employed	0.01	−0.02	1.10*	0.05
Neighborhood disadvantage	−0.01	−0.04*	−0.03	−0.02
Procedural justice	0.09*	0.05*	—	0.13*
Problem solved	−0.04*	0.24*	—	—
Deserved outcome	0.07*	0.27*	—	—
Perceived response time	−0.02*	0.06*	2.17*	0.10*
Call: violent crime	−0.01	0.08	−0.38	−0.04
Call: nonviolent crime	−0.02	−0.00	1.64*	−0.24*
Call: interpersonal conflict	−0.06	−0.00	−0.19	−0.12
Call: suspicious circumstance	0.01	0.05	−0.78	0.01
Call: traffic	−0.02	0.09**	2.53*	0.13
Call: dependent person	−0.06	0.08	0.77	0.23*
Call: medical	0.01	0.28*	−1.38	0.11
Call: other assistance	0.05	0.11**	0.54	−0.11
Call: other	0.15**	0.16	−4.47*	0.21
Call: unknown	0.07	0.20**	−0.44	−0.01
Arrest: felony	0.09	—	−3.27	−0.10
Arrest: misdemeanor	0.14	—	−3.02	−0.22
Arrest: violation	0.25**	—	−3.10	−0.03
Appearance ticket	−0.01	—	5.93*	0.11
Arrest: released	−0.07	—	4.16*	0.09
Arrest: warrant	−0.03	—	3.55*	−0.06
Arrest: crime in progress	−0.04	—	0.54	−0.13
Search/frisk person	0.09	—	−7.56*	0.22
Search vehicle	−0.06	—	−3.97*	0.03
Citizen consent search/frisk	−0.29*	—	8.31*	0.24
Citizen consent search of vehicle	0.06	—	2.70	0.12
Platoon 2 (day)	0.00	−0.08*	0.54	−0.03
Platoon 3 (evening)	−0.02	−0.08*	0.32	−0.06
Adjusted R^2	0.75	0.72	0.22	0.57

* $p < .05$
** $p < .10$

an independent relationship to response time (our measure of which captures the celerity of the response relative to citizens' expectations, and is therefore itself subjective), but for the most part, citizens' satisfaction is not explained by the objective features of police-citizen encounters that are measured here.

Citizens' judgments about procedural justice are shaped by a number of the factors analyzed here. Citizens who called for service and citizens contacted at police initiative tended to rate procedural justice more positively, compared with those whose contacts with the police were initiated by a third party. Response time affects procedural justice (or both judgments might be affected by another factor, such as prior attitudes). But some of the largest effects stem from the exercise of police authority. Searches detract from citizens' sense of procedural justice: among citizens who were stopped, those who were searched or frisked tended to rate the procedural justice of the police less favorably—3 to 7 points lower.[7] But citizens who consented to a search or frisk were more favorable, though not quite correspondingly so. Among arrestees, those who were either released in the field or issued an appearance ticket were more positive about procedural justice, and those who were arrested on warrants were more positive, relative to those who were held and those who were arrested on complaints, respectively.

Citizens' backgrounds are also related to procedural justice, all else being equal: citizens who were employed judged procedural justice more favorably, as did men; blacks tended to judge procedural justice less favorably. Assessments of procedural justice improved with age.

Subjective outcomes—whether the citizen believed that s/he got the outcome s/he deserved—are largely a function of the perceived procedural justice. With procedural justice omitted from the equation for subjective outcome, citizens' backgrounds and the situational context together account for just 14 percent of the variation in subjective outcomes. The addition of procedural justice to the equation increases the explained variance to 57 percent. Remarkably, the objective features of outcomes—even whether or not the citizen is arrested and held—have fairly weak effects on subjective outcomes. Even with procedural justice excluded from the equation, the effect of arrest is substantively modest and statistically insignificant.

PROCEDURAL JUSTICE AND TRUST

Procedural justice and trust are associated in Schenectady and Syracuse, as in previous survey research. Half of those who judged procedural justice in the most favorable terms exhibit the highest level of trust, while more than half of those who judged procedural justice in the least favorable terms exhibit the lowest level of trust. Nearly half of those with the greatest distrust judged procedural justice in the least favorable terms, and nearly 90 percent of those with high levels of trust assessed procedural justice in very favorable terms. The two (continuous) indices are correlated at 0.64, with virtually identical coefficients in the two sites. (Procedural justice is more weakly related to obligation; the two indices are correlated at 0.36.) This cross-sectional association reflects the reciprocal effects of procedural justice on trust and of trust on procedural justice.

SUMMARY

Using survey items identical to those used in previous survey research, we find in Schenectady and Syracuse patterns of subjective experience similar to those reported in previous research. First, citizens overall reported fairly high levels of satisfaction with their contacts with police, with 70 to 75 percent very or somewhat satisfied with how police treated them and how police handled their problem, and fairly high levels of procedural justice, with 60 to 65 percent in the high range of scores on the procedural justice index and nearly 80 percent on the favorable side of the scale. As we detail in chapter 8, this was a stable pattern throughout the eighteen-month survey period, and so each department had a rather high baseline level of satisfaction and procedural justice at the outset of survey-based measurement of police performance.

Second, procedural justice is comprised of a set of tightly associated features of subjective experience—that is, the components of procedural justice, as they are captured by the various survey items, exhibited the same strong intercorrelation here that they have displayed in previous research. One factor was distilled from a factor analysis, and the additive index formed by the nine survey items has a high level of reliability. The measurement properties of the procedural justice index appear quite satisfactory.

Third, these features of subjective experience—procedural justice and the two forms of citizens' satisfaction—bear strong relationships to one another, as in previous research, and they are also related to other factors that previous research has reported as correlates of subjective experience: whether the contact is police- or citizen-initiated; citizens' race, age, and education; police response time. Not all of these associations are the product of independent influences on subjective experience, however. The effects of citizens' backgrounds and even of situational context on satisfaction and subjective outcomes are apparently mediated entirely by citizens' judgments about procedural justice.

Finally, and notwithstanding the modest differences between the two departments in trust that we reported in chapter 3, levels of subjective experience with police-citizen encounters were very similar across the two sites, and patterns of relationships between procedural justice and other hypothesized correlates were, with only a few exceptions, comparable.

We analyze subjective experience further, and in terms of the actions taken by officers, in chapter 7, and we examine the longitudinal patterns in subjective experience in each site in more detail in chapter 8. But now we turn to a qualitative analysis of citizens' subjective experience, going beyond citizens' responses to closed-end survey items and tapping dissatisfied citizens' own words to describe the reasons for their dissatisfaction.

5
———

Citizens' Dissatisfaction in Their Own Words

Procedural fairness addresses how authority is exercised, and how people experience it, which affects their views about the legitimacy of authorities. We know that when citizens assess their subjective experience in an encounter with the police, their judgment turns to a large degree on process-based criteria about the quality of decision-making and the quality of treatment they received. But we also know that factors beyond the immediate interaction influence citizens' subjective judgments about the immediate interaction.

Our police services survey gave respondents who were reportedly dissatisfied an opportunity to describe the reasons for their dissatisfaction in their own words. Our description of the sources of dissatisfaction with police treatment stem from the responses of 824 respondents (363 of whom called the police for assistance and 300 of whom were arrested). While there are differences in the overall number of individuals in each contact type, nearly all who were dissatisfied (ranging from 90 to 97 percent) went on to attempt to articulate the source of their dissatisfaction, regardless of contact type. Those who called the police for assistance and who reported that they were not satisfied with the way the police handled their problem were likewise given the opportunity to explain the source(s) of their dissatisfaction. Here again, nearly all of those who stated they were dissatisfied attempted to articulate why (677 of 700).

The findings we derived from our analysis of respondents' views provide further evidence that assessments of police are influenced by factors beyond the immediate encounter. These include preconceptions about law enforcement as well as judgments about the interaction that are triggered at (and colored by) the earliest stages of the process, prior to interaction with the police (i.e., impressions of dispatch).

We took an inductive approach to the textual analysis, as respondents' own words led us to the categories we formed. We identified ten main categories of sources of dissatisfaction, several of which include subcategories under the main theme. While we organize the discussion around the individual themes we identified, we also tie them to one or more elements of procedural justice typically discussed in the literature. Our review of studies that have examined procedural justice (most of which are quantitative) suggests that the same or similar items have not consistently been applied to the same subscales that make up elements of procedural justice. Our approach to coding and presenting the textual data enables us to place a theme we identified in one or more of the domains of procedural justice commonly identified in the literature.

In doing so we are able to better understand the factors that influence citizens' reported dissatisfaction. The closed-end items summarized in chapter 4 are corroborated by respondents' own words, indicating that the perceived character of the immediate interaction does shape citizens' satisfaction. In addition, respondents' stated reasons for dissatisfaction shed light and provide further support for the view that citizens' judgments are also shaped by forces outside of the immediate encounter, and often beyond the involved officers' control.

We turn now to a discussion of the categories that emerged when we content-analyzed stated reasons for dissatisfaction without discriminating by the nature of the contact. Any one respondent could cite more than one reason for his/her dissatisfaction.

STATED REASONS FOR DISSATISFACTION

In order of descending frequency, the categories we identified included dissatisfaction stemming from: (1) the outcome of the contact; (2) perceived disrespect/loss of dignity; (3) perceived lack of concern; (4) inability to have one's voice heard; (5) perceived disparity in treatment and/or decision-making; (6) failure to provide information; (7) failure to respond to the scene; (8) failure to respect rights; (9) negative image of the police in general; and (10) external forces.

Outcome

When asked to provide a description of why they were not satisfied with how their problem was handled or how they were treated, many respondents focused on the outcome that followed the interaction. Within this category we identified two primary concerns: the officer was perceived to have not done enough (or even anything) to resolve the problem, or the ultimate resolution was not appropriate. The comments below exemplify those we characterized as typifying the "did nothing," "did not do enough," or "failed to resolve the problem" sentiment. Here, displeasure with the outcome seemed to rest on the perception that the police simply did not expend adequate energy or do enough toward problem resolution.

> *Nothing was done about the situation. Somebody had broke into my car they wrote a report and that was it.*
>
> *They didn't do anything.*
>
> *I had a break-in and I thought a report was going to be made but nothing has happened. They were polite but other than that it was a waste of time.*
>
> *For one, I've been calling the police department with proof of what my neighbor was doing. Neighbor's son and herself have damaged my property and neighbor woman came up in my porch and spit in my friend's face. Police said couldn't do anything, they didn't have proof.*
>
> *Because I am a homeowner and I have someone living in my apartment. The person had someone in the apartment that was destroying the property. They didn't do anything. They won't do anything.*
>
> *I was assaulted by a former employee and they said there was nothing they could do.*
>
> *I called several times about this problem, and still no tickets have been issued yet.*
>
> *Because he tells me that they have to see it with their own eyes if my girlfriend had my baby in the car without the car seat. The officer overreacted when I showed them the car seat as proof that she took the baby without it and he got in my face and said, "I'll arrest you right now."*
>
> *I called the police about my truck being stolen, they done nothing. I have made complaints.*
>
> *They come to the scene and tell me there is nothing they can do about the drug dealers selling drugs in front of my business. I would appreciate if they would at least question the drug dealers. My property has been destroyed because the drug dealers know I'm calling the police, but the police don't do anything about it.*
>
> *They left and left the problem there.*
>
> *Because the problem wasn't handled they just swept it under the rug.*
>
> *It was kids on my roof of my business and they were vandalizing my business. They said they could not do anything about it.*
>
> *The work they did was superficial.*
>
> *Because I feel further action should have happened with the situation, it makes you feel like why bother calling the police.*

For others, the dissatisfaction turned not on police effort but on the outcome itself. Here, citizens felt that the officers' determination of how to handle the problem was incorrect. The quality of the decision was deemed unsatisfactory because its outcome was not the outcome the citizen felt he/she deserved.

> *They told me that they would arrest my neighbor and they didn't.*
>
> *They should've charged someone with assault and no one was charged.*
>
> *What happened was I gave the guy a ride and he stole my wallet out of the truck. It was on the dash. I was already driving away when I noticed it was gone and rushed back. I called the police when I noticed it was gone . . . I confronted him about the wallet and he gave it back. I was still on the phone with the police and they said because I got*

the wallet back they didn't need to do anything. I still wanted him prosecuted through and the police would [not] do anything.

The lady that was supposed to be arrested has not been arrested yet.

Among those who were not satisfied with the outcome, some went on to cite extenuating circumstances or justifications that should, in their opinion, have factored into the officer's decision.

I felt like I could have been given a warning since it was the first time I had been pulled over for that certain offense.

I wasn't trespassing and they wrote me a ticket for it and court was on a Saturday and I didn't know and then they issued a warrant for my arrest.

I went through a stop sign unknowingly. When the police stopped me he ask "just didn't feel like stopping at the stop sign today." I told the officer that I didn't see the sign and he just gave me a ticket.

Just don't understand why they had to put me in the cell when I had turned myself in for a warrant and I was honest enough to go in. I don't think that was necessary for them to do.

Respect/Dignity

We know that satisfaction is shaped by the extent to which officers interact with citizens in a manner that is perceived to be respectful and affords citizens the ability to maintain their dignity. And, indeed, this emerged in the open-ended responses. The respect category we formed captures the views of respondents who indicated that the basis for their dissatisfaction stemmed from their view that the officer(s) belittled them, were rude, and failed to show respect. In their own words:

He was being very rude and arrogant . . .

They treat you like an animal. I'm not used to being looked down on.

They talked to my mother and I and my sister like below human levels, like they didn't care about us. Bad mouthing my mother which was uncalled for . . .

They were very impolite and they threatened me.

They were rude and conceited and aggressive.

They were taking a personal attitude instead of a professional attitude.

When he made me walk home instead of riding with my friend as I walked away he said "You're a fucking liar." I turned around and said "excuse me." He said "don't walk up at me." He said "you're going to jail." The other one was motioning me just to go on like he knew the other guy is a jerk, I turned around to walk away and he said it again and I just kept on walking.

They talked down on me like I am a piece of shit.

The way I was treated. Like I was a second class citizen.

One of them was extremely rude and I told them that . . . One of the officers said he didn't have time to argue and got in his car and left . . . I was really surprised how rude he was.

. . . Very rude and very nasty . . .

*The way they treated me in broad daylight. He walked up to me and said, "I.D."
They were very disrespectful. I know I did the wrong thing and threw a ticket on the
ground. He started asking inappropriate questions, like how many tattoos I have and
how many teeth are missing in my mouth and stuff that had nothing to do with what
I was stopped for.*

*They always say something about my son, they laugh at him, they say, 'oh you got
your son dressed like a little gangster', says the cops . . . I feel like they're treating my
family like crap.*

Expressing Care and Concern

Some citizens' dissatisfaction stemmed from the perception that police did not
care about the problem and so minimized the seriousness of the respondents'
views. When citizens perceive that their own needs and concerns are viewed as
a "waste of time" by either the officer or the department, this is a source of displeasure. Many times, citizens appear to draw this inference from specific actions
or inactions (e.g., not getting out of the police car when speaking to the citizen).
Similarly, department policy around response priority sends a signal about the
worthiness of the problem; regardless of whether or not the citizen is able to disentangle department policy on response priority from an individual officer's decision to take his/her time to the scene, the citizen is left unhappy. Responses in
this category closely overlap with other themes we identify, particularly "respect,"
"outcome," and "voice." However, we captured this category separately because it
serves to explain directly *why* certain decisions or actions leave citizens questioning the motives of officers.

*Showed no compassion. It was a very emotional situation, no human side of their selves
showed, no compassion.*

*They were very unsympathetic with me. I felt they didn't care at all about [my] being
attacked in my own home.*

*They disregarded my state of mind and there were thirteen cop cars all men no
women and I'm telling the officers I'm on parole and on house arrest and that I needed
to go home and asked for a ride. When I was walking home the officer drove by me and
honked the horn trying to be funny.*

*Because they didn't think it was important enough for them to come. They don't like
to be bothered . . .*

*Because obviously they didn't care about my call and they would probably be at
Dunkin' Donuts.*

They acted like I was bothering them bringing it to their attention.

The regard and the seriousness of my situation was disregarded as non-important.

*Didn't care about the incident at all . . . We asked for assistance getting a tow truck
and he told us it was on us to get one, and he was more worried about getting to where
he was at and not concerned about the situation at all.*

*Because they should have gotten out of the car and spoken to her instead of just
watching me fight with her.*

Because the officers didn't get out of the car or anything. They sit and do nothing but play with computers and then do nothing.

Response time can depend on a variety of factors including staffing, call volume, and call type, and it includes both dispatch delays and patrol units' travel time. Citizens' satisfaction with response time is also influenced by their expectations, which may not be realistic. While the department should do what it can to manage citizens' expectations regarding response time, it is surely the case that there will be those whose expectations cannot be met.

The response time, in trying to get an intoxicated person off the road, they never stopped by to even talk to me.

Because they don't care about other people. I mean we got into an accident and they never showed up. It took hours before they showed up. That's not right. He could have gotten hit again.

It took too long for them to arrive, and they were not helpful. It seemed like they did not want to be here and wanted to leave as soon as they could.

They never showed up for like three hours, and actually in that time span I saw some officers hanging out in a parking lot chitchatting.

My car was broken into and the cops didn't show up until 3–4 hours later. Told me I was a low priority.

Voice

Citizens assess the quality of the service provided by police, at least in part, by the opportunity they are given to tell their side of the story, be heard, and to explain themselves. Several examples of respondents' comments along these lines provide richer detail on why this is important to citizens and what they experience when they believe they have been denied the opportunity to express themselves.

Did not care about us or the situation . . . Didn't ask any questions.

Because when they came up to my door after 911 call they wouldn't let me tell my story. The officers told him that he should call CPS, said that they didn't want to hear his side of the story . . .

They don't like, listen to what you're trying to explain to them about what's going on. And they automatically jump to conclusions about how to best handle the situation.

They weren't listening, not paying attention . . .

For some citizens, the issue was not simply that the officer failed to listen or get their input, but more so that they were perceived to have given more opportunity for other involved parties to be heard. The officers' neutrality was in question. Displeasure stems from the belief that the officer gave more weight or input to the other party (in effect "taking the other person's side").

They wouldn't let me explain my side of the story. I never once said anything wrong to them and they ignored me when I asked them questions . . .

The police don't take the time out to listen to both side of the story.

I can't figure out why he would take a pedophile's word over mine, the officer, he blew me off.

After I got hit by the car I bought by my ex-girlfriend they were totally on her side because she called before I called. They did not take a statement from me at all. I haven't signed anything yet. They did take a statement from my ex-girlfriend after the acci-dent . . . They were taking the other person's words over mine which was not right.

The female cop was sort of real cocky. She wasn't listening to my side and I had every right to talk to the people, and she took their side and she wouldn't listen to me.

Listened to the other guy more and took down his statement as gold and mine wasn't.

Disparity

Satisfaction can turn on the extent to which a person believes they are treated fairly and shown neutrality. When the decision an officer makes or the way s/he treats a citizen is believed to be biased, citizens are dissatisfied. Citizens feel they have been treated unfairly when they believe that they are singled out for "special" treatment (e.g., stopped or ticketed) by virtue of personal attributes or perceived stereotypes inferred from such things as the type of neighborhood in which the citizen lives or the sort of car he or she drives. The following comments provide further detail:

. . . Very racist. I don't remember exactly what it was but the officer was being very racial.

Because they seemed racist.

Because they don't treat you like people. I feel because I'm black they treated me differently.

They told me to get out of the ambulance and then he said something I couldn't understand and to me they were trying to be racist or something like that . . .

I feel like I was treated unfairly because I'm a black female.

It was more common for respondents to question the fairness or legitimacy of police actions or the officer's honesty than it was for them directly to suggest racism. Respondents clearly believe they were singled out improperly (a violation of their rights) and received police attention they did not deserve.

Because they treated me differently from the way they were treating other people.

They know I'm on parole, they treat us like scavengers. So they pick on me . . .

I felt like I was being targeted. They didn't have a legitimate reason to stop me . . .

The cops know me from previous times so they target me.

Because I was in a not so nice area on the west side. I was treated like a criminal and I was being called names and treated not so nice.

Failure to Provide Information

Dissatisfaction also turned on the perception that officers failed to provide infor-mation and explain themselves. We know that people want to understand what they are experiencing, and in order to make sense of experiences they tap into available information, filling in missing information (accurately or inaccurately). Responses in this category encompass three related basic issues: (1) a failure to explain decisions and actions; (2) a failure to follow up to provide information after the immediate incident; and (3) the provision of incorrect information.

In some cases, the issue seems to be straightforward displeasure around not knowing what is happening or why decisions are being made as they are. In other cases, there is a deeper underlying issue. A failure to provide information opens the door for citizens to question the trustworthiness of officer motives. Specifically, when officers fail to explain themselves (at all or enough) to citizens' satisfaction, respondents question the basis for the police action or question the veracity of the explanation given for the action.

> *I feel like if you give someone a ticket you should be able to explain why.*
> *My view is when you have rookies they always try and take control. When I asked what my charges were they wouldn't tell me what they were. They need to fight real crime, not little petty crime.*
> *The police gave me a ticket and could not explain why he gave me the ticket . . .*
> *They would not tell me what I was being arrested for they just manhandled me. And didn't explain until after I was in handcuffs. The one officer was somewhat under control. The other was a young punk and was above the law that was full of himself. I would have cooperated if they would have just tell me what was going on.*
> *Very unprofessional, didn't explain anything, I was completely unaware why I was stopped.*
> *They did not inform me of anything.*
> *They did not explain themselves.*
> *I didn't get an idea if anything was going to be done or not.*

Perceived failure to follow up with citizens and provide information after an incident (setting aside the issue of whether follow-up is warranted) is a source of dissatisfaction with the quality of police services. Some citizens simply described the problem as "no follow-up," while others went on to explain how the failure to follow up made them feel. Here, displeasure is rooted in uncertainty about the outcome of an incident. It may be that satisfactory problem resolution need not involve an arrest or lengthy investigation. For some, it may be that managing their expectations (e.g., regarding the likelihood of a follow-up call or a full investigation) could have a positive impact.

> *I don't know what the outcome was.*
> *I reported a situation that was rather dangerous and no one did any follow-up. It was a child that might have been endangered.*
> *I was very unsatisfied because the police officer that took my info didn't follow up with anything . . .*
> *They never called me back. They said a lot of stuff . . .*

I called the police about fireworks being set off in the neighborhood. No way of knowing if things were dealt with . . .

A gun was pulled out on my son. They told me that they would contact me back to let me know what they find out about the incident, and they still have not contacted me back.

He took a report and said that the detective would get back to me, and I still haven't heard nothing.

Failure to Respond to the Scene

Dissatisfaction also stemmed from the belief (correct or incorrect) that no officer ever responded to the citizen's call for assistance.

Because the dispatcher told us to stay in an area where I was in harm's way and then the police didn't show up. I was willing to put myself in danger to help someone, but the police were not.

Because the police never showed.

No one responded at all.

Personal Rights Violated

The belief that one's rights were violated was a source of dissatisfaction. Responses in this category centered on either the use of force, failure to read an individual his/her rights, or perceived improper searches of a person or vehicle. Citizens in this category do not draw favorable inferences about officer motives. The following examples illustrate the use of force issues we characterize under perceived violation of rights. The perceived use of force fell along a continuum from unnecessarily tight handcuffs to displays of physical force including pushing and hitting.

When I was in the back of the car, my handcuffs were on extremely tight and I was losing feeling in my fingers, and I told the officer and when we were at the station he went and started talking to someone else when I felt that he could have loosened them up . . .

When the police pulled up on the scene I was injured and one arm and hand was injured, and I was put in cuffs anyway. When I requested to be handcuffed in the front they would not listen. I didn't know how bad the injury was. I bled all over the police car . . . The guy in the ambulance saw how bad the injury was and he put the cuffs in the front.

They slammed me up against the wall, bent me over the railing and then pulled my arms behind my back and handcuffed me. I am only 5'6" and weigh 115 lbs. They were both over 6 feet . . . They just manhandled me . . .

They stun-gunned me. I fell to the ground. I was not resisting anymore and they almost pulled my arm out of the socket. Two officers jumped on me, and I had cuts and bruises all over me. I weigh 165 and two 240 pound [officers] jump on me. I was not resisting at this point. Pushing my face into the concrete.

For others, a baseless police action was at the root of the perceived rights violation. In this category we capture comments from which we inferred the citizen was getting at the issue of reasonable suspicion:

> *He acted like I was a felon and there was no reason to pull me over. I was behind two 45 degree angles, claiming I ran a light but he was 500 yards behind me. You don't have to lie, and pull me out of my car.*
>
> *Because they took me out of the car and I wasn't the driver. Also because there was no reason to pull us over.*
>
> *I was stopped for supposedly the tint on the window, but when I was on X— street it was dark . . .*
>
> *I wasn't speeding, and they said I was. He was filling his quota.*
>
> *I felt it was an inappropriate stop and the evidence of it being an inappropriate stop there was no ticket or warning.*
>
> *They just arrested me just to make an example for my friends. I deal with this cop all the time.*
>
> *I feel that they lied. He was not speeding when he was stopped at the traffic stop. His foot was not on the accelerator at all . . .*
>
> *I didn't like it when I was pulled over for an improper cause saying my lights didn't work.*

Some believed their rights were violated when the officer allegedly failed to read them their rights:

> *They had no reason to arrest me. They did not read my rights to me until in front of the judge.*
>
> *They never read me my Miranda rights . . .*

Also included in rights violation category were comments highlighting the citizen's belief that s/he had been subjected to an improper search, perhaps because s/he did not give consent or, even with consent, the search seemed unnecessary given the nature of the incident that gave rise to the police contact:

> *They didn't ask to search my person and they had no right to search my person . . .*
>
> *They pulled me over for a loud muffler which I didn't have, and they searched my vehicle and that was kind of unfair to me.*
>
> *There has been a few occasions that I have been stopped because my music is too loud and they have to search the vehicle, I don't think that is right.*
>
> *They wanted to search the vehicle. I said no and they said either they can give me tickets or they can search my vehicle.*

Last, the personal rights category captures references to dissatisfaction driven by a belief that one's privacy was violated. For example, respondents who called the police to report a neighbor for loud music or to report drugs being sold in the area and who perceived that the police violated their right to confidentiality.

When we call them to tell about drugs they go back and tell the people we called them on. I worry we could get killed. They tell the drug people and they know where I live.

Negative Image of the Police Generally

What emerged when some people described their dissatisfaction with how their contacts were handled were negative feelings about law enforcement in general. The responses in this category lend support to research findings that citizens enter an encounter with preconceived views of law enforcement. We can suppose that these are people whose subjective experiences with the police are determined by their prior attitudes toward the police, and whose attitudes are probably not susceptible to change as a result of even superior police performance in an encounter.

Two primary issues emerged within the category of generally negative views of the police. The first centered on police officers and their perceived shortcomings as a group, and the second focus was at the specific department-level and its practices more generally:

I don't really know. I just don't like cops period.

The police have an attitude that they are always right no matter what the situation is. Frankly, I would not call them unless someone was being stabbed or flashing a gun.

Because they are just fucking assholes. They like to push you around and tighten handcuffs too tight. They are just known to be crooked SOBs. They are just as guilty as we are.

Because the police are a bunch of idiots.

Well for one, the majority of the officers cheat you. They have a problem. They judge you.

Police have the right for discretion, but regardless of the situation they need to maintain composure, respect, and self-dignity. If police go around acting like high school bullies then they are ignorant. Police need to be proactive not reactive. If they act like the criminals they apprehend then what makes them so different?

A lot of them like to take their badge and abuse their authority.

I just don't like the way they talk down to you, they disrespect you and are forceful. I don't have a high regard for the police department.

I believe that when [investigating] a break-in or vandalism that they should keep track and then inform you of the crimes in your neighborhood . . . they should take a proactive view.

External Forces

For some respondents dissatisfaction was shaped by other actors in the process. Among those who expressed dissatisfaction with the police, a number specified that their initial contact with dispatch was the cause of their dissatisfaction. Some respondents even went so far as to distinguish that they did not have an issue with the responding officer or actions taken after they placed the call to dispatch. Others appeared to be dissatisfied with how they were treated at the jail subsequent to an arrest:

> *The dispatcher was also very rude to my wife.*
> *The dispatcher . . . he disrespected me by the tone of his voice.*
> *Dispatchers were very indifferent about it, "Well we will try to get over there."*
> *While I was in jail they treated me terribly and it was cold . . .*
> *When I was in the holding tank they put nine girls in one small tank, it's dirty, we complained about something biting us . . .*
> *They would not let me call my family. There were people in the jail that were there for something more serious than what I did and they were treated better than I was.*

SUMMARY

The findings discussed above reveal the salient influences on dissatisfaction, shed light on why they are sources of dissatisfaction (the logic citizens apply when they judge an interaction), and how seemingly discrete factors "feed or fuel" one another. With respect to factors associated with the immediate encounter, respondents' own descriptions of what shaped their dissatisfaction fit within categories previously identified in the literature. Further, respondents' own words substantiate findings from quantitative measures that while outcomes matter, satisfaction is also driven by elements of procedural justice, including voice and the quality of interpersonal treatment, and also the perceived quality of decision-making. We further find that citizens' assessments of how they were treated or how their problem was handled are shaped by influences that are beyond the responding officer's control.

One of the "values added" through letting respondents frame their experience in their own words is that the data provide a level of detail and context not generally available through quantitative data. This level of detail shows the concrete factors citizens attend to when assessing the quality of their interaction with the police and, moreover, shed light on why they matter to citizens. This level of detail can give purchase to police managers and trainers striving to provide specific guidance to law enforcement on how to move toward a more procedurally just model of policing. They also "simplify" and reduce ambiguity around common procedural justice concepts and phrases.

Secondly, the open-ended responses corroborate what quantitative data has found, primarily through surveys of citizens. In addition, they reveal that citizens do not separate the behavior of the officer with whom they interacted from others in the process or from law enforcement more generally. While this is not surprising, it is important to draw out. Feedback from citizens is considered an important piece of assessing police performance at both the department level and the individual officer level. However, survey data offer citizens' perceptions that are only partially shaped by officers' performance. Also, departments seeking to promote more procedurally just policing could, perhaps, achieve more demonstrable success were these values to be inculcated among their own personnel, as well as among actors from other involved agencies including, but not limited to, dispatch and jail staff. Even with that, moving the dial on improvements in citizens' perceptions of the procedural justice with which police perform is a difficult task.

6

Procedural Justice in Police Action

Previous research on citizens' subjective experiences in their encounters with police has relied almost exclusively on surveys of citizens, and so extant evidence leaves as an open question the extent to which citizens' reported perceptions are congruent with what officers actually do (and do not do) in those interactions. In addition to surveying citizens who had contacts with the Schenectady police, we observed a subset of the encounters about which citizens had been interviewed, relying on the video and audio recordings of police-citizen encounters that are routinely made as a matter of police department procedure. In this chapter, we summarize findings about the procedural justice with which Schenectady police were observed to act, based on the judgments of trained independent observers who applied a standardized coding protocol to measure officers' behavior.

We build on previous efforts to measure police behavior, in general, and officers' procedural justice behavior in particular, and so first we review previous research that has informed our study. Then we explain how we conducted the observations and, on that basis, measured procedural justice, and we summarize our observations in those terms. We also present information on other pertinent forms of police behavior, and on features of the context in which officers act—for example, the resistance that citizens offer. Finally, we estimate the parameters of a model of officers' procedural justice in order to better understand the factors in the immediate situation that influence the procedural justice with which officers act.

MEASURING PROCEDURAL JUSTICE BEHAVIOR

Notwithstanding the volume of research on police behavior that has accumulated over the past five-plus decades, we know very little about the procedural justice with which police routinely exercise their authority, except insofar as citizens' subjective experiences are reliable indicators. Official police records do not open a window on these aspects of police performance, of course; offense and arrest reports do not normally include information on officers' adherence to the principles of procedural justice, and even if they did, officers' self-reports of these behaviors would not generally be considered reliable for scientific purposes. But even though a number of studies have provided for direct, in-person observation of police officers at work in its natural setting, with copious data on police-citizen interactions, this research has dwelled much more on the forms of authority that officers exercise and the circumstances under which that authority is applied than on the procedural justice with which authority is wielded.

Furthermore, survey-based measures of citizens' judgments about procedural justice are much better developed than observation-based measures of officers' overt behavior. It is not only that most previous research using systematic social observation of police did not use procedural justice concepts, as such, to guide the construction of observation instruments. Part of the challenge, we surmise, stems from the fact that the distinctions among the four widely accepted elements of procedural justice—voice/participation, quality of interpersonal treatment, trustworthy motives, and neutrality—are not as clearly demarcated in forms of police action as they are in citizens' interpretations of their experiences. Tom Tyler explains, for example, that "authorities can encourage people to view them as trustworthy by explaining their decisions and justifying and accounting for their conduct in ways that make clear their concern about giving attention to people's needs." But the same actions by police—explaining their decisions—from which citizens can infer trustworthy motives also offer transparency, from which citizens can infer neutrality: "evidence of factuality and lack of bias suggest that those procedures are fair" (Tyler 2004, 94).[1] This may help to account for the lack of a consensus among researchers about the translation of officers' actions into procedural justice constructs.

We review this small but important body of empirical evidence here, and as much as possible build on that foundation. All of this research is based on systematic social observation (SSO) of police.[2] Albert Reiss Jr. pioneered the application of SSO to the study of police in 1966, and the instruments that Reiss developed have since been elaborated through several major studies and a number of smaller-scale, more focused studies. SSO has employed in-person observation of patrol officers as they perform their work in its natural setting, with researchers accompanying selected officers during their regular work shifts. SSO is *systematic* in two respects. First, the selection of officers to be observed is subject to probability sampling, so that inferences from analytic results can be drawn with the benefit of known statistical properties. Second, observers are all guided in their observation by a single structured coding protocol that is formulated prior to the field research and directs observers' attention to specified features of police work; thus their observations are captured in the form of standardized measurement categories, which are quantifiable and replicable. This research has been invaluable in describing and understanding how often and under what circumstances officers use various forms of police authority, including their authority to make arrests, use physical force, and stop, detain, and search citizens.

SSO research on the police has been less informative about the procedural justice with which police authority is wielded, but some advances have been made in putting observational data to use in measuring procedural justice, and the development of the observation instruments for coding the Schenectady encounters capitalized on the rich tradition of SSO-based research and on the recent advances with respect to measuring procedural justice. One study examined disrespectful behavior by officers toward citizens, which is of course a form of procedural injustice. Several studies have attended to the role of procedural justice in shaping citizen compliance with police requests, and the measures formed for these studies are instructive. One of those studies not only analyzed the data for which the structured observation instrument provided, but in addition exploited narrative accounts of police-citizen encounters prepared by observers, to derive indicators of procedural justice for which coding instruments did not provide. Finally, one recent study (Jonathan-Zamir et al. 2015) expressly built indicators of procedural justice into its coding instrument.[3]

Disrespect

In 2002, Stephen Mastrofski, Michael Reisig, and John McCluskey analyzed data collected in Indianapolis and St. Petersburg, Florida, for the Project on Policing Neighborhoods (POPN) to describe and account for police disrespect toward citizens. They found that in 9 percent of the observed police-citizen encounters involving suspected offenders, the officer was disrespectful to the citizen. Such disrespect encompassed "name calling, derogatory statements about the citizen or the citizen's family, belittling remarks, slurs, cursing, ignoring the citizen's questions (except in an emergency), using a loud voice or interrupting the citizen (except in an emergency), obscene gestures, or spitting" (Mastrofski et al. 2002, 529–30).[4] They also found that in many of these instances, the officer was responding in kind to disrespect by the citizen; only 4 percent of the respectful citizens were subjected to "unprovoked" disrespect by police. Moreover, this study also found that officers did *not* respond in kind to displays of disrespect by citizens *two-thirds* of the time. Officers in these cities more often than not maintained a professional (i.e., civil) demeanor even in the face of citizens' discourtesy.

This study is very helpful, to be sure, but we should not mistake police disrespect for procedural justice. Disrespect is a form of only procedural injustice, and officers are not respectful by virtue of not being disrespectful; they can be neither disrespectful nor respectful. Police are respectful when, for example, they use titles (e.g., "mister") or other terms of deference (e.g., "sir" or "ma'am") to address citizens. In addition, of course, police performance in their encounters with citizens can be described in terms of other elements of procedural justice: actively listening to citizens, explaining what they are doing and why, expressing concern or sympathy for citizens' situations, and asking citizens for their accounts of events.

Police Requests and Citizen Compliance

Observations in Richmond, Virginia (Mastrofski et al. 1996), in Indianapolis and St. Petersburg, Florida (McCluskey et al. 1999; McCluskey 2003), and in Cincinnati (Dai et al. 2011) have formed the basis for analyses of the procedural justice of police actions as a factor that conditions the success with which police obtain citizens' compliance when they make requests of citizens. The requests made of citizens were for them to leave the scene or leave another person alone, discontinue their disorderly behavior, or discontinue their illegal behavior. All but one of these studies relied on the data coded by observers according to the observation instrument, and so the indicators of procedural justice were somewhat limited. For example, the initial study (Mastrofski et al. 1996) and the replication of that study (McCluskey et al. 1999) both operationalized voice or participation in terms of whether a citizen rather than police initiated the encounter (e.g., by flagging down the officer in the field, or placing a phone call to 911 or another police number); this of course leaves open the extent to which the citizen is given an opportunity by the officer at the scene to tell his/her story. The quality of interpersonal treatment was measured only as police disrespect toward the citizen, and trustworthy motives were captured only as police treating the citizen as having a situational status other than that of suspected offender. Mengyan Dai et al. (2011) did somewhat better—for example, voice reflected officers' reactions to citizens' requests—but was nevertheless limited by the coding instrument, which was not designed with procedural justice in view.

McCluskey (2003) escaped the limitations of the coding instrument by tapping the narratives prepared by observers to capture elements of the interactions that were not coded originally, and he thus was able to construct indicators that individually enjoyed greater face validity and that together better represented the range of actions that comprise procedural justice. So it was that McCluskey took into account displays of respect as well as disrespect, whether officers sought information from citizens and explained their actions. He found that, in encounters in which police requested compliance from citizens, displays of respect were nearly twice as common as disrespect, although neither respect nor disrespect was displayed in about three-quarters of the encounters. Citizens were given "voice"—that is, communicated facts about the situation to police—about one-third of the time, and had their voice terminated—officers "silenced" the citizen—in only 4 percent of the encounters. In 12 percent of the encounters, officers explained to citizens that the circumstances of the case provided them with authority to invoke the law of which they chose not to avail themselves.

Since the focus of these studies was on citizen compliance, and not on procedural justice as such, they analyzed only the subsets of encounters in which officers made a request for citizen self-control, and so of course they shed no light on the procedural justice with which police act more generally. The subsets were not large. McCluskey 2003, for example, focused mainly on 1,022 of the 5,623 citizens who interacted with observed officers across the two research sites. The degree to which officers' behavior in these encounters is representative of their behavior more generally is impossible to say.

We would also note that in the context of this analytical framework, citizens' interpretations of the justice with which police act are presumptively intervening but unmeasured variables, and we infer that associations between police actions, on the one hand, and citizen (non)compliance, on the other hand, reflect an effect of the former on the latter that is mediated by the subjective experience of citizens. Overall, citizens complied in 69 percent of the encounters. But compliance was nearly twice as likely when police showed respect, and about 60 percent as likely when they showed disrespect, as when police displayed neither respect nor disrespect. The termination of voice cut compliance rates by half, while seeking information about the situation doubled compliance.

Procedural Justice

Tal Jonathan-Zamir, Stephen Mastrofski, and Shomron Moyal (2015) recently completed a small-scale observational study whose purpose was to develop and validate an instrument with which the procedural justice of police behavior could be measured. They built, as we did, on the protocols of previous observational studies of the police, but they also added items to the observation form to more completely describe procedural justice. Moreover, they offer a particularly careful and thorough assessment of previous studies—including those discussed above—to advance the discussion about how to operationalize procedural justice in terms of data on police behavior. We should examine their study very closely, for it is the only previous effort to translate structured observations into a full complement of measures of procedural justice.[5]

Their study provided for observations of the pseudonymous "Everdene" police, who serve a small suburban city. Four trained observers accompanied twelve patrol officers on thirty-five work shifts, capturing information on 233 police-citizen encounters with 319 citizens.[6] From these data they construct a measure of behavior in each of the four domains of procedural justice and, in addition, combine those measures to form an overall index of procedural justice.

Jonathan-Zamir and her colleagues argue for the use of formative measures of procedural justice in action. They maintain that although survey items are properly treated as various reflections of an underlying perceptual construct when citizens' subjective experiences are measured, such that the items can be expected to exhibit strong associations, officers' behaviors are not the manifestations or products of an underlying construct. Instead, they contend, officers' behaviors *form* a measure of procedural justice: "because measures of procedural justice are not expected to develop from a single latent variable, and the various procedurally just behaviors are viewed as tapping different facets of the construct, they are not expected to be intercorrelated and are not interchangeable" (Jonathan-Zamir et al. 2015, 852). We agree with this assessment, and we would add as further justification the situationally contingent nature of police action, as a consequence of which we might expect to observe in different situations different manifestations of neutrality or trustworthy motives or quality of treatment.

For each of the four procedural justice domains, Jonathan-Zamir et al. formed a five- or six-point scale. Two of the scales (neutrality and trustworthy motives) were each a simple sum of binary individual actions, such as explaining why police became involved and explaining the choice of resolutions. One (participation) was in effect a weighted sum, weighting officer's requests for information and citizens' provision of information by the attentiveness with which police listened. And one scale (dignity) captured degrees of respect and disrespect, respectively, based on the duration or frequency of such behaviors, though disrespect was so infrequent that such distinctions were needed only for respect. The four scales were combined to form a single (unweighted) index of procedural justice.

They found a fairly high level of participation, with 43 percent of the police-citizen interactions at the high end of the scale (4), and an additional 25 percent nearly so high (3). This would imply that officers asked for information and/or citizens provided information, with officers listening passively or actively. Neutrality exhibited the opposite pattern, with 38 percent of the interactions in the "very low" category and an additional 43 percent in the "low" category. Dignity was more or less normally distributed, with only 5 percent of the interactions at the low (disrespectful) end and 6 percent at the high end (at which the officer showed "dominant" respect). Finally, the distribution of trustworthy motives resembled that of the neutrality scale, with nearly half of the interactions at the low end. The four scales were all positively intercorrelated, though fairly modestly, with correlations ranging from .10 to .30. Each was correlated with the overall index, with correlations ranging from .59 to .70.

Jonathan-Zamir et al. (2015) estimated the correlations of the index of procedural justice and each of its subscales with the "citizens' behavioral manifestations of satisfaction with the police," as judged by the observers. In this way they were able to assess the criterion-related validity of their measure of procedural justice. Their observers were able to assess citizen satisfaction in about half of the cases, and among those, they found a substantial association between satisfaction and procedural justice overall. They also found statistically significant associations between satisfaction and three of the four subscales.

SCHENECTADY OBSERVATIONS

The Schenectady Police Department's use of in-car cameras afforded us an opportunity to collect observational data on police-citizen encounters, and in that way to not rely exclusively on survey data to describe officers' procedural justice. At the conclusion of the police services survey, we sampled from among incidents about which we had completed an interview with the citizen, and we requested copies of the video/audio files, with which the Schenectady Police Department obliged us.

To our knowledge only one previous effort has been made to conduct "armchair" observation of police by using video recordings of police-citizen encounters, rather than conducting in-person observation, to collect systematic information about police actions for analytical purposes (Dixon et al. 2008). That study focused on traffic stops only, and in addition, it was designed to examine the influences of citizen and police officer race on communication patterns, and particularly "communication accommodation"; it did not extend to the wide range of citizen and officer behaviors on which SSO of police has dwelled, or on procedural justice as such. However, this study affirmed the feasibility of coding police-citizen interactions from video and audio recordings, and the theoretical constructs and operational measures that it formulated were useful additions to extant SSO protocols in capturing how police authority is exercised.

Thus we drew from both lines of research to form observation instruments that are rooted in previous inquiry but also suited to the measurement of procedural justice. Like previous SSO research, we provided for information on the encounter as a whole, for example, the type of location in which the interaction transpired, and the nature of the problem that was the focus of attention. The instruments departed in some respects from previous SSO instruments, however, insofar as we were particularly interested in the officers' behavior toward one citizen in each encounter—the citizen who was the respondent to our survey, and on whose subjective experience we wanted to estimate the effects of officers' behavior. Hence we designated as the "primary citizen" the citizen whose name appeared in the police record, and whom we interviewed after his/her contact with the police, and we instructed observers to try in each incident to identify the primary citizen and code items accordingly. For each incident, observers

TABLE 2 Observation Instruments

Encounter-level
primary citizen x primary officer
primary citizen x other officer(s)
other citizen(s) x primary officer
other citizen(s) x other officer(s)

were provided with some identifying information to facilitate this task: the primary citizen's name, race, and sex, as well as the nature of the contact (arrest, call, field interview). Citizens other than the primary citizen were treated as a single group for coding purposes. The "primary officer" was the officer who was assigned to the patrol unit that was dispatched to a call, or whose name appeared on the arrest report or field interview card, and whose microphone recording was included with the video; this was the officer who is analogous to the officer to whom an observer would be assigned in the context of an in-person SSO study. Other officers, like other citizens, were treated as a single group. Items concerning the primary citizen's dyadic interaction with the primary officer comprised one instrument, and items concerning the primary citizen's interaction with other officers (if any) at the scene comprised a separate instrument. (See table 2.) Other citizens' interactions with the primary and other officers, respectively, were captured in less detail on separate instruments. Thus we can describe the interaction of the primary citizen with the primary officer and with other officers; we can likewise describe the interaction of other citizens with the primary officer and with other officers.

Based predominantly on the observation instruments used for the Project on Policing Neighborhoods (POPN) in 1996–97, the instruments captured information on requests that citizens made of officers and how police responded to those requests, requests or commands by officers and how citizens responded to those requests or commands, officers' use of police authority (e.g., searching or frisking the citizen, the use of physical force, arrests, citations), and forms of disrespect by citizens and/or officers. In addition, observers were prompted to make summary characterizations of selected features of the interaction, such as how much patience officers exhibited, how well officers listened to citizens, and how much consideration the officers showed for the citizens' point of view.

Each sampled incident was assigned to two observers,[7] who independently watched and listened to the recorded incident, took notes, and worked through the computer-guided data entry process, clicking on selected response options or, in some instances, entering information in a free-field format.[8] An observer could watch all or a portion of any incident multiple times as needed.

Sampling

The major SSO studies of the police have sampled patrol units, to which observers are assigned for the duration of an entire work shift, such that the observed police-citizen encounters are those in which the officer assigned to that unit became involved. Sampling has been structured spatially, by police beats, and temporally, by work shifts or tours of duty; normally, observations are concentrated somewhat on the more active beats, in which police-citizen interactions are more numerous. Some more focused observational studies have instead sampled first among officers and then, for sampled officers, among their work shifts, again observing the encounters in which those officers became involved.

Our sample was based on the sample of incidents about which we surveyed citizens, and so it was structured neither spatially nor temporally. We observed encounters that took place in any of Schenectady's eight patrol zones and on any of the three platoons. We observed many individual officers multiple times—eighteen officers at least ten times each, and one in as many as twenty-one incidents, as the primary officer. Our sample was not confined to the more active parts of the city. However, among the 1,800 incidents about which citizens were surveyed, we oversampled arrests and field interviews, on the assumption that these are the kinds of incidents in which procedural justice may be less readily practiced, and to ensure as much as possible that the subsamples would support separate analysis.[9]

Armchair observers need not negotiate access, as observers sometimes must do in the field when officers resist having an observer assigned to them, but officers can in effect resist observation by failing to activate the recording equipment, which we consider below in conjunction with our discussion of sample attrition. We also note here that not all of the incidents were recorded, because some of them involved foot or bicycle officers, and some transpired at the station desk. In addition, some incidents that involved the dispatch of a patrol unit did not involve a face-to-face interaction between the primary citizen, who called for assistance, and the primary officer; given our interest in the primary citizen's subjective experience, we instructed observers not to code incidents in which the officer had no interaction with the primary citizen.

Our observers coded 539 encounters from among those that we sampled and obtained recordings of from the Schenectady police. We assessed the similarities and differences among the population of incidents we sampled for observation, the sample, the set of incidents for which we obtained recordings, and the set of incidents that were coded by both observers. Few noteworthy differences appeared among comparisons including the nature of the contact (call for service, arrest, or field interview), the survey wave, the patrol area in which the incident transpired, the time of day, the nature of the incident about which callers contacted the police (as recorded in CAD records by dispatchers), features of the arrests, and the recorded race and sex of those who were arrested and field interviewed. The principal source of disparities between the population and the sample of incidents, on the one hand, and the incidents for which we obtained recordings and successfully coded, on the other hand, stemmed from the fact that ninety-nine of the sampled arrests took place at the police station when the arrestees turned themselves in on an arrest or bench warrant. These incidents were not captured on in-car cameras, of course, and so the incidents that we observed, compared to the incidents that we sampled, underrepresent arrests. In addition, and as a consequence, the observed incidents underrepresent incidents that took place in patrol area 1 (in which police headquarters are located), felony-level arrests, and arrests based on warrants. In all other respects, the observed incidents bear a strong resemblance to the population. Among the recordings that we received, the sources of case attrition were (1) a mismatched event (i.e., the event captured in the recording was not the sampled incident—eight cases);[10] (2) the poor quality of the recording, especially the audio (seventy-five cases); (3) no detectable interaction between police and a citizen (twenty-one cases); and (4) other idiosyncratic problems (five cases).

Armchair Observation: Advantages and Disadvantages

As it has been conducted since 1966, SSO of the police places an observer in the field to see and hear directly what transpires in a police-citizen encounter. The observer accompanies the officer to whom s/he is assigned as a part of the sampling plan, and is normally able to see and hear what that officer says and does, as well as what citizens say and do to the officer. At times, when multiple officers and citizens are involved, an observer may not see or hear what other officers say or do to other citizens, whose interactions may take place in other rooms of a house, say, or in other nearby locations. But in-person observation generally affords the observer a good opportunity to hear what is said around the observed officer and also to take note of nonverbal behavior as well. The limitations stem mainly from, first, the inherent ambiguity of some elements of a police-citizen encounter, as observers map the specific words and actions of the participants into analytic categories, and second, the capacity of the observer to later recall and reconstruct the encounter, for which no replay is available, of course. The notes that observers take in the field are sparing, and the task of reconstructing the exchanges between officer and citizen— or among multiple officers and/or multiple citizens—across a number of encounters observed during a full patrol shift is hard work. Since it is rare for researchers to be able to compare the observational data to other kinds of information about the same encounters, we lack evidence about the success with which observers capture the interactions in their entirety.[11] And since the logistics (and costs) of in-person observation prohibit the placement of two observers in the same patrol unit, there are no (published) estimates of the inter-coder reliability of observational data.

"Armchair" observation that relies of recorded video and audio has advantages and disadvantages relative to in-person observation. One advantage is that it is

surely much less onerous a burden for the department than in-person observation. The department's burden is borne mainly by the personnel whose duty it is
to provide the recordings of sampled incidents; it was a time-consuming task in
Schenectady to locate the specified incidents among the voluminous recordings,
finding the right date and unit and then finding the right incident.

Another advantage concerns reactivity: the observer's presence cannot alter the
behavior of the officer if the observer is not present. Inasmuch as Schenectady's
police department has provided for in-car cameras since 2003, and recording is
done *routinely* as a matter of policy and not on an episodic basis, we believe that
officers have become accustomed to the fact that their interactions with citizens
are captured on video and audio.[12] The recordings are seldom reviewed absent ex-
ceptional circumstances, for example, to resolve a citizen complaint, and so with
few exceptions, officers' recorded behavior is not subject to adverse consequences
for them.[13] The SPD command staff was aware that we would review a sample of
incidents about which citizens had been surveyed, but so far as we can tell, patrol
officers were unaware of (or at least unconcerned about) our plans for such observation; no one mentioned (or complained about) it in our interviews with patrol
officers and supervisors.

Still another advantage is that the observer is not limited to the real-time event:
the dynamics of the police-citizen interaction can be replayed as many times as
necessary. Furthermore, resources permitting, multiple observers can code the
encounter according to the same observation protocol, without having to navigate
the logistical challenges of deploying two in-field observers to a sampled patrol
unit. Consequently, the observers' respective judgments can be compared to one
another, and their judgments on any one item can be combined, such that what
one observer may miss the other observer may capture.

The disadvantages of armchair observation stem mainly from the limited field
of vision that the camera affords, and this limitation is more pronounced for the
dash-mounted cameras Schenectady provides than it would be for the body-worn
cameras with which many departments are now outfitting their officers. For urban
police, many of whose encounters with citizens—other than traffic stops—do not
transpire in front of the patrol vehicle, much of what officers do is off-camera.
In Schenectady, the audio was generally quite good (impaired mainly on windy
days), but insofar as police-citizen interaction occurred outside the range of the
camera, observers were limited to what they could hear, and so they missed nonverbal behavior. We assessed our observers' capacity to detect what transpires in
the sampled police-citizen encounters in several ways:

· whether the primary citizen and/or the primary officer were visible and,
   whether or not they were visible, could be identified;
· the observer's estimate of how much of the audio portion of the recording was
   unintelligible;

- the frequency with which observers coded items as "not determinable"; and
- how much confidence the observer felt in his/her coding.

The methodological appendix includes details of these assessments. As we discuss there, the audio proved to be of greater value than the video, and for the purposes of measuring procedural justice, which is mostly verbal behavior, we believe that armchair observation was up to the task. We also evaluated the reliability of the measures of procedural justice based on these data, which we describe below.

PROCEDURAL JUSTICE IN SCHENECTADY POLICE ACTION

We observed 539 police-citizen encounters drawn from among the 1,800 about which citizens had been interviewed. Arrests and field interviews are somewhat overrepresented in our observed encounters, based on the premise that such incidents represent, on average, somewhat more challenging dynamics for officers to manage; overall results are weighted to represent the entire population of contacts during this time period.

Using the four domains of procedural justice as a guide to actions that signify procedural (in)justice, we will first describe the actions of Schenectady police in each of four domains, but we thereupon combine those domains for analytical purposes, as Jonathan-Zamir et al. (2015) did. However, unlike Jonathan-Zamir and her colleagues, we distinguish behaviors that are procedurally just from behaviors that are procedurally unjust, forming two distinct measures of the procedural justice with which police act. Officers may take only procedurally just actions in their interactions with citizens, only procedurally unjust actions, or both (or neither) just and unjust actions, in any of the domains of procedural justice. Moreover, there is good reason to suspect that procedurally unjust actions have a greater (negative) effect on citizens' subjective experience than procedurally just actions have a (positive) effect, as we discussed in chapter 3. So we believe that it is useful to separate the just and the unjust and specify two behavioral constructs: procedurally just action, and procedurally unjust action.

We exclude from measures of procedurally (un)just action those forms of behavior whose theoretical status is ambiguous, such as the overt use of police authority—conducting searches or frisks, using physical force, or even issuing commands. We agree with Jonathan-Zamir et al., who "regard force as an inappropriate indicator of dignity or any other procedural justice element. Force is an action that may aggravate or provoke a citizen, but the character of the social status that it signals to those at the scene is not inherently clear simply by knowing that some degree of coercion was applied" (2015, 856). Commands can be issued rudely or disrespectfully, of course, but the rudeness or disrespect is captured in the measures of the quality of treatment.[14] We do not exclude any of these actions from our analysis, hence we take them up below.

We also exclude from measures of procedural justice features of the context of police-citizen interactions, though we describe and include contextual characteristics that may be relevant in our analysis. For example, the evidence of criminal wrongdoing, especially when it is sufficient to constitute probable cause for arrest, may be important in shaping a citizen's interpretation of police actions, but is not intrinsic to the action. Another feature of context is how the encounter begins: at the initiative of police, acting on their own authority, or at the behest of a citizen who requested police assistance—a difference that turns partly on the actions of a party other than the police.

Below we examine the frequency with which actions are taken in each of the domains of procedural justice, forming in each of the four domains a subscale of just action and a subscale of unjust action by summing across the coded actions in that domain. Then we form indices of procedural justice and procedural injustice by summing the respective subscale scores, and describe the distributions of scores along each construct. We focus mainly though not exclusively on the "primary citizen"—the citizen whom we interviewed, and whose subjective experiences we will examine in the next chapter. Furthermore, we examine only the 411 cases in which both observers were able to identify the primary citizen, and so we exclude 59 cases in which only one of the two observers was able to identify the primary citizen, and an additional 63 cases in which neither observer was able to identify the primary citizen.[15]

The primary citizen might interact only with the primary officer, that is, the officer whose unit was dispatched to a call for service, or whose name appeared on an arrest report or field interview card; the primary officer was in most instances the lead officer. We form a procedural justice scale and a procedural injustice scale for the actions of the primary officer toward the primary citizen in each encounter, averaging the two coders' scores. Other officers were present and interacted with the primary citizen in 90 of the 411 encounters, and, as we show below, these officers tended to serve as backup, but primary citizens could also interact with officers other than the primary officer. Thus we also form corresponding scales of procedural justice and procedural injustice for other officers' actions toward the primary citizen. Finally, inasmuch as officers' actions toward other citizens in the encounter could influence the subjective experience of the primary citizen, we also construct scales for police actions toward other citizens.

We formed the subscales and the scales for each of the two observers for each encounter, and then formed subscales and scales for the encounter by averaging the individual observers' scores. We assessed the level of inter-coder agreement in terms of the interclass correlations, which we report below in connection with each of the scales.[16] When agreement was less than perfect, the averaged scale scores are not integers.

Voice/Participation

Citizens want to have an opportunity to explain themselves and their circumstances to police—to tell their side of the story, and to participate in decision-making even if they cannot determine the outcome. Hence police are procedurally just when officers ask citizens to tell them what happened, to explain their actions, or to explain what they want the police to do. Police are procedurally just also when they listen to citizens and pay attention to them, and when they indicate that they are considering the citizen's views. Observers characterized overall how well the officer listened to the citizen on a scale from 0 to 5, and they also characterized the extent to which the officer considered the citizen's view on a similar scale; scores of 4 and 5 on those scales were treated as procedurally just.

Furthermore, when officers make requests of citizens, or offer suggestions, or even try to persuade or negotiate, they are allowing citizens to make choices and in this way to participate in the decision-making, so we treat such actions by police as forms of procedurally just treatment. For example, an officer might ask a citizen to stop his/her disorderly or illegal behavior. Or an officer might try to persuade a citizen to leave the scene. (In previous research that was concerned with citizens' compliance with police requests, such requests were a defining feature of the encounters and so could not be treated as a component of procedural justice.)

When these actions are combined to form a scale, the scores range from 0 to 8, and the intraclass correlation of the scale is 0.54. The actions that contribute to these scores especially include officers paying attention to what citizens had to say, asking citizens what happened, listening (at least 4 on a 0–5 listening scale), and considering citizens' views (4–5 on a 0–5 scale).[17] Across all of the contacts, the mean score is 3.43, as shown in table 3, with somewhat higher mean scores in encounters in which the citizen had called for police assistance and somewhat lower scores in encounters in which the citizen had been stopped or arrested. Even so, the scores for the different types of contact are not widely disparate.

By contrast, police are procedurally unjust when the officer does not pay attention to what the citizen had to say, does not listen, and does not consider the citizen's views. We also treat as procedurally unjust instances in which the officer interrupted the citizen. When these actions are combined to form a scale, the scores range from 0 to 4, and the intraclass correlation of the scale is 0.64. The most frequently observed actions were the officers interrupting citizens, not considering the citizens' views (below 2 on a 0–5 considered views scale), and not paying attention to what citizens had to say. Officers were seldom observed to act in any of these ways, however, though it was more common among encounters in which the citizen was arrested than in either calls for service or stops, as shown in table 3.

TABLE 3 Scales of Procedural Justice and Procedural Injustice in Action

	Range	All contacts*	Calls	Arrests	FIs
Just: voice	0–8	3.43 (1.42)	3.64 (1.38)	2.76 (1.39)	2.69 (1.24)
Just: quality of treatment	0–3.5	0.56 (0.72)	0.55 (0.68)	0.57 (0.82)	0.57 (0.83)
Just: neutrality	0–3.5	0.92 (0.76)	0.85 (0.70)	1.29 (0.91)	0.89 (0.85)
Just: trustworthy motives	0–6.5	2.08 (1.20)	2.25 (1.18)	1.69 (1.19)	1.04 (0.72)
Procedurally just action	0–15	6.99 (2.96)	7.30 (2.81)	6.30 (3.30)	5.19 (2.88)
Unjust: voice	0–4	0.33 (0.56)	0.26 (0.48)	0.67 (0.79)	0.26 (0.41)
Unjust: quality of treatment	0–6.5	0.23 (0.73)	0.15 (0.54)	0.51 (1.10)	0.50 (1.20)
Unjust: neutrality	0–1	0.03 (0.14)	0.02 (0.12)	0.06 (0.19)	0.07 (0.18)
Unjust: trustworthy motives	0–2.5	0.09 (0.29)	0.07 (0.28)	0.17 (0.35)	0.01 (0.08)
Procedurally unjust action	0–12.5	0.68 (1.35)	0.51 (1.09)	1.41 (2.06)	0.85 (1.48)

*Weighted results

Quality of Treatment

Citizens want to be treated with dignity and respect, and such treatment can take several forms. If officers greet citizens at the outset of their encounter, they can do so in ways that signal respect—for example, by using generically formal terms, such as "sir" or "ma'am," or if the officer knows the citizen's name, addressing him or her as Mr. or Ms. ---, or using the citizen's first name. Similar considerations apply when the officer and citizen part ways at the end of the encounter. Furthermore, officers can through a friendly "manner" signal that the status disparity that stems from police authority need not be observed. We also consider as respectful treatment officers' use of polite terms, such as "please" and "thank you."

When these actions are combined to form a scale, the scores range from 0 to 3.5, and the intraclass correlation of the scale is 0.61. The most frequent such action is use of polite terms (e.g., "please" and "thank you"), followed by a friendly manner. We seldom observed these actions in any type of police-citizen contact, though, and the scores on this scale are very similar across types of contacts, as shown in table 3, above.

Officers' treatment of citizens is procedurally unjust when officers greet or leave citizens in an insulting way (with name-calling abuse, for example), when officers' "manner" is hostile, when the officer makes derogatory remarks or is otherwise disrespectful to the citizen, and when officers act in a patronizing, sarcastic, or angry way toward citizens. When these actions are combined to form a scale, the scores range from 0 to 6.5, and the intraclass correlation of the scale is 0.80.

Neutrality

Citizens believe that decisions are made fairly when they see evidence that decision-makers have considered objective facts and are evenhanded in their treatment of the parties involved. That does not imply slavish equality of treatment, as Jonathan-Zamir et al. (2015) point out. One way that citizens can infer that police are basing their judgments on facts, and not on prejudices or biases, is in hearing officers explain their actions and decisions.[18] This can take several forms. An officer might explain to the citizen how the officer's resolution is based on legal standards or requirements, or how it is that the officer is giving the citizen a "break," with less punitive action than the law allows. Or the officer could explain, in response to a specific citizen request, why the officer cannot or will not oblige the request. Or an officer might explain to the citizen why s/he is conducting a search or frisk. Lest we fail to take account of the myriad other explanations that an officer might provide to a citizen, observers also characterized more generally how well the officer explained the reasons for the officer's decisions or actions to the citizen, on a scale from 0 to 5; scores of 4 and 5 were treated as procedurally just.[19] When these actions are combined to form a scale, the scores range from 0 to 3.5, and the intraclass correlation of the scale is 0.59. The scores on this scale are fairly low overall, but they are higher in arrests and stops than in calls for service, as shown in table 3 above. Indeed, an explanation of some kind(s) is modal in arrests and stops.

We rely on observers' characterizations of how well the officer explained his/her reasons for decisions and actions to the citizen, treating as procedurally *unjust* a score of 0 or 1 on the 0–5 continuum. Such low scores were infrequent. In thirty-four encounters one but not both of the coders placed the officer's actions in this respect at the low end of the continuum, and in five encounters both coders agreed on such a characterization. It was somewhat more common in arrests. The measure that we form, then, ranges only from 0 to 1, and the intraclass correlation of the scale is 0.38.

Trustworthy Motives

Citizens perceive that decisions are fair when they believe that authorities care about their well-being and are taking their needs into account. Police can exhibit such care and concern in several ways. An officer can comfort a citizen, promise to give the citizen's situation special attention, tell or ask the citizen to call if the citizen's problem recurs, or—at the officer's initiative—provide information or physical assistance, or contact an agency for assistance on the citizen's behalf. An officer also exhibits care and concern in fulfilling (or promising to fulfill) citizen's requests, for example, to file a report, to provide information, or to have another citizen leave the scene. We also treat patience as an outward sign of such concern; observers characterized officers' impatience with the citizen on a scale of 0 to 5, and we treat scores of 0 and 1 as procedurally just patience. When these actions are combined to form a scale, the scores range from 0 to 6.5, and the intraclass correlation of the scale is 0.73. Some such action was nearly ubiquitous in calls for service and modal in arrests and stops, as shown in table 3.

When officers ignore citizens' requests, or refuse to fulfill them without expla-nation, they do not exhibit trustworthy motives, leaving citizens to draw unfavor-able inferences about the fairness of police decisions. When an officer tells a citizen not to call police if the problem recurs in the future, s/he may be taken to imply a disregard for the citizen's concerns, as the officer does when s/he is impatient. When these actions are combined to form a scale, the scores range from 0 to 2.5, and the intraclass correlation of the scale is 0.58. These actions were seldom ob-served in any of the types of contacts, as shown in table 3.

Scales of Procedural Justice and Injustice in Action

Like Jonathan-Zamir et al. (2015), we are persuaded that formative measures of procedural (in)justice are more compatible with the situationally contingent na-ture of police work, in the context of which only some but not other types of ac-tions fit the circumstances. In order to capture the levels of procedural justice and procedural injustice that officers' actions represent, respectively, we map the coded actions onto the two conceptual constructs, and arithmetically sum across the ac-tions in each category.

The scale of procedurally just action, which is formed by summing across the procedurally just subscales, ranges from 0 to 15 with a mean of 6.99, and it has an intraclass correlation of 0.73. This overall scale exhibits correlations with indi-vidual subscales ranging from 0.50 to 0.85, respectively, with a mean correlation of 0.67. The scale of procedurally unjust action formed by summing across the proce-durally unjust subscales ranges from 0 to 12.5 with a mean of only 0.68, and it has an intraclass correlation of 0.80. This overall scale exhibits correlations with indi-vidual subscales ranging from 0.4 to 0.86, respectively, with a mean correlation of 0.70. Table 3 displays the scale means and standard deviations for the contacts as a whole and for each type of contact: calls for service; arrests; and field interviews.

The correlation between the two scales is, as expected, negative and of moder-ate magnitude: -0.26. Scale scores are for the most part jointly concentrated in moderate-to-high procedurally just categories and none to low procedurally un-just categories, with two-thirds of the cases in these four cells of a cross-tabulation.

Other Officers' Actions

The primary citizen interacted with an officer other than the primary officer in ninety encounters, and so we should take account of those officers' behavior in order to describe and understand the procedural justice that citizens experience. Both scales' scores tend to be low, because other officers served as backup and thus seldom took action. In the ninety encounters in which other officers were present and interacted with the primary citizen, the mean score for other officers' procedurally just action was 4.33, and the mean score for procedurally unjust ac-tion was 0.72.

Action toward Other Citizens

Police took action toward citizens other than the primary citizen in 60 percent of the encounters, and of course these actions could affect the subjective experience of the primary citizen. However, we would expect that the impact of police behavior—just or unjust—toward other citizens would be weaker than that of actions directed toward the primary citizen, and depending on the relationship of the primary citizen to the other citizen(s), even procedurally unjust action toward other citizens might not be unfavorably received by the primary citizen. The mean of procedurally just action toward other citizens was 4.49, while the mean of procedurally unjust action was 0.72.

OTHER POLICE ACTIONS IN SCHENECTADY

How police use their authority matters, but we might also expect that *whether* police use any of a variety of forms of authority matters as well. Officers may issue commands or warnings, use physical force, pat citizens down or conduct full-scale searches of citizens' persons or vehicles, whether or not they are procedurally just or unjust.

Verbal "force" is one form of police authority, and the form that, as previous research shows, is the most commonly exercised. Here we treat as verbal force any occasion on which one or more of the officers: commanded or explicitly threatened a citizen to leave the scene, cease disorderly or illegal behavior, or provide information; threatened to charge or cite the citizen, notify another agency, or to use physical force. Physical force encompasses the use of physical restraints (exclusive of handcuffing), the use of pain-compliance techniques, or the use of impact force. (No firearm discharges were observed.) Searches or frisks/pat-downs of persons were treated as a single category, as were searches of vehicles.

Verbal force was seldom used toward the primary citizen in the context of encounters prompted by the citizen's call for police assistance (3.2 percent), as one would expect, and other forms of authority were rarely exercised in those instances—physical force in just 0.8 percent, and a search or frisk in 0.4 percent. In arrests and field interviews, however, each of these actions was much more common. Verbal force was used in nearly half of the arrests and more than one-fifth of the field interviews, physical force in slightly more than one-third of the arrests and one in seven field interviews, and a search or frisk was observed in nearly half of the arrests (not all of which were custodial) and 30 percent of the field interviews.

All of these actions are associated with procedural justice and injustice. In encounters involving verbal or physical force, the procedural justice scale score is 1 to 2 points lower than in encounters with no force, and the procedural injustice scale averages about 2.5 (compared to 0.5 in other encounters). In encounters in which officers conducted a search, the procedural justice scale score is 1 point lower than in encounters with no search, and the procedural injustice scale averages about 1.5 to 1.7 (compared to 0.6 in other encounters).

We did not ask observers to make judgments about the legality of searches or the reasonableness of officers' use of physical force; the practice of systematic social observation has prompted observers only for concrete description and not for legal opinions that they are not trained to make. Neither did we ask lawyers to make these assessments (see, e.g., Gould and Mastrofski 2004), and if we had, we might have found that it is illegal searches and unreasonable force that are associated with procedural justice and injustice. But some recent evidence—the only empirical evidence on the question—indicates that citizens' assessments of the propriety of police behavior are not based on officers' compliance with the technical requirements of Constitutional law, but rather on citizens' perceptions of procedural justice (Meares et al. 2012). We return to this issue when we reexamine citizens' subjective experience in chapter 7.

THE CONTEXT OF POLICE ACTION

More than three-quarters (78 percent) of the field interviews (FIs) and almost half (44 percent) of the arrests were police-initiated encounters. Citizen-initiated incidents could have been initiated by the primary citizen or by another citizen. The highest levels of procedural justice, on average, and lowest levels of procedural injustice were observed in calls for service. Among FIs and arrests, the procedural justice with which officers acted was somewhat greater in police-initiated encounters than in citizen-initiated encounters, perhaps because police-initiated encounters call for some explanation of officers' interventions. The procedural *in*justice with which officers acted was also somewhat greater in police-initiated arrests and FIs.

Officers' procedural justice and injustice varies some across different types of problems. Both procedural justice and procedural injustice are highest in encounters that concerned violent crime, and also fairly high in interpersonal conflicts. Procedural justice was lowest in encounters that involved suspicious circumstances.

Based on the observations (and hence exclusive of information contained in police records), and following the practice of previous observational research established in the mid-1990s (Mastrofski, Worden, and Snipes 1995), we formed a scale of legal evidence of criminal wrongdoing by the primary citizen. The scale is a weighted combination of several pieces of coded information: whether the officer observed the citizen commit an offense; whether there was physical evidence implicating the citizen; whether the citizen gave a full confession to an offense; whether the officer heard eyewitness testimony implicating the citizen; and whether the citizen gave a partial confession. Assigning two legal "points" to each of the first three factors and one point to each of the last two factors, the evidence scale can range from 0 to 8; in general, and somewhat loosely, we could consider scores of 2 and above to represent probable cause for arrest. In the encounters that we observed in Schenectady, the scale ranges from 0 to 5. Procedural justice declines and procedural injustice increases with increasing evidence between 0 and 3 on this scale, though this simple association could be driven by the citizen's role in the encounter (as, e.g., suspect or complainant); this pattern reverses at the higher levels of evidence, though the numbers of cases become rather small.

Part of the context for police action is whether and how citizens resist or challenge officers' authority or display disrespect toward police. Resistance can take different forms: passive resistance, by refusing or ignoring officers' questions or commands; defensive resistance, by fleeing or trying to evade officers' grasp; and aggressive resistance, by attacking or threatening to assault officers. Resistance in any of these forms was very infrequent in the Schenectady sample of encounters, and it was with rare exceptions limited to arrests and field interviews. Among arrests, observers recorded passive resistance by the primary citizen in 17 percent (i.e., twenty-two encounters), defensive resistance in 7 percent, and aggressive resistance in only two cases. Disrespect was more common, observed in 12 percent of the encounters, including 8 percent of the calls for service, more than one-quarter of the arrests, and one-sixth of the field interviews. Disrespect can consist of derogatory comments about police and/or any of a variety of actions that would be widely interpreted as disrespectful in any social setting.[20] Multiple forms of resistance can occur in the same encounter, of course, and resistance can overlap with disrespect, but 78 percent of the occasions of citizen disrespect were *not* observed in conjunction with citizen resistance of any detected kind. Overall, neither resistance nor disrespect was observed in 86 percent of the encounters.

The demeanor of a suspect has been a consistent predictor of police action in previous studies—officers respond punitively to those who show a disregard for their authority and thereby flunk the "attitude test." This has remained true despite a debate among researchers regarding the appropriate definition and operationalization of "demeanor." David Klinger (1994) first questioned the measurement of demeanor in previous research, arguing that prior studies had failed to adequately isolate and control for crime committed by suspects during their encounter with police (in particular, crime *against* the police). Although subsequent research found that the original findings regarding the influence of demeanor hold (e.g., Lundman 1994, 1996; Worden and Shepard 1996; Klinger 1995, 1996; Worden et al. 1996), Klinger's critique pushed research to exercise greater care in the conceptualization and measurement of demeanor (and its separation from suspect resistance). However, despite all of the research conducted to date, the demeanor/resistance question has still not been conclusively answered. That officers react to negative behavior on the behalf of a citizen is not in dispute. The forms that such behavior takes, however, and the ways in which officers interpret representations of "attitude," remain open questions if we approach police behavior as the outcome of a decision-making process. Although some forms of resistance (e.g., passive) are legal, officers may not make such a distinction in the field. It may be that officers view both disrespect and forms of resistance as equal affronts to their authority.

Resistance and disrespect are associated with the procedural justice and especially injustice with which officers act. Procedural justice is somewhat lower (less than 1 point lower on the scale) when citizens are disrespectful, and all three forms of resistance are associated with still lower levels of procedural justice. But it is procedural injustice that is more strongly associated with resistance and disrespect. Whether resistance or disrespect are cause or effect—a feature of the situation to which officers respond or a response by citizens to officers' behavior—is a question that cannot be entirely resolved by these data, but we can at least partially disentangle the citizens' disrespect toward the police and officers' disrespect toward citizens. Citizen disrespect followed police disrespect of the citizen in seven of sixty-one (unweighted) cases of citizen disrespect toward police; citizen disrespect was reciprocated by police in sixteen and not reciprocated in the remaining thirty-eight encounters. In sixteen other (unweighted) cases, police disrespected the citizen and the citizen did not reciprocate. In seventy-seven encounters in which one or both parties disrespected the other, police initiated the disrespect in twenty-three, or about 30 percent of the time. From these data we can infer with some confidence that more often than not, citizen disrespect is a context for officers' behavior and not an effect of officers' disrespect.

Another facet of the context for police action is the condition of the citizen with whom officers interact. We might expect that officers' behavior would be affected by elements of the citizen's capacity to communicate and act rationally, and so citizens who exhibit signs of mental disorder or intoxication might be treated differently. Mental disorder was infrequent, observed in only eight encounters, in five of which the citizens were arrested. Intoxication was a condition observed somewhat more frequently, in just under 8 percent of all contacts, but was fairly prevalent among arrests, as more than one quarter of the primary citizens in arrest encounters exhibited mild (15 percent) or strong (12 percent) intoxication. The procedural justice with which police act does not appear to be strongly associated with any of these conditions, with scale scores averaging 6.2–6.4, but the procedural injustice with which police act is considerably greater under each of these circumstances, with scale scores of 1.6 to 2.3, than when citizens exhibit none of these conditions (an average scale score of 0.6).

TALES FROM THE FIELD

The virtue of quantitative analysis is in breaking police-citizen interactions into discrete pieces so that they can be carefully examined, piece by piece, but a sense of the texture of behavior and interpersonal dynamics can be compromised by such fragmentation. It might be instructive, therefore, to consider some examples of the police-citizen encounters that we have analyzed above. For some of the observed encounters, an observer prepared a narrative description of the event; we draw on those narratives here. In each case, the primary officer appears as "O1," and other officers as "O2," "O3," while citizens are "C1," "C2," and so on.

In one incident (case 6–1, below), police responded to a 'keep the peace' call shortly after 5 p.m. A landlord had called on behalf of one of his tenants, who had a guest stay past his welcome; but under state law, the guest had stayed long enough to claim the apartment as his legal residence. The officer listened to the tenant's explanation of the situation, asked some clarifying questions, and explained that under the circumstances, the police could not take legal action. The officer also expressed his sympathy for the tenant's predicament, and offered some advice about how not to make the situation worse. The entire encounter took only six minutes, but in that space of time, the officer's actions manifested each element of procedural justice: he gave the citizen voice in explaining the situation; he sought additional information, so that his decision about how to proceed would be based on facts; he expressed concern for the citizens' needs and well-being; and he treated the citizens with dignity and respect. The score on the procedural justice scale was 13; the procedural injustice score was zero.

CASE 6–1

O1 was initially greeted by C1 (male) on the sidewalk of a residential neighborhood. After O1 asked who called, C1 identified himself as the landlord and C2 (male) as his tenant. C1 explained that a friend of C2 and C2's wife had recently moved in, despite not being on the lease. O1 inquired about the location of this person, and C1 says he is off scene.

C1 stated that his tenants wish for this person to leave. O1 asked C2 exactly how long their friend has lived there, as that is the main issue. After C2 stated his friend has lived there for "about a month," O1 respectfully described to both citizens that C2's friend legally lives in the residence, and C1 must have him legally evicted. O1 explained that under different circumstances (if the "friend" did not have proof of residence) he could provide assistance in getting him to leave the property.

It is evident that O1 understands it is an unfair situation, and he expressed this understanding to the citizens. O1 explained that despite the fact the "friend" is not paying rent or helping C2 and C2's wife, he is unable to help due to NYS law.

O1 advised the citizens to avoid the "friend" in the meantime in order to not turn the situation into a domestic dispute. O1 also advised C2 to respect the clause in the lease agreement that states no one may live with them in order to avoid the current situation. Before leaving O1 suggested that the citizens call the police when the "friend" returns so the police may talk to him, but they must start the eviction process in order to make him leave.

In another case (6–2), an officer is called to a convenience store at nearly 11 p.m., where he encounters a man in a strongly inebriated state:

CASE 6–2

O1 arrived at a convenience store and parked before walking toward the back of the building. O1 greeted C1 (male) by asking him, "What's up?" C1 was noticeably intoxicated, and told O1 he was tired. O1 then asked C1 where he lived, and C1 asked him if he was a cop, to which the officer responded that he was indeed a cop. C1 then gave O1 his address, and O1 asked what he was doing at the convenience store; C1's response was inaudible. O1 then asked C1 who he lived with, and C1 said he lived with his cousins and his mother. O1 then asked why C1 was drinking, and C1 said he had "a lot of problems on his mind." C1 then began to tell O1 that "God told me it is better to be truthful," and O1 patiently let C1 talk. C1 then told O1 he would be truthful with him, so O1 asked what C1 would be truthful about, but C1 said he did not know. C1 then repeatedly asked O1 if he had a problem, and O1 simply said, "No." O1 then asked C1 how long he had been at the convenience store, and C1 said he thought he had been there for about an hour. O1 then asked C1 if he knew what time it was, and after C1 said he did not know, O1 told him to guess. C1 then asked the officer if it was morning (it was in fact 22:59). O1 said no, and told C1 the time. O1 then pointed out to C1 that he had an open container of alcohol, and asked C1 if he had ever gotten an open container ticket. C1 said no before standing up to retrieve his ID. C1 spoke unintelligibly for a few minutes while O1 examined his ID.

After several minutes C1 asked the cop if he had a warrant, and O1 told him that's what he was waiting to find out. O1 also told him he was there because people had called and C1 was making people nervous. O1 suddenly asked if something that C1 had in his possession was cologne or pills. C1 ignored the question and again asked if he had any warrants. O1 told C1 he did not have any warrants, and asked twice more if C1 was holding pills or cologne. C1 spoke unintelligibly while handing the item to O1, who determined it was cologne. O1 told C1 to wait where he was while he returned to his car.

After a few minutes O1 asked C1 if there was anything left in the alcohol container. O1 asked multiple times before C1 said it was empty. O1 then asked C1 if he was supposed to be at the convenience store, and C1 said he did not know. O1 told him he was not allowed to be at the convenience store due to prior incidents. O1 proceeded to write C1 a ticket, and asked him various questions such as name, date of birth, etc. while doing so. When asked how old he was, C1 told the officer he was older than him. When O1 asked again, C1 replied by asking the officer, "How old do you want me to be?" O1 asked him why he was making the information gathering process so difficult, and warned C1 that he could take him to the station. C1 asked O1 where his car was, and O1 pointed to his car and said with a light tone, "That one, with the big dog in the back. It will bite your ass." O1 then told C1 he had to take down C1's information and then he could send him on his way. C1 then asked O1 if he liked him, and O1 told him "So far, yeah." O1 lightly joked about C1 being "a little difficult." C1 did not give O1 much trouble for the remainder of the questions. Any lack of attention exhibited by C1 during O1's questions could be attributed to his inebriated state.

O1 returned to his car to complete paperwork and returned to C1 with a ticket and told him he had a court date the next Monday. O1 told C1 he was not supposed to be at the convenience store, and he needed to think about being "passed out and intoxicated." C1 repeatedly told O1 he was "supposed to be his friend."

O1 stayed for a few minutes after giving C1 his ticket to make sure he took his keys and his bike. O1 reminded C1 of his court date and that he was not allowed at the convenience store before leaving.

The officer is clearly very patient with the man, shows concern for his welfare, treats him with respect, and explains why he is there, what he is doing and why. The procedural justice scale score was 8.5; procedural injustice registered 2.5 on the scale.

Less procedural justice, and greater procedural injustice, can be seen in case 6–3, as officers responded to a call for service in the late afternoon:

CASE 6–3

O1 and O2 stopped on a residential street in front of a house with four citizens standing outside on the sidewalk. O1 and O2 approached the citizens on the sidewalk and O1 asked which of the citizens called. C1 (male) told the officer he called because C2 (male) had insulted him and a dispute had developed. As C1 explained, O1 then asked for the citizens to make a long story short and explain why the police were contacted. C2 told the officers that C1 had held a knife to him. O1 asked what he wanted the police to do and C2 told the officers he wanted C1 to leave. As C1 was standing in the doorway of the house, O1 assumed he lived there and told C2 he could not make him leave. C2 then told the officer C1 was not on the lease, and O1 replied by telling him if he has been there for thirty days he must be evicted. C2 attempted to tell the officers that C1 had not been there for thirty days. O2 did not believe this, as he had been to the same address two months earlier and knew that C1 had been there for at least thirty days. O1 turned to C1 and asked how long he had lived there, and C1 said he had been there for five months. Upon hearing this C2 began to argue with C1. As they were arguing, O1 said C1 must be evicted if C2 wanted him out of the residence. C1 then said that C2 had forced his way in and had put his hands on C1's neck. After a brief moment of arguing between the citizens, O1 announced that he and O2 were going to leave, and C2 needed to have C1 evicted. C1 then said, "That guy [C2] attacked me and you're just going to leave?" O1 simply said, "Yeah." After a few moments of complaining by both citizens O1 told them to "cry about it." The citizens continued to argue with the officers about not honoring their complaints, and O2 told them the officers must honor either both or neither complaints. Both officers left without any parting remarks.

The conflict between the citizens clearly makes the situation an emotional and perhaps volatile one. The officers showed little interest in learning about the situation or concern about either citizen's well-being, however. One citizen claimed to be the victim of an armed assault, but the officers seemed quick to seize upon a definition of the situation that called for no police action, and even mocked the citizens' disgruntlement with the limited police response. The procedural justice scale score was 4.5; procedural injustice scored 7.0.

Finally, case 6–4 illustrates what observers captured as (predominantly) procedural injustice by police in the context of citizen resistance and disrespect, likely owing at least partly to inebriation. In a 45-minute encounter that began just after midnight:

CASE 6–4

O1 and O2 were driving through downtown and responded to a call at a bar. O1 and O2 approached C1 (male) on the sidewalk who was arguing with someone inside the bar. There were also approximately four other citizens standing outside around C1. C1 told the officers as they approached that a person in the bar had choked him and thrown him on the floor. C1 alleged that he was thrown out because his friend had thrown up inside the bar. C1 told the officers he had hurt his arm during the incident, and that the person involved with him in the incident tried to fight him. C1 told the officers his friend had a video of the encounter on his phone and that he wanted to press charges against the bar. At this point C1 was very agitated and began to argue with O1 and O2 as they told him he needed to calm down and listen. O1 asked C1 for his name, and C1 told him his name before continuing to shout about previous incidents he had at the bar. C1 was not responding to the officer's requests to calm down and lower his voice, and after repeated requests by the officers, C1 quickly said he was sorry before continuing to yell. O1 said he did not believe he was sorry and told him to shut his mouth. O1 told C1 he had lost his talking privileges, and C2 (male) told the officers he wanted to ask them a question. O1 asked C1 and C2 if they wanted to do jail time before both officers walked inside the bar while C1 and his friends stayed on the sidewalk.

Inside the bar O1 asked C3 if he worked there, and C3 (male) said he was the bartender. O1 asked C3 what happened, and C3 told him C1 was in the bar with a friend, and the friend was falling asleep. C3 had told C1's friend to either get up or leave, and he threw up two minutes later. C3 had then told C1 and the group C1 was with they had to leave. C1 refused to leave, so the doorman put him in an armlock and pushed him out the door.

The officers returned to the sidewalk and O1 asked C1 and C2 if they had been asked to leave. C2 then said, "This is the United States of America, I don't have freedom of speech?" O1 again asked C1 and C2 if they had been asked to leave, to which C2 said yes, but for the wrong reasons, and C1 said he still wanted to press charges for assault. O1 asked C2 why they were asked to leave, and C2 told him it was because their friend was sick. C2 then said the bouncer had no reason to choke out his cousin (C1). O1 told C1 and C2 to listen, and told C2 it was apparent C1 was very intoxicated, very argumentative, and unable to keep quiet. O1 then said that C2 was having a hard time not talking over him. O1 then told C2 everyone inside the bar said C1 and his friends had been asked to leave, and everyone had also cited C1 as the main problem as he refused to leave and said the bouncer would have to make him leave. O1 then told C2 that because the bar is a private establishment, they may ask anyone to leave for any reason. O1 then told C1 and C2 they had to leave. C1 then yelled about being choked out, and O1 warned him if he swore at the officers one more time he would be locked up. C1 angrily asked O1 if it was illegal to swear, to which O1 said it was, and C2 told O1 it was not illegal to swear. At this point O1 told the citizens to go. They did not leave, and C2 said he was in the Marine Corps and knew his rights. O1 told C2 he was in the military too, and that just because C2 was in the Marine Corps did not mean he would not get locked up. C1 then said he needed new cops. O1 told C1 he could either leave or go to jail, and C1 began to argue about what he would be arrested for. C2 managed to get C1 to walk down the street before the officers arrested him. C2 asked the officers if he could tell them a story, and O2 said no and summarized the situation by telling C2 that C1 was acting like an idiot and everyone in the bar said C1 was asked to leave but refused. O1 said the officers were not having a conversation with C2. The citizens continued to argue with the officers about how C1 was assaulted, and O1 continuously asked the citizens to leave. Before leaving O1 warned C1 and C2 if they came back that night they would be locked up for trespassing. C2 continued to argue so O1 cuffed him. At this point C1 was also arrested. C2 complained of the handcuffs hurting his wrists and said he was politely asking the officer to remove them. O1 sarcastically asked C2 why he all of a sudden wanted to be polite. O1 frisked C2 in front of his vehicle before putting him in the back seat. O1 returned to the front of the bar and asked C4 (male) to recount what he had seen. C4 told the O1 approximately the same story O1 had already heard, but included that C1 had ripped his shirt off and spit on a girl. O1 thanked C4 and returned to his car to leave with C2 in custody.

After arriving at the police station C2 continued to argue with O1, and O1 refused to listen and told C2 to shut his mouth.

Officers are doubtless challenged to act with procedural justice in an emotionally charged situation, and with people who are intoxicated and not entirely in control of themselves. The officers' patience is severely tested in this incident. The procedural justice scale score was 1.5; procedural injustice was 8.5.

A MODEL OF PROCEDURAL JUSTICE IN ACTION

We can describe more succinctly the respects in which procedural justice and injustice are shaped by the characteristics of the situations in which officers become involved and the citizens with whom they interact, and we can better isolate the independent effects that these factors have on officers' behavior. Previous research (see especially Mastrofski, Jonathan-Zamir, et al. 2016) would lead us to hypothesize that the (in)justice with which police act is influenced by:

- The race, ethnicity, sex, age, and social status of the citizen;
- The role that the citizen plays in the encounter—for example, as suspect, victim/complainant, or something else (a third party);
- Indications of mental disorder or intoxication, which affect the citizen's capacity for communication and rational behavior;

TABLE 4 Regression Analysis of Procedurally Just and Unjust Action Scales

	Procedurally Just Action Scale	Procedurally Unjust Action Scale
Constant	5.83*	0.06
Citizen a suspect	−1.20*	0.65*
Citizen a third party	−4.64*	0.64*
Citizen resistance: passive	−0.68	1.87*
Citizen resistance: defensive	−3.49*	0.44
Citizen resistance: aggressive	−0.17	0.28
Citizen disrespect	0.60	0.76*
Citizen mentally disordered	−0.98	0.56
Citizen mildly intoxicated	−0.10	0.62**
Citizen very intoxicated	−0.15	−0.07
Citizen male	−0.25	0.23**
Citizen's age	0.01	0.00
Citizen Black	0.73**	−0.34*
Citizen Hispanic	−0.74	−0.06
Citizen's education	0.12	−0.08
Citizen employed	0.27	0.04
Other citizen present	0.18	0.09
Police-initiated	0.24	−0.07
Evidence	0.24	0.02
Neighborhood disadvantage	0.05	0.08
Platoon 2	0.43	0.01
Platoon 3	0.19	0.15
Call: violent crime	1.70*	0.50
Call: nonviolent crime	0.23	0.12
Call: interpersonal conflict	1.07*	0.13
Call: suspicious circumstance	−1.34**	0.34
Call: traffic	0.48	−0.26
Call: dependent person	0.47	0.40
Call: assistance	−0.42	0.23
Adjusted R^2	0.15	0.27

NOTE: Weighted results
* $p < .05$
** $p < .10$

- Citizen resistance and/or disrespect for police;
- The nature of the problem;
- Whether the encounter was initiated by police or a citizen;
- Evidence of criminal wrongdoing.

Operationalizing these variables (excepting the initiation of the encounter) with the observational data, we find that a number of these hypotheses are supported. See table 4 above.[21]

Procedural justice is greater when the situation involves a violent crime or interpersonal conflict, and when the citizen is black. Procedural justice is lower when the citizen is a suspect or a third party, and when the citizen defensively resists police authority. Procedural injustice is greater when the citizen is a suspect, a male, disrespectful, or passively resists police authority. Procedural injustice is lower when the citizen is black.

The citizen's role in the encounter has a clear bearing on how officers act. Suspects, relative to victims and complainants, are accorded less procedural justice and greater procedural injustice, even holding constant the actions—resistance or disrespect—or conditions—mental disorder or intoxication—that might be expected to affect officers' behavior. Third parties are shown lower levels of procedural justice, presumably because they are given less attention.

Treating resistance and disrespect as factors to which police respond, resistance matters, but different forms of resistance affect procedural justice and injustice differently. Defensive resistance evokes lower levels of procedural justice, while passive resistance evokes greater procedural injustice, even controlling for disrespect. Disrespect evokes greater procedural injustice, but does not have a detectable effect on procedural justice.

Black citizens, compared with whites, are treated better on both dimensions of police behavior: other things being equal, blacks are accorded greater procedural justice and less procedural injustice. These estimated effects are in the unexpected direction, and they defy our attempts to account for them.

SUMMARY AND CONCLUSIONS

Building on previous observational research on the police, we formed measures of police behavior that capture the elements of procedural justice. We formed separate measures of procedural justice and procedural injustice, allowing for officers to exhibit either or both in a police-citizen encounter, and also allowing for the possibility that the effects of procedural justice on citizens' subjective experience (which we estimate in the next chapter) would differ from the effects of procedural injustice not only in direction but also magnitude.

The construction of each of these two measures proceeded first by forming a subscale for each of the domains of procedural justice: voice/participation; quality of treatment; neutrality; and trustworthy motives. We classified officers' actions, as observers coded them, in terms of these domains, and we assessed the level of consistency between observers by calculating the intraclass correlation for each subscale. We formed scales of procedural justice and procedural injustice, respectively, by summing the subscale scores for each observer, and we estimated the intraclass correlations of the summed scales (0.70 or higher). We constructed these measures to capture the behavior of the primary officer and other officers toward the primary citizen—the citizen whom we interviewed about the encounter—and we also constructed measures of the procedural justice and injustice with which officers acted toward other citizens in the encounter.

We examined the mean and distribution of each of the two scales in all contacts and in the three types of contacts, finding differences of the expected nature: higher levels of procedural justice in calls than in arrests or field interviews, and higher levels of procedural injustice in arrests and field interviews than in calls for service.

We also formed measures of other actions by officers that might affect citizens' subjective experiences, including the use of verbal or physical force, respectively, searches and frisks of citizens, and searches of citizens' vehicles. We formed measures of the context in which police took action, including the availability and strength of evidence of criminal wrongdoing, resistance by the citizen, and disrespect of the police, and we found the expected patterns of procedural justice and injustice across these contexts, for example, greater procedural injustice when citizens are disrespectful to the police.

Finally, we estimated the parameters of a regression model that includes the factors that previous research suggests might affect procedural justice, finding that procedural justice and injustice bear readily interpretable relationships to a number of situational factors. These analyses offer further evidence that the scales of procedural justice and injustice are valid measures.

With these measures of procedural justice and injustice, derived through observations by trained observers and independent of citizens' survey responses, we are prepared to examine citizens' subjective experience in terms of officers' behavior. To that examination we turn in chapter 7.

7

Citizens' Subjective Experience and Police Action

When previous survey research has analyzed the effects of procedural justice in police-citizen encounters, it has with few exceptions been with the (usually implicit) presumption that citizens' subjective experience bears a fairly strong relationship to what police officers actually do in those encounters. When citizens report that police treated them with dignity and respect, respected citizens' rights, and paid attention to what they had to say, research has generally taken those reports at face value. When citizens report that police were impolite, did not consider their views, or did not make their decision based on facts, research has again taken those reports at face value. Inferences have been drawn from this body of evidence that if police were to improve their performance in these process-based terms, then citizens would have more positive experiences, police legitimacy would improve, and citizen cooperation and compliance would in turn improve. In this way, presumably, police can "create" legitimacy through their interactions with citizens.

Some previous research gives us reason to question this presumption, though any doubts about the strength of the connection between subjective experience and procedural justice in action are seldom reflected in the conclusions drawn from the evidence. As we discussed in chapter 3, panel surveys have shown that legitimacy and other global attitudes toward the police tend to be stable over time. A single contact with the police has a fairly modest impact on subsequent attitudes; the subjective experience in that contact, however, is substantially shaped by the citizen's prior attitude. The effects of prior attitudes could reflect the operation of selective perception by citizens, seeing what they expect to see—for better or for worse—from the police, and/or the effects of prior attitudes on citizens' behavior in their encounters with the police, to which officers respond. Most extant evidence does not extend to whether and how subjective experience is affected by the overt behavior of police.

Some empirical evidence on this question has recently accumulated in experimental studies of traffic enforcement. In the first study of this kind, the Queensland Community Engagement Trial (QCET), police were directed to follow scripts in their administration of roadside breath tests at traffic checkpoints; the scripts were formulated to provide for the elements of procedural justice. To date, the QCET design has been replicated in two published studies (and a third unpublished study of which we are aware), though its findings have not been replicated. Notwithstanding the inconsistent findings, this body of research warrants our attention, and we will consider it first.

We thereafter turn to our analysis of the subjective experience of citizens who were interviewed about their contacts with Schenectady police, and whose encounters were captured in video and audio recordings that we used to code features of the interactions. We begin by reexamining the relationships estimated in chapter 4, for all 1,800 sampled contacts, among only the 411 encounters for which both of our observers were able to identify the primary citizen. We reestimate the same model of subjective experience, using the additive index of procedural justice formed from the survey items. We then examine the relationships between citizens' subjective experience, on one hand, and the scales of procedural justice and injustice in action—hereafter simply officers' procedural justice and injustice—and other actions of the police, on the other hand. We thereupon build a more complete model of subjective experience, which incorporates the observed behavioral constructs, so that we can further contribute to filling the gap in extant evidence on the effects of police procedural justice.

EXPERIMENTAL STUDIES OF PROCEDURAL JUSTICE

The Queensland Community Engagement Trial (QCET) was a randomized controlled trial that provided for an experimental treatment in the form of scripted traffic checks for drunk driving. Officers were trained to follow a protocol designed to maximize the procedural justice of the brief interactions occasioned by the random breath testing (RBT). Scripts were formulated to incorporate the components of procedural justice into officers' administration of the RBT; during half of sixty RBT operations, officers were directed to use the experimental script, and senior officers monitored their compliance with the protocol. Ordinarily these RBT encounters were brief—about twenty seconds long—and "very systematic and often devoid of anything but compulsory communication" (Mazerolle et al. 2013, 40). The scripted procedurally just encounters were longer, at ninety-seven seconds on average, but still quite brief. Each driver who was stopped during these sixty RBT operations was given a survey to be completed later and returned to the researchers. Response rates, for both experimental and control drivers, were about 13 percent. The procedural justice treatment had the hypothesized effects on citizens' judgments, and of course a randomized trial has the unique virtue of strong controls for the effects of citizens' prior attitudes and other potentially confounding factors. The QCET's design but not its results have been replicated, however (Alpert 2015; MacQueen and Bradford 2015; Sahin 2014).

An experimental treatment applied randomly, as in QCET, allows us to assume that the confirmation biases in citizens' subjective judgments are distributed evenly across treatment and control groups and thereby isolate the effect of the procedural justice treatment. How much potential everyday policing allows for experimental scripting and direction is questionable. Traffic checkpoints that involve very brief encounters between police and citizens are susceptible to such prescriptions, but police-citizen encounters in most domains of police work—and especially in those with the potential for contentious interactions—do not lend themselves to such experimental manipulation. The QCET and studies like it cannot be written off as irrelevant eccentricities of police research, but we believe that a properly grounded understanding of the dynamics and outcomes of police-citizen interactions, including but not limited to the subjective and (more) objective features of procedural justice, will require the application of nonexperimental approaches that provide for two forms of data: data on citizens' subjective experiences, the likes of which have been collected through postcontact surveys of citizens; and data about police and citizen behaviors independently coded by observers.

A MODEL OF SUBJECTIVE EXPERIENCE, REVISITED

In chapter 4 we estimated the parameters of a model of subjective experience, based on survey responses and police records (e.g., concerning the nature of the call, arrest charges, and the like) for all of the encounters in Schenectady and Syracuse about which we interviewed citizens. Our analysis, however, omitted the behavior of police. It revealed that citizens' satisfaction is driven by subjective procedural justice and subjective outcomes, and holding those factors statistically constant, satisfaction is only weakly related to citizens' background characteristics or characteristics of the situation. Subjective outcomes are shaped by and large by subjective procedural justice. Finally, subjective procedural justice is driven mainly by how the encounter is initiated and especially by the use of police authority: searches or frisks, and the type and disposition of an arrest. Citizens' race, employment, and age also affect procedural justice.

We estimated the parameters of that same model of subjective experience for only the contacts in Schenectady. The regression coefficients are very similar—many are identical—to those based on an analysis of both sites. One of the few exceptions is the estimated effect of the citizen's race on subjective procedural justice; among encounters in both sites, Blacks rated procedural justice less favorably than whites did, other things being equal, but among the Schenectady encounters, race bears no independent relationship to subjective procedural justice.

Our assessment of the observation sample against the larger survey sample suggested that the observed encounters resembled the incidents from which they were sampled (see the methodological appendix). As reassuring as that is, we also estimated the parameters of the model for only the observed encounters in Schenectady.[1] The pattern of effects in the observed subset of Schenectady encounters is very similar to that found among all of the Schenectady encounters, though a number of the coefficients that achieve statistical significance in the latter analysis do not achieve statistical significance at a conventional level among observed encounters, given the smaller N, and a few differences among call types emerge that were not found among all of the Schenectady encounters. But the story remains much the same in this subset of encounters: satisfaction is driven by citizens' judgments about procedural justice and about outcomes, which explain all but a small fraction of the variation in satisfaction. Subjective outcomes are for the most part a function of citizens' perceptions of procedural justice. Subjective procedural justice is shaped mainly by how the encounter is initiated and the use of police authority, among the observed encounters as among all of the contacts about which citizens were interviewed. Thus this comparison of regression results further suggests that the observed encounters are fairly representative of police-citizen contacts in Schenectady, aside from the underrepresentation of routine traffic stops.

AN EXTENDED ANALYSIS

Our analysis of subjective experience in chapter 4 omitted a construct of signal importance: the behavior of police, and particularly the degree to which officers' actions toward the citizen either conform to or violate principles of procedural justice. Like previous research that relies mainly or exclusively on citizens' responses to survey questions about their experience, we must make assumptions about the correspondence of citizens' judgments to officers' behavior in order to draw inferences about how police can enhance police legitimacy through their contacts with citizens. With data on how officers act that are independent of citizens' reports, however, we can instead treat as testable empirical propositions the connections between officers' behavior and citizens' subjective experience.

The model first presented in chapter 4 includes officers' procedural justice (see figure 6). We have already considered some of the hypothesized relationships between features of the situational context and citizens' backgrounds, on the one hand, and officers' procedural justice, on the other hand, in the analyses presented in chapter 6. Here we consider, not the antecedents of officers' procedural justice, but rather its consequences. We posit that the most immediate effects of officers' procedural justice are on citizens' subjective procedural justice and outcomes. We further posit that the effects of officers' procedural justice on citizens' satisfaction are mediated by subjective procedural justice and outcomes, though we will later allow for the possibility that officers' procedural justice has direct effects on citizens' satisfaction, in addition to any indirect effects that it may have. We begin with a detailed examination of the relationship between officers' procedural justice and citizens' assessments of procedural justice.

Subjective Procedural Justice

Measured by the procedural justice index, the procedural justice that citizens perceive and experience—which we simply call "subjective procedural justice"—correlates in expected ways with the procedural justice that we observed in police-citizen encounters, but the correlations are only of rather weak-to-moderate magnitude. The correlation of subjective procedural justice with the procedural justice with which the primary officer treated the primary (surveyed) citizen is only 0.14. Subjective procedural justice is inversely correlated, at -0.31, with the procedural injustice with which the primary officer acts. As previous research on citizen satisfaction might be taken to imply, the inverse correlation of subjective procedural justice with procedural injustice is larger in magnitude than the positive correlation of subjective procedural justice with procedural justice. Subjective procedural justice is also inversely correlated with procedural injustice by other officers, and correlated with procedural injustice toward other citizens in the encounter, though the coefficients (-0.15 and 0.11, respectively) are weaker still. Subjective procedural justice is also inversely correlated with the use of police authority—verbal and physical force, searches of persons and vehicles—with coefficients ranging from -0.2 to -0.27.

The modest magnitude of the correlations between subjective procedural justice and procedural justice seems to stem mainly from rather generous characterizations of officers' performance by citizens. Figure 7 shows a cross-tabulation of citizens' subjective judgments about procedural justice and the primary officers' behavior, in bar-chart form, such that each segment of each bar depicts a cell in a cross-tabulation. Comparing subjective procedural justice (along the vertical axis) to officers' procedural justice (along the horizontal axis), more than 40 percent of the cases overall are found in four segments (the blue and green in the upper left of the figure) that encompass police behavior of low-to-moderate procedural justice and subjective assessments of high-to-very-high procedural justice. In 50 percent of the cases of *low* procedural justice by officers, citizens rated procedural justice *very* highly. In nearly two-thirds of the cases of only moderate procedural justice by officers, citizens assessed procedural justice as very high. Conversely stingy judgments—low-to-moderate subjective procedural justice despite high-to-very-high procedural

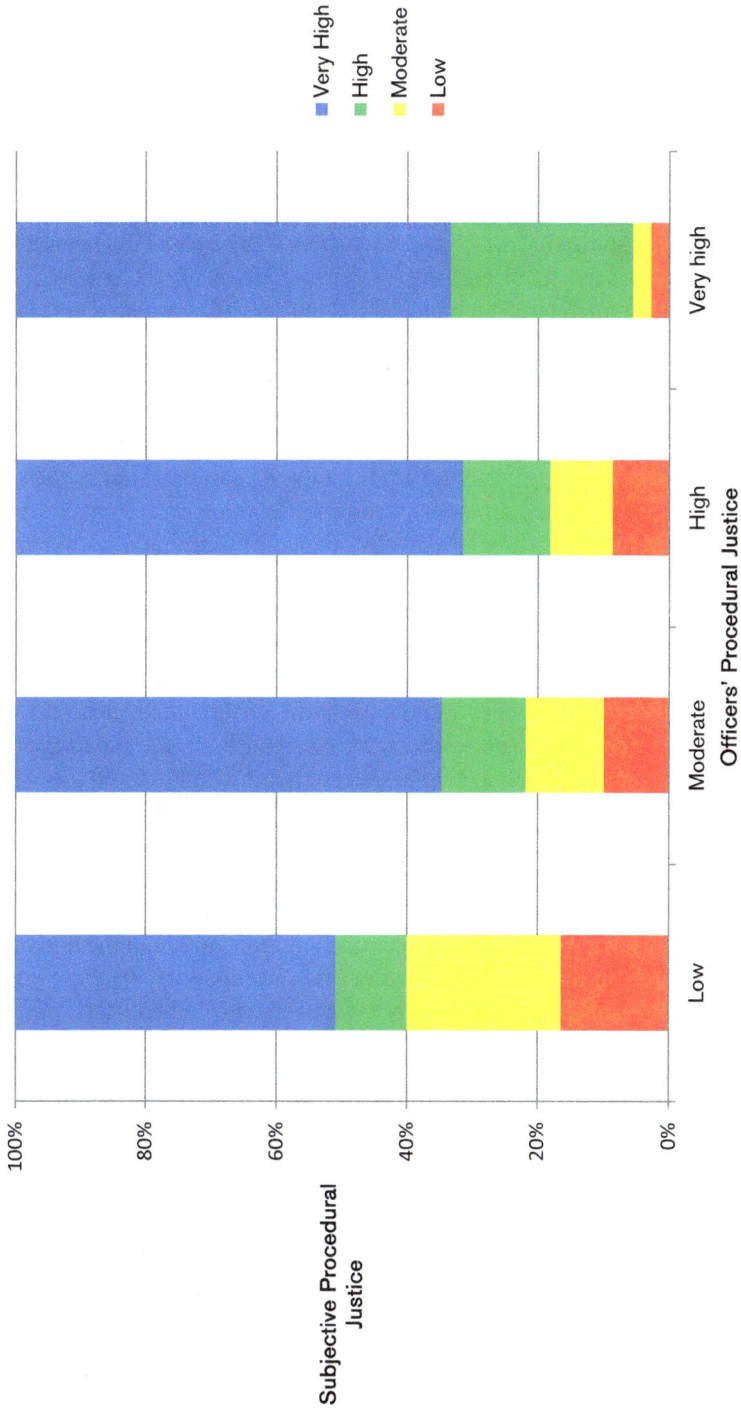

FIGURE 7. Subjective Procedural Justice by Officers' Procedural Justice.

justice by officers—were much less common (7 percent of all of the cases), found in the lower right segments. Overall, in these bivariate terms, positive ratings of procedural justice by citizens do not appear to be very responsive to officers' overt behavior, inasmuch as half to two-thirds of the citizens rated procedural justice very highly regardless of officers' observed behavior.

Citizens were somewhat less likely to overstate the procedural justice with which officers acted when officers behaved in procedurally *unjust* ways. When officers acted with moderate-to-high procedural injustice (the two bars in the right of figure 8, below), citizens rated procedural justice as high or very high about half of the time.

Arrestees, as a group, are less generous in their assessments, and their scores on the subjective procedural justice index bear a closer correspondence with police behavior. Among cases in which observations showed procedural justice to be low, less than one-quarter of the arrestees rated procedural justice very highly, while nearly one-third judged it to be low. Positive ratings of procedural justice among arrestees appear more closely tied to overt behavior, with a larger spread in the proportion of very high ratings, from 23 percent to 58 percent.

Overall, these results contradict the phenomenon to which Wesley Skogan (appropriately) draws our attention: that negative experiences with the police have more powerful detrimental effects on global attitudes than the beneficial effects of positive experiences, and more generally that "bad is stronger than good." If we think of citizens' perceptions that are incongruent with observed procedural justice as errors, then the false positive errors are far more numerous than the false negative errors. Our data allow us only to speculate on why many citizens make what appear to be overly charitable characterizations of how police performed in their contact with them, but piecing together these findings with those in chapter 3 on the generally favorable attitudes of the survey respondents, and the findings of previous research on the powerful effects of prior attitudes on subjective experience, we could reasonably, albeit only very tentatively, attribute the false positives to citizens' prior attitudes.

We can examine false negative errors more closely, though the subsample is small and the information limited. Fourteen (unweighted) respondents have scores on the procedural justice index that place them in the "low" category, yet the officers' procedural justice was high or very high and procedural injustice was low or moderate. Thirteen of the fourteen answered open-ended questions about their reasons for dissatisfaction. The most common reason, cited by five, concerned outcomes. Two of those five, and one other respondent, cited listening, and three other respondents cited respect.

Regression analysis shows that together the scales of officers' procedural justice and injustice explain no more than 12 percent of the variation in subjective procedural justice; see the column for model I in table 5. Such explanatory power as

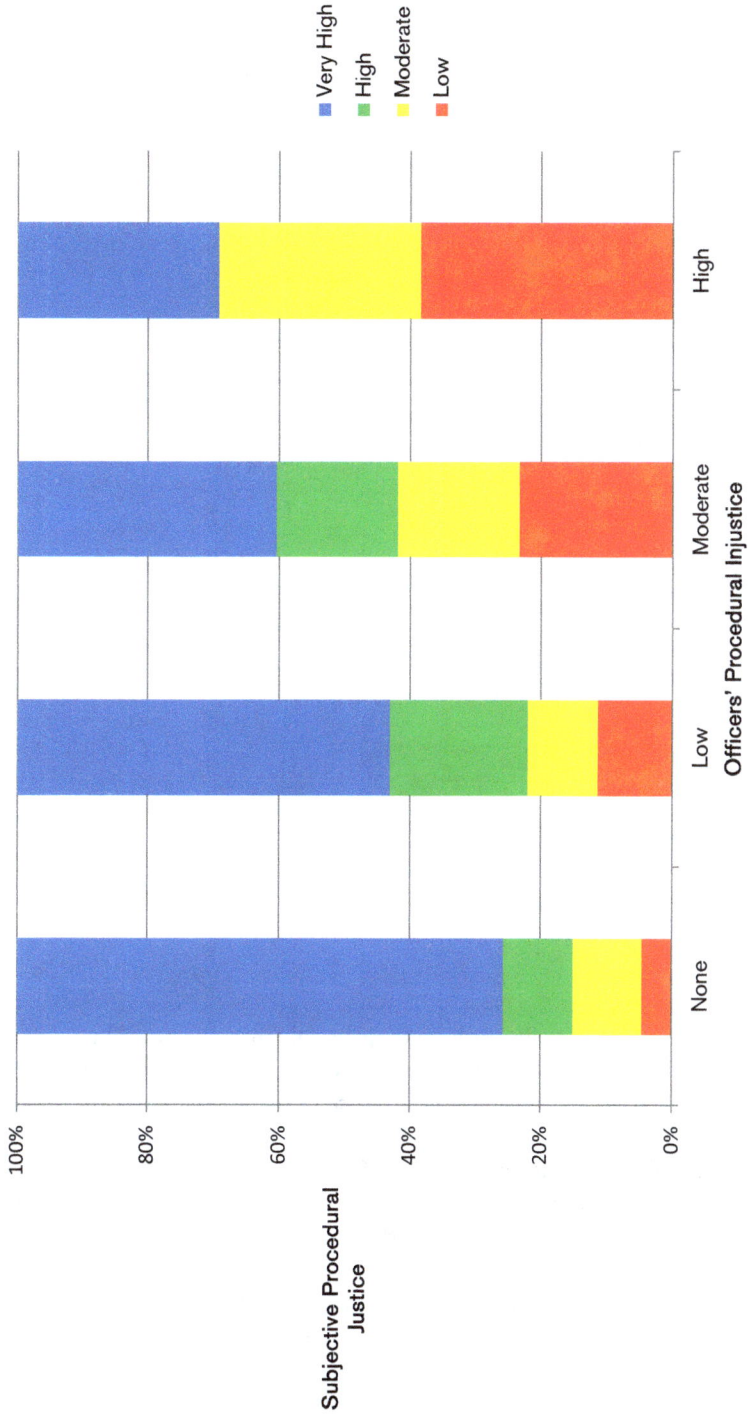

FIGURE 8. Subjective Procedural Justice by Officers' Procedural Injustice.

TABLE 5 Five Models of Subjective Procedural Justice

	I	II	III	IV	V
Constant	6.37*	5.27*	4.81*	3.56	3.70
PC x PO: procedural justice	0.40*	0.33*	0.28**	0.20	0.20
PC x PO: procedural injustice	−1.73*	−1.31*	−1.01*	−1.16*	−0.72**
PC x OO: procedural justice	−0.38	−0.28	−0.30	−0.31	−0.24
PC x OO: procedural injustice	−0.84	−0.59	−0.45	−0.38	−0.45
OC: procedural justice	−0.11	−0.14	−0.07	−0.12	−0.06
OC: procedural injustice	−0.33	−0.40	−0.55	−0.64	−0.45
Citizen called for service	—	3.39*	3.54*	2.27	1.51
Police-initiated	—	0.58	1.42	2.46	1.50
Citizen arrested	—	−3.53**	−1.29	−1.46	−0.86
Search/frisk person	—	—	−3.56**	−4.33**	−4.57*
Search vehicle	—	—	−6.21*	−6.07*	−5.97*
Citizen consent search/frisk	—	—	5.88*	5.19*	4.94*
Citizen consent vehicle search	—	—	4.92	4.40	3.31
Verbal force	—	—	1.29	1.39	1.16
Physical force	—	—	−2.06	−1.95	0.45
Evidence	—	—	−0.96	−1.00	−0.99
Citizen male	—	—	—	2.11*	2.41*
Citizen's age	—	—	—	0.04	0.05
Citizen black	—	—	—	−0.23	0.32
Citizen Hispanic	—	—	—	−0.90	0.12
Response time	—	—	—	1.96*	1.95*
Neighborhood disadvantage	—	—	—	−0.38	−0.46
Citizen disrespect	—	—	—	—	−3.24*
Citizen resistance	—	—	—	—	−6.58*
Adjusted R^2	0.12	0.18	0.21	0.25	0.28

NOTE: PC = primary citizen; PO = primary officer; OO = other officer(s); OC = other citizen(s)
* $p < .05$
** $p < .10$

can be attributed to what officers do stems primarily from the procedural *in*justice with which they act, which has fairly strong effects when those actions are directed toward the primary citizen. Procedural *justice* in this model has a substantively modest but statistically significant effect. As modest as these relationships are, they could be partially spurious, inasmuch as officers' procedural justice is associated with other factors that drive citizens' subjective experience. The effects of procedural injustice are attenuated some by the inclusion of how the encounter was initiated and especially arrest in model II; all else being equal, subjective procedural justice is more favorable when the citizen calls for police assistance and less favorable when the citizen is arrested. The estimated effect of procedural injustice is further attenuated by the inclusion of officers' use of authority in model III; subjective procedural justice is less favorable when police search the citizen and/or his/her vehicle (without consent) and when they use physical force.[2] But even controlling for these actions by police, procedural *in*justice toward the primary citizen affects that citizen's judgments. Model IV adds the assessed response time and demographic variables: the citizen's sex, age, race, and ethnicity, and the level of neighborhood disadvantage. Among the demographic variables, only sex has a large or statistically significant effect on citizens' subjective procedural justice, and response time has a substantively significant effect.[3]

Finally, model V adds indicators of citizen resistance and disrespect, respectively, both of which have a large bearing on subjective procedural justice.[4] The inclusion of these variables attenuates but does not eliminate the estimated effect of the officer's procedural injustice on citizens' judgments about procedural justice, however, from which we would cautiously infer that the effects of prior attitudes on subjective experience found in previous research may reflect the combined influences of citizens' selective perception *and* of citizens engaging in behavior that evokes from police a response that citizens judge unfavorably. If resistance or disrespect by citizens who hold negative attitudes toward the police were the mechanism that accounts for the relationship between prior attitudes and subjective experience, then the inclusion of these variables in a model of subjective experience would substantially reduce or eliminate altogether the estimated effect of officers' procedural justice. When citizen resistance and disrespect are added to the model, the coefficients for procedural injustice are reduced in magnitude to a degree but not eliminated; the coefficient for the use of physical force is also substantially reduced, as one would expect insofar as resistance is the factor that (should) prompt the use of physical force. Citizens who resist police authority tend to evoke the use of physical force by police and thus to rate the procedural justice of their contact less favorably. But holding resistance and disrespect constant, the pattern of other relationships is largely unchanged.

The use of police authority, and particularly searches, has a powerful impact on citizens' subjective procedural justice. One previous study, Meares et al. 2012, suggests that it is not the legality of the search but rather the procedural justice with which police act that shapes citizens' assessments of the propriety of police action. We might expect, therefore, that citizens' judgments that the police search was legitimate mediate either the effects of searches on citizens' subjective procedural justice and/or the effects of officers' procedural justice. When citizens' judgments that the search was legitimate are included in model IV, however, we find that the estimated effects of citizens' consent to searches are attenuated, but otherwise the pattern of effects is not altered. The search or frisk of the citizen continues to have a large coefficient (-4.92, compared with -4.33 in model IV), as does a vehicle search (-5.70, compared with -6.07). The primary officers' procedural injustice remains significant (a coefficient of -1.06, compared with -1.16 in model IV). We infer that citizens' judgments about the propriety of police searches are associated with citizens' *perceptions* of procedural justice, but they do not mediate the effect of officers' use of authority or their procedural justice on citizens' subjective procedural justice.

We note that we have approached tests of statistical significance in a conservative fashion, using two-tailed tests. If instead we applied one-tailed tests when the direction of expected effects was clear, the citizen's consent to a vehicle search and procedural injustice toward other citizens would be significant at the .10 level in model IV. We also acknowledge that all of these estimated relationships are attenuated due to measurement error. The survey data contain error, just as the survey data collected in previous research contained error. The observational data contain error, just as observational data collected in previous studies using systematic social observation contain (inestimable) error. So we could suppose that the effects of procedural justice and injustice are somewhat greater than the estimated effects, and we could suppose that the effects of other variables—the use of physical force, searches, consent to search—are also understated in these results as a consequence of measurement error. But even taking account of attenuation due to measurement error, the strength of the relationships between subjective procedural justice and officers' procedural justice is modest—much too modest to support the inferences that have been drawn from previous analyses that rest on only survey data.

The weak to null effects of officers' procedural justice on citizens' subjective procedural justice probably has to do with the high ratings that citizens tend to give police even when officers' behavior represents low-to-moderate levels of procedural justice. At the margin, better performance in procedural justice terms by the police cannot improve citizens' subjective assessments very much.

Officers' procedural justice might be expected to have different effects on subjective procedural justice in different types of police-citizen contacts; in particular, we might expect that procedural justice would have pronounced effects in police-initiated contacts and encounters involving an arrest. Analyzing each subset of encounters separately allows us to check for effects that are contingent on the type of contact, though it also compromises the statistical power of the analysis. Few effects that are contingent on the type of contact emerge from those analyses.

Among citizen-initiated contacts, and contrary to our expectations, procedural injustice has stronger effects than it has in either police-initiated contacts or in those ending in arrest. Some differences in subjective procedural justice can be seen across types of calls, which in this analysis rest on measures derived from the observational data; compared with citizens who called about public nuisances, citizens who called for assistance with respect to nonviolent crimes, interpersonal conflicts, suspicious circumstances and traffic problems were more positive, while those who summoned police with respect to a violent crime were less positive.[5] Men who called for assistance were more positive about procedural justice than women. Response time was also a factor in citizens' judgments about procedural justice in citizen-initiated contacts.

Among those whose contacts were initiated by police, neither procedural justice nor procedural injustice by officers has a detectable impact on citizens' subjective procedural justice. Searches, however, detract from subjective procedural justice. Among those who were arrested, regardless of how the encounter was initiated, searches detracted from procedural justice. Procedural injustice toward other citizens in the encounter detracts from arrestees' sense of procedural justice, though officers' procedural justice toward other citizens has no effect.

A somewhat more complicated picture emerges when subjective procedural justice (the procedural justice index) is regressed on the procedural justice subscales in lieu of the combinatory scales, allowing for the four domains of procedural justice to have varying effects. When the subscales are included in the analysis, we find, first, that the effect of procedural injustice by the primary officer is comprised of the effects of three of the four procedural justice domains. Untrustworthy motives have an unexpectedly positive coefficient, but the estimate is statistically unreliable and not significant. Second, and moreover, the procedural justice subscales have detectable but countervailing effects, as trustworthy motives and quality of treatment improve subjective procedural justice, while neutrality detracts from it, though only two of the effects achieve statistical significance.

The negative effect of neutrality is anomalous on its face, but it may reflect the situationally contingent nature of police behavior, as officers act in accordance with the demands of individual situations, and the fact that procedural justice in action is not entirely an exogenous variable. Higher scores on the neutrality subscale mainly reflect officers' efforts to explain their decisions, in general, and to a lesser extent their efforts to explain more particularly the legal standards on which they based their actions. Higher scores on this subscale are associated with police-initiated encounters, problems concerning either traffic or interpersonal conflict, arrests, and evidence of criminal wrongdoing by the citizen. Scores on this subscale are higher when the citizen is a suspect or disputant, and lower when the citizen is a victim or service recipient. We would speculate that officers act in these more procedurally just ways when the situation demands it, and that these situations are by their nature situations in which citizens are less likely to be pleased with the contact; indeed, officers might extend themselves to explain when citizens send signals that an explanation is expected. As plausible as this account may be, and although the primary citizens' requests for leniency (for him/herself or others) have a fairly substantial relationship to subjective procedural justice, it does not appear that citizens' requests mediate the effect of neutrality, the estimated magnitude of which is largely unaffected by the inclusion of citizens' requests.

These effects are of fairly modest magnitude, and together the procedural justice subscales together (and alone) explain no more than 12 percent of the variance in subjective procedural justice. These results indicate that what officers do—that is, both the justice and the injustice with which officers act—is not entirely lost on citizens as they assess their contacts with police, but as we found previously, the effects of officers' procedural justice on citizens' subjective experience are quite modest. When further controls are added for the nature of the situation and officers' exercise of authority, the estimated effects of several subscales are attenuated somewhat, though the addition of controls for citizens' backgrounds does not alter the pattern of effects.

In view of previous research, we have compelling reason to suppose that the omission of citizens' prior attitudes from these models leaves them misspecified; prior attitudes toward the police generally have a strong effect on subjective procedural justice. Thus we added our measure of legitimacy—the trust index—to the model in order to gauge the extent to which the estimated relationships are biased by the omission of prior attitudes. It is of course true that the trust index is not a measure of *prior* attitudes, as it is based on responses to the survey that followed the encounter in question, and it could instead be specified as an effect of subjective procedural justice rather than its cause. But based on previous research, it is fairly safe to say that the postcontact trust score is nearly the same as the precontact trust score, since global attitudes like this one tend to be stable, and moreover, the effect of the citizen's subjective procedural justice on trust is likely much weaker than the effect of trust on subjective procedural justice.

With only the officers' procedural justice and the trust index in the model, the pattern of procedural (in)justice effects resembles that estimated earlier: procedural injustice detracts from subjective procedural justice, while procedural justice contributes little. Trust bears a moderately strong relationship to subjective procedural justice, controlling for the officers' procedural (in)justice. The coefficient for trust is unaffected by the addition of controls for the officers' use of authority. Furthermore, the estimated effect of trust is stable with the addition of controls for citizens' characteristics and for citizens' behavior (resistance and disrespect), respectively. The effect of trust is not diminished by the addition of citizen resistance and disrespect, suggesting that the effect of global attitudes on subjective experience is mainly a matter of selective perception by citizens, and is not mediated by citizens' behavior.

The coefficient for trust, like those in all of the cross-sectional research, reflects the reciprocal effects of prior attitudes (for which we treat the trust index as a proxy) and subjective procedural justice on one another, but given the much greater magnitude of the effect of prior attitudes, we can surmise that most of this relationship is probably attributable to that effect. Moreover, the effects of officers' procedural (in)justice on subjective procedural justice remain asymmetrical and, on balance, fairly small.

TABLE 6 Five Models of Subjective Outcomes

	I	II	III	IV	V
Constant	0.47*	−0.58*	−0.43**	−0.10	−0.03
PC x PO: procedural justice	0.04	0.01	0.02	0.02	0.02
PC x PO: procedural injustice	−0.21*	0.06	0.07	0.05	0.07
PC x OO: procedural justice	−0.08*	−0.02	−0.02	−0.05**	−0.05*
PC x OO: procedural injustice	−0.08	−0.01	−0.02	−0.02	−0.00
OC: procedural justice	0.02	0.02	0.02	0.02	0.02
OC: procedural injustice	0.11	0.10	0.11*	0.09**	0.10**
Subjective procedural justice	—	0.13*	0.14*	0.14*	0.14*
Citizen called for service	—	—	−0.44*	−0.41**	−0.46*
Police–initiated	—	—	0.44	0.44	0.40
Citizen arrested	—	—	−0.36	−0.37	−0.36
Search/frisk person	—	—	0.34	0.38	0.34
Search vehicle	—	—	0.29	0.25	0.16
Citizen consent search/frisk	—	—	−0.01	−0.10	−0.11
Citizen consent vehicle search	—	—	−0.53	−0.47	−0.41
Verbal force	—	—	−0.33	−0.26	−0.22
Physical force	—	—	0.10	0.07	0.15
Evidence	—	—	0.04	0.04	0.02
Citizen male	—	—	—	0.05	0.07
Citizen's age	—	—	—	−0.01	−0.01**
Citizen black	—	—	—	−0.24	−0.22
Citizen Hispanic	—	—	—	−0.17	−0.16
Response time	—	—	—	0.07	0.07
Neighborhood disadvantage	—	—	—	0.04	0.04
Citizen disrespect	—	—	—	—	−0.52*
Citizen resistance	—	—	—	—	0.05
Adjusted R^2	0.03	0.55	0.58	0.61	0.62

NOTE: PC = primary citizen; PO = primary officer; OO = other officer(s); OC = other citizen(s)
* p < .05
** p < .10

Subjective Outcomes

Our model posits that officers' procedural justice shapes citizens' judgments about their outcomes. For the most part, however, subjective outcomes are not a function of procedural justice: together the scales of procedural justice explain 4 percent of the variation in citizens' assessments of whether the outcome they received was the outcome they deserved; see table 6. The primary officer's procedural injustice detracts from citizens' judgments to a modest degree, and other officers' procedural justice also (and independently) detracts from the citizen's judgment that the outcome was deserved. But in the main, citizens' assessments of outcomes are not a reflection of officers' procedural justice.

Citizens' judgments about procedural justice, however, have a powerful impact on subjective outcomes, independent of the officers' procedural justice, and when subjective procedural justice is controlled, officers' procedural justice has no effect on citizens' judgments about their outcomes (see model II in table 6); the effect of officers' behavior—and especially the injustice with which they act—is mediated entirely by citizens' subjective procedural justice. The nature of the situation affects citizens' judgments only to a small degree, and officers' use of authority (controlling for subjective procedural justice) has no detectable effects (in model III). Likewise, citizens' backgrounds add little to the explanation (model IV), and the inclusion of citizen disrespect and resistance (in model V) also does not alter the pattern of effects. The hypothesized effect of subjective procedural justice on subjective outcomes is confirmed, but the hypothesized effects of officers' procedural justice on subjective outcomes are not confirmed.

Citizen Satisfaction

Our model holds that the effect of officers' procedural justice on citizens' satisfaction is mediated by citizens' judgments about procedural justice and outcomes, but we nevertheless estimate the parameters of regression equations that include officers' procedural justice; insofar as officers' behavior has effects on citizens' subjective experience, we think it valuable to have a full accounting of them. Officers' procedural *in*justice affects citizen satisfaction; that effect is mediated for the most part, but not entirely, by citizens' subjective procedural justice. Officers' procedural justice, by itself, accounts for no more than 11 percent of the variation in citizens' satisfaction. The addition of subjective procedural justice pushes the explained variation up to 78 percent. Further additions to the model—for example, officers' use of authority and citizens' backgrounds—add nothing further to the explanation of satisfaction.

TALES FROM THE FIELD

Since percentages and coefficients can tell only part of the story of police-citizen interactions, as we commented in chapter 6, we offer here a couple of illustrations of incongruence between observed police behavior and citizens' subjective experience, which may serve to put some descriptive flesh on the numerical skeletons of charts and regression parameters. We begin with a case in which the observations were indicative of fairly high procedural justice (a score of 11), no procedural injustice (a score of zero), and a citizen's judgment that represented an unfavorable subjective experience (with an index score of -11).

CASE 7–1

O1 (male) was driving through a residential neighborhood during daytime. O1 stopped next to a house and greeted C1 (female) by saying, "How are you doing, hun?" O_1 asked how C_1 was doing and asked if she wanted to talk to him away from C_1's children. O_1 asked C_1 what was going on and C_1 told him she was picking up her daughter from her ex-husband/boyfriend and an altercation ensued. C_1 said her ex was flagrantly insulting her, and she responded by pushing him. He pushed her back, and C_1 said she punched him in the face after being pushed. C_1 told O_1 he hit her back, and followed that statement with showing the officer her reddened ear. C_1 then said she hit him a "good number of times" after being hit by her ex. O_1 then told C_1 he would be honest with her, and told her that because there was no visible injury and because she had told O_1 she had hit her ex multiple times while holding her child, she was going to be arrested. C_1 was noticeably confused, and asked the officer if he was serious. O_1 told her she was endangering the welfare of a child. C_1 protested by saying her ex had put hands on her as well, and O_1 responded by saying she had no visible injuries and from her story, she was the primary aggressor. O_1 told C_1 he would not arrest her in front of her children, and asked who was home with C_1 at the time. C_1 said her stepfather was home. C_1 asked if she was going to stay the night in jail, and O_1 said there was no bail. O_1 then called to another police car to have them contact the ex so he could pick up his child. C_1 calmly told the officers her actions were in self-defense, and O_1 told her that was not the case according to her description of events. O_1 told C_1 that after seeing both C_1's face and C_1's ex's face, and because he knew C_1 was holding her child during the incident, the police determined C_1 was the primary aggressor. O_1 sympathized with C_1 and explained as best he could why C_1 was being arrested.

O_1 was explaining the basis for C_1's arrest when C_2 (male, C_1's stepfather) came to speak to C_1 and the officers. C_1 told C_2 she was being arrested for endangering the welfare of a child, and C_2 seemed confused and slightly angry. He said, to no one in particular, that C_1's ex had pushed her first. O_1 said it did not matter. C_2 then said C_1 was holding the baby, and O_1 told him that was what mattered. C_2 told O_1 that C_1's ex had a history of being abusive. O_1 explained to C_2 that C_1 had caused substantial physical injury to C_1's ex while holding her child, which was a greater offense than C_1's ex's actions. C_2 began to bring up other possible scenarios in which C_1's ex may have been determined to be the primary aggressor, and O_1 told him he was not going to discuss it any further. C_2 said the officer had to talk to him, and O_1 said he did not.

O_1 asked C_1 to give her child to her father so O_1 could speak to her for a minute. O_1 told her if she wanted to press harassment charges against her ex, she may do that. O_1 warned her that if she were to press harassment charges, Child Protective Services would get involved and may remove the child. O_1 continued to explain to C_1 that he fully understood the situation, and he understood that C_1's ex was not a good person. O_1 said he was going to call his sergeant to see if they could press the issue of harassment. O_2 (male, unknown arrival time) began to speak to C_1 and slowly went over the sequence of events during the incident. O_2 pointed out that C_1 hit her ex first, and continued to hit him after he hit her back. C_1 then told the officers that her ex had accidentally hit her child as well.

O_1 explained to C_1 that NYS laws stated that when a child is endangered in a situation that at least meets the criteria for a misdemeanor, an arrest must be made. O_1 told C_1 the officers would have had more flexibility if the child had not been involved. C1 then said her ex should be facing the same charges, and O1 told her that was not the case as C1 was holding the child during the incident.

C1 asked to change clothes before being taken to the police station, and O1 said they were not worried about her fleeing, and that she could go inside and speak to her stepfather about the situation.

C1 went inside to speak to her father. O1 and O2 spoke to each other about what options there were that would allow them to arrest C1's ex. While talking to C1 both officers demonstrated their understanding of the situation, and stressed to her that her descriptions of events forced them to make the decision that she was the primary aggressor.

O1 went inside and asked C1 for her child's identifying information. O1 asked C2 if he could take care of the child after they left. O1 told C2 he was going to try to put the issue of child endangerment on C1's ex, but it was not a promising option. O1 told C1 that he did not want to arrest C1, and that he wished the laws of New York were different. O1 also told C1 that he appreciated her honesty.

O1 told C2 they were going to leave C1's daughter with him. O1 said that the officers talked to their supervisor and C1 must be considered the primary aggressor. O1 said he had to contact Child Protective Services to let them know about the incident, but he would explain to them that C1's actions could have been in defense of herself and her child. O2 then confirmed that C2 could take care of the child while C1 was in jail. O1 then asked C2 for his identifying information. O1 explained where C1 would be arraigned in the morning and that he may bring an attorney for C1 if he wished.

O1 asked C1 if she had anything in her pockets, to which she said she did not, before putting her in the back of his vehicle and leaving the scene with O2 in the passenger seat.

During the ride C1 told the officers she believed she had an order of protection against her ex that expired the day of the incident. O1 told C1 he did not think she was a bad person, or that she did more wrong than her ex during the incident, and he said he believed she was the better parent when compared to her ex. C1 told the officers she thought her mother was going to her house to pick up her daughter, and O2 said that her father would be taking care of C1's daughter that night. C1 made a small joke by asking the officers if she could ride in the car with them while on patrol instead of spending the night in jail.

Considering the circumstances, both officers made a considerable effort to comfort C1 and assure her they were doing everything in their power to help her. They were friendly, calm, and honest with C1 about every aspect of the situation.

The officers were courteous and sympathetic toward the citizen, explained the constraints of the law, showed concern for her (and her child's) welfare, and showed other consideration in allowing her to change her clothes. Yet the citizen's judgments, as they are captured in her survey responses, reflect none of these elements of procedural justice.

On the other hand, and as we noted above, sometimes citizens' judgments give police more credit for procedural justice than independent observation suggests is warranted. Consider case 7–2, in which the observation-based scores for procedural justice and injustice were 4.5 and 5.5, respectively, and in which the primary citizen gave police high ratings:

CASE 7–2

O1 and O2 stopped on the street in front of a house with three citizens on the porch and another citizen walking by. O1 got out of his vehicle and he immediately shouted, "Yo bro, get over here" to the citizen walking down the street (C1). As the officers approached C1 he attempted to give a name, but did so with exceptionally slurred speech. O1 told C1 to put his hands behind his back and handcuffed him. C1 asked what happened and O1 responded by saying C1 was drinking on the street, which is illegal, and he was harassing people for money. C1 asked who he was harassing, and O1 responded by telling him people had called about C1. O1 asked C1 if he had anything in his pockets before he frisked C1. C1 did not respond. O1 frisked C1 and found two daggers. When asked what he needed the daggers for C1 told the officers he found them in his girlfriend's house. C1 told the officers he was fixing the house for his girlfriend, but most of C1's words were slurred and unintelligible. O1 further restrained C1 by putting him on his knees, and C1 told O1 he was not going to fight back. O1 asked if he had any ID or warrants, and C1 produced an ID and said he did not have any warrants. C1 handed the ID to O2, who briefly tested C1 on the information from the ID. C1 apologized for drinking on the street. O1 then walked C1 over to the police vehicle and poured out C1's alcohol. O1 told C1 he was going to get a ticket and then placed him in the back of the car. The officers then left the scene with C1 in custody.

Approximately a hundred feet down the street the officers were hailed by two citizens on the side of the street. The officers told them they had someone in the back and if the citizens wished to make a complaint they must contact the station. The officers then continued towards the police station. C1 asked if he was being brought in for the drinking, to which O1 replied he was bringing him in to give him a ticket, but he would not be locked up. C1 told the officers his name, and asked for O1's name. O1 gave C1 his name, which was the same name as a popular video game. Upon hearing this C1 told the officer, "No disrespect, but I'm sorry." O1 then told C1 the main issue was not the fact that he was drinking on the street, but that he did not tell the officer he had two daggers. O1 told him he was going to let him go until he found the daggers. C1 attempted to explain how he came across the daggers in his girlfriend's house and took them because he liked them. C1 continuously told O1 he understood and he was being honest. O1 reprimanded C1 for lying about the daggers, to which C1 told him he did not lie, and only did not answer.

The video ended when they arrived at the station.

It is certainly possible that, in responding to our survey a few weeks after the sampled incident, the citizen in case 7–2 suffered greater memory decay than the average respondent, given that he had been drinking. Memory decay can affect any respondent's judgments, even with the passage of only two or three weeks' time. We would suppose that any gaps in citizens' recollection tend to be filled by their prior attitudes toward the police, to either the benefit or the detriment of the police, and that citizens who are intoxicated at the time of their encounter with police would be all the more susceptible to such bias.

SUMMARY

Extant empirical evidence leaves as an open question the degree to which officers' behavior in police-citizen encounters affects citizens' subjective experience; instead, such hypotheses are typically treated as assumptions, because research has relied exclusively on survey data on the citizens. We subjected these hypotheses to empirical testing here. We found that officers' procedural (in)justice has effects on citizens' judgments about procedural justice, though the effects are fairly modest in magnitude and they are asymmetrical: procedural injustice has substantially greater negative effects on citizens' judgments than procedural justice has positive effects. The procedural justice with which officers act accounts for a rather small fraction of the variation in subjective procedural justice. Furthermore, officers' procedural justice has very small effects on citizens' judgments about outcomes, and they are mediated by subjective procedural justice. Similarly, officers' procedural justice has little direct effect on citizen satisfaction.

These findings are quite compatible with the findings of previous research concerning the effects of citizens' prior attitudes on subjective experience; moreover, the effects of officers' procedural justice on subjective experience do not appear to be mediated to a large degree by citizens' behavior, in the form of resistance or disrespect, suggesting that previous findings about the effects of prior attitudes stem from citizens' selective perception and not from citizens' behavior toward police.

This is not to say that officers' behavior has no effect on subjective experience. The use of police authority has a bearing on subjective experience, independent of the procedural justice with which authority is exercised. Searches especially have a strongly negative effect on subjective experience, which is by and large neutralized when citizens consent to a search, and the use of physical force also appears to influence citizens' subjective experience.

The asymmetrical effects of procedural (in)justice do not spring from a negativity bias, however. To the contrary, it appears that citizens are rather generous to police in their judgments about procedural justice, relative to the more concrete accounts of officers' actions by trained, independent observers. Insofar as citizens tend to overstate the procedural justice of their interactions with police when officers do not exhibit high levels of procedural justice, we do not find that subjective experience is responsive when police act with higher levels of procedural justice. Police can detract somewhat from the subjective experience of citizens through procedural injustice, but they do not add substantially to subjective experience through procedural justice.

8

Procedural Justice and Management Accountability

As we observed in chapter 1, police systems of management accountability do not normally measure all of the outcomes that are important, and one of the outcomes that is omitted is the procedural justice with which police act in their encounters with citizens. We sought to rectify this omission, if only for a finite period of time, by administering the police services survey and summarizing results on a monthly basis at departmental Compstat meetings. With these survey-based figures, we supplemented the departments' continuing attention to crime as an outcome. The survey measures each month served both as inputs to Compstat and as the previous month's outcomes; we analyze change over time below.

We heard, albeit unsystematically at Compstat meetings, from mid-level managers—captains in Syracuse and lieutenants in Schenectady—about the efforts that they made to manage these outcomes. But we also conducted two waves of semi-structured interviews with patrol officers and patrol supervisors about what their commanders were doing to manage these dimensions of police performance. We analyze their responses to understand the managerial efforts that were made to affect officers' performance, which we discuss here, and also to understand their interpretations of the administrative priority—that is, the sense that they made of the push toward procedurally just policing, which we discuss in chapter 9.

MEASURING WHAT MATTERS

The police services survey included numerous items on citizens' subjective experiences with police. We thought it better to present the counts of citizens' responses to specific questions—for example, whether police were polite— with which respondents could agree or disagree, either strongly or somewhat, rather than a summary scale like the procedural justice index (introduced in chapter 4), on the assumption that the command staff would find concrete response categories for specific survey items more readily interpretable than artificial scores on a derivative indicator, and that specific items might offer them some clues about what officers were doing and not doing that could be better managed. But we did not want to overload the command staff with information, and so we looked for a way to economize in reporting survey results. Upon compiling a baseline of survey results (seven survey waves in Schenectady and ten in Syracuse), we analyzed citizens' satisfaction in terms of process-based factors to identify those that appeared to be particularly important in citizens' overall subjective experience. From those analyses we distilled eight items that we thereupon treated as the measures around which future reporting would revolve:

- Satisfaction with treatment by police
- Satisfaction with how police handled the problem
- How helpful police were
- Whether police took care of the problem
- Whether police considered the citizen's views
- Whether the police treated the citizen with dignity and respect
- Whether police made their decision based on facts
- Whether police respected the citizen's rights

All but the fourth listed item above allowed for four categories of response, so that stronger or more intensely held views could be distinguished from less intensely held views; only whether the police took care of the problem was a binary yes/no item.

Performance Measures in Compstat

We introduced the project to the command staffs at Compstat meetings in September, 2011; the survey was under way at that time, but we did not report results then. On December 21, 2011, we appeared at the Schenectady Compstat meeting to present the summary of baseline survey findings, and to illustrate the survey items that we would be charting for them month-to-month. We summarized a larger number of items at that time, in order to place the focal items in context and explain the rationale for making those items the recurring indicators on which we would concentrate. We also broke survey results down by contact types—calls for service, stops, and arrests—and summarized the distributions on several measures of legitimacy. Our corresponding appearance at the Syracuse Compstat meeting was on January 11, 2012.

Figures 9 and 10 below are excerpts from the PowerPoint presentations at Compstat meetings. These charts are typical of those that we routinely shared at

Police Treated Me with Dignity & Respect

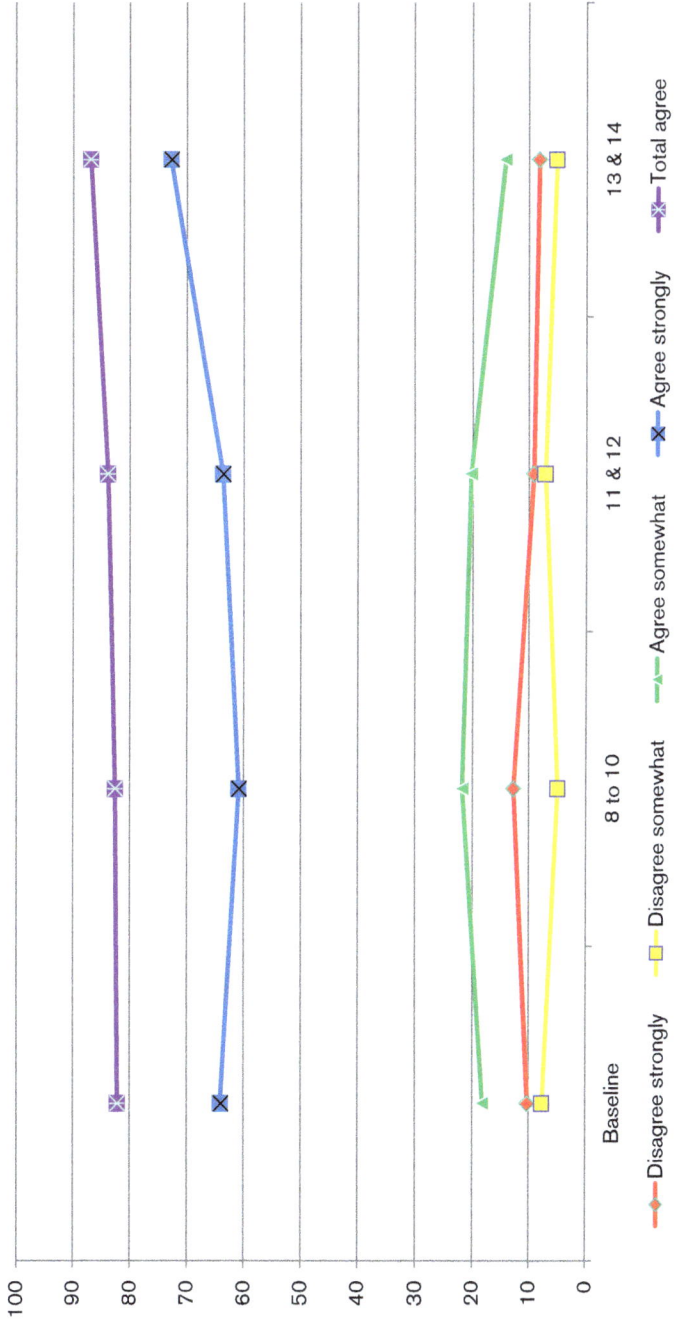

FIGURE 9. Schenectady Compstat Excerpt.

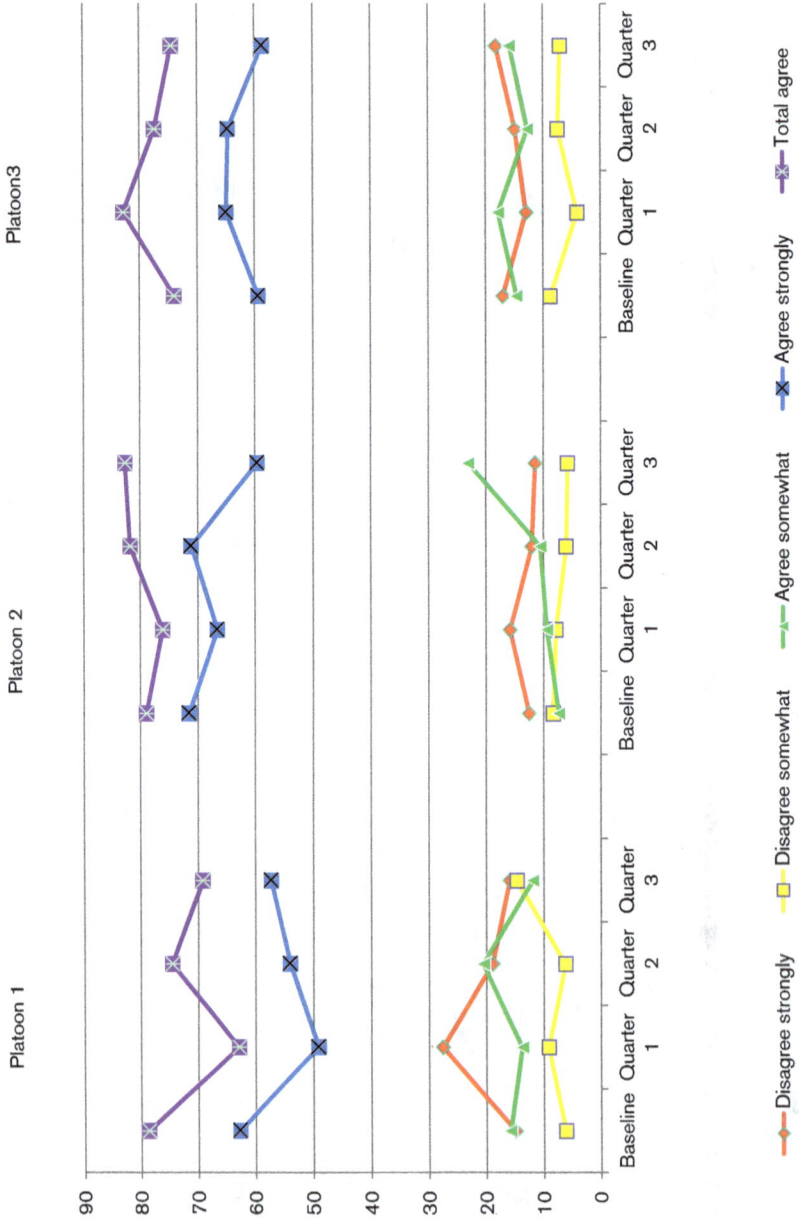

Police Made Their Decision Based on Facts

FIGURE 10. Syracuse Compstat Excerpt.

Compstat meetings; we also converted the PowerPoint slides to pdf documents and sent copies to our department liaisons. Each chart depicts the baseline levels of performance and subsequent monthly levels (labeled as survey waves).

We supplemented these routine reports with additional analyses at times. In order to provide measures of outcomes for which platoon commanders might feel a greater sense of individual responsibility, we provided for quarterly breakdowns by individual platoons, as shown in figure 10. We also undertook additional analysis as command staff raised questions about the patterns, for example, in Schenectady, we summarized the measures by patrol zone and by (CAD-recorded) response time. Both departments' command staffs expressed curiosity about how the results for their department compared to those for other cities, in response to which we shared with them the comparisons (to, e.g., Chicago) summarized in chapter 4.

Interim Reports

In addition, we prepared interim reports for each department. One report summarized survey findings in more detail than we did in Compstat meetings, based on the first twenty waves of surveys. Much as we reported in chapters 3 and 4, we summarized findings on trust and subjective experience, and also provided breakdowns of subjective experience by contact type, call type, and patrol zone or beat. We also summarized a qualitative analysis of open-ended survey responses about the reasons for citizens' dissatisfaction, as we reported in chapter 5.

A second report for each department was based on information gathered through interviews with patrol officers and supervisors. Detail on the interview methods is included below. The report focused on the views of the rank and file regarding the emphasis on customer service, how (if at all) expectations were being communicated down through the ranks, and potential sources of resistance to a customer-service orientation. In addition, we provided recommendations to address the barriers to efforts to manage these aspects of police performance.

MANAGING WHAT'S MEASURED

We anticipated a priori several reasons why measuring procedural justice performance would not result in detectable improvements over time. First and perhaps most basically, both of the study departments exhibited high baseline levels of subjective experience, leaving only so much room for improvement. The high baseline levels were received quite favorably by the command staffs, respectively, at the meetings at which the baseline results were reported. The Syracuse command staff, recognizing that 100 percent satisfaction was not an achievable goal, seemed satisfied that their officers were doing quite a good job of meeting citizens' expectations and treating them properly. These high levels of subjective experience, citywide, are not unique to our study departments, of course, and even without reference to our findings about the tenuous relationship between officers' procedural justice and citizens' subjective experience, they raise questions about how much the implementation of a procedural justice model could increase measurable subjective experience.

There are a number of other reasons to doubt that change would be observed once police managers were given measures of procedural justice performance, some of which are specific to this project. First, the measures based on the survey reflected the performance of the entire department and only occasionally that of individual platoons, which we would suppose had the effect of vitiating individual commanders' sense of personal responsibility. It was only on a quarterly basis that we could summarize the performance of individual platoons, and quarterly measures of performance are probably not sufficiently frequent to motivate managers to attend to the outcomes in question (Behn 2008). Second, everyone on the departments' command staffs was aware that the project provided for surveys that would extend over only eighteen months, and so performance measurement was a fixed-term proposition. Neither city had the funds to continue such surveying indefinitely; indeed, we are aware of no city that does (or has done) such ongoing surveys with sufficient frequency that they are useful for management accountability. The fixed-term nature of the measures of procedural justice could be expected to compromise the investment of effort that managers would make with a view to this outcome. Third, and finally, we were given the task of reporting on the procedural justice performance measures each month, which may have made it seem like an academic interlude to the Compstat meeting, and not an outcome that the departments' executive staffs embraced.

Yet another reason to be doubtful that change would be observed, and which is probably not confined to the study departments or this project, is that Compstat as executed did not stress accountability. As in Compstat mechanisms in other departments (Willis et al. 2007; Weisburd et al. 2003), platoon commanders and other unit heads did not succeed or fail by results, and we might suppose that as in other departments, Compstat was loosely coupled with street-level performance. We interviewed commanders in the study departments to learn more about current expectations of those involved in Compstat. In both departments the perception of platoon commanders was that the assessment of police performance was nearly exclusively numbers-driven (e.g., number of tickets, number of drug buys, number of field contacts, number of arrests, number of crimes). They described expectations for their role as it relates to Compstat in terms of "being on top of the numbers," "identifying patterns," and being prepared to explain during the meeting what they had done to address the patterns or numbers. While the introduction of feedback on citizens' subjective experience with police represented an additional set of numbers, interviewees did not anticipate this would have implications for how they managed their subordinates or for their role in Compstat. Most went on to explain that they already managed this aspect of police performance on an individual basis and they already knew the character and ability of their officers. Independently and systematically collected information (the survey) was seen as a potentially positive development insofar as it could reinforce or confirm what they already knew (akin to the purpose we see many in law enforcement attribute to crime mapping). Commanders correctly anticipated that feedback on officers' performance would not alter expectations for their role in Compstat. In neither department was Compstat used to hold commanders accountable for achieving results in the ends of policing (crime reduction, disorder control, or improvements in the quality of life), and it was not a mechanism for holding commanders accountable for improvements in outcomes measured through the survey. We seldom heard administrators ask unit commanders to explain what steps they had pursued to manage and promote procedurally just policing.

All of these obstacles to the management of street-level procedural justice arguably pale by comparison to the larger structural obstacles in American police departments. As Michael Brown observes, "police administrators and supervisors are caught between demands for loyalty to the men on the street and demands from the public that police power be used in a specific way or even curtailed" (1981, 91). On the street, police work is performed in an environment marked by uncertainty, ambiguity, and danger, in the face of which officers cope by pulling together. Administrators must depend on officers to perform this arduous work satisfactorily, and as Brown points out, "the pressures for loyalty and solidarity are refracted throughout the police bureaucracy" (90), with norms that prohibit second-guessing and micromanagement.

The implementation of community policing in Chicago hit a cultural "wall" whose foundation is set on these structural conditions. Wesley Skogan (2006, 81) describes the reluctance of police officers to perform tasks that are seen as not "real police work," and also their "aversion to civilians playing any role in telling them what to do or evaluating their performance." Officers do not believe that anyone who has not done police work can understand it, and they tend to dismiss police administrators who introduce change as "out of touch" with the street (also see Skogan 2008).

The intrinsic demands of the work on the street and of cultural norms probably account for the limited success of training that is geared toward shaping how officers relate to police clientele. In her study of the effects of a recruit training curriculum into which the concepts and skills of community and problem-oriented policing had been integrated, Robin Haarr (2001) found positive changes in recruits' attitudes, which subsequently dissipated as the new officers went into the field and were exposed to the work and to cultural norms. More to the point of the procedural justice model, the Quality Interaction Training Program of the Chicago police had limited and mixed effects in the context of the academy (Schuck and Rosenbaum 2011; Rosenbaum and Lawrence n.d.), and modest effects in its in-service form (Skogan et al. 2014); we might expect that even these effects would decay over time without consistent reinforcement. Many departments have offered training in "verbal judo," and although we are aware of no empirical evaluations of the impacts of such training, anecdotal evidence suggests that it is not always well-received by officers. The content of training along these lines—"quality interaction" or "verbal judo"—is for many officers not compatible with the multiple and conflicting demands of the work as they experience it.[1]

Managerial options are, then, limited. Platoon and other unit commanders could exhort their officers, directly and indirectly through first-line supervisors, to be more mindful of the utility and propriety of interacting with citizens with procedural justice. They could explain the benefits in the form of citizen compliance with police direction and citizen cooperation, as well as the standing of the department with the community. Armed with information on citizens' subjective experience, they could reinforce the exhortation with measures of police performance. Ultimately, however, the efficacy of such exhortation turns on the sense that supervisors and officers make of commanders' expectations.

Commanders and supervisors could engage in greater direct oversight of officers' interactions with citizens. This takes time, of course, and moreover, it carries other risks. Violating the norm of not second-guessing the judgments of the officer who is handling a situation, direct oversight risks antagonizing officers and undermining the routine, day-to-day cooperation of subordinates in performing basic police tasks. Schenectady supervisors are expected to routinely complete a Service Quality Control Report (SQCR) as a means of exercising oversight over the quality of interactions between officers and citizens. This practice did not appear to be resisted by supervisors or to be objectionable to officers. We suspect this could be because sergeants did not appear to use them as a means to prove that an officer had done something wrong or to show them how they might do something better (which would violate the norm of not second-guessing officers' judgments), and the occasions on which officers were the subject of a report were few (policy calls for four SQCRs per sergeant, per month).

Administrators have some additional options. In-service training could be offered. Indeed, Schenectady planned to make procedural justice the subject of in-service training in the fall of 2012, but those tentative plans were derailed when the assistant chief of the Field Services Bureau sustained an injury and was out of work for some time. Syracuse contemplated a podcast by the chief to be played at roll calls. As we recounted above, however, the content of training and exhortation is filtered through officers' understanding of the requirements of their work.

Still other administrative options for managing street-level procedural justice are administrative rule-making and early intervention systems. Rules could be promulgated—for example, rules that require officers to explain to those whom they stop the reason(s) for the stops, and to give citizens an opportunity to explain themselves. As we explained in chapter 2, however, the capacity of police administrators to enforce such rules is directly proportional to the visibility of the conduct to which the rules apply, and the procedural justice of officers' actions is of decidedly low visibility. Early intervention systems could be structured to flag repeated citizen complaints about discourtesy and other forms of procedural injustice, but citizen complaints are of dubious validity as indicators of procedural injustice, and early intervention takes the forms of either training or counseling, whose impacts on officers' performance depend on the sense that officers make of the content.

Patrol Interviews

We conducted interviews with patrol sergeants and patrol officers in order to assess the views of the rank and file regarding the emphasis on customer service, how (if at all) administrative expectations were reverberating down through the ranks, and any sources of resistance to a customer-service orientation. In our conversations with uniformed personnel, we did not use the term "procedural justice," which would likely not have been recognized by or meaningful to them. Instead, we framed "customer service" and "citizen satisfaction" with police performance as the topic of the interviews. In retrospect, the term "customer" may have set a less neutral tone for the interviews than, say, "citizens' assessment of the quality of police service" or "the quality of police citizen interactions" might have done. However, we and the command staff used the term "customer service" from the outset of the project, and so the use of that term during the interviews was consistent with prior practice.

Two waves of interviews were conducted in each department, the first in June 2012, after five to six months of survey feedback to command staff, and the second in February 2014, well after the final feedback. We asked sergeants what, if anything, they and their platoon or unit commander had done to direct officers' attention to the importance of customer service. In addition, we asked patrol officers what, if anything, their field supervisors had done to direct attention to the importance of customer service. The structured interview protocol also assessed perceptions of the extent to which customer service is an organizational priority, how officers' performance in terms of customer service was measured, awareness of the ongoing surveying of citizens, and the extent to which respondents felt citizen input was an appropriate means to monitor police performance. We conducted a total of eighty-seven interviews with patrol sergeants and patrol officers in the study departments: fourteen and eleven sergeants in Syracuse and Schenectady, respectively; thirty-one patrol officers in each department. We did not detect meaningful differences in the nature of the responses between waves 1 and 2. The wave 2 instruments paralleled wave 1, with the exception of a question to determine whether the respondent had been interviewed during the earlier wave (seven respondents indicated they were interviewed two times and two were uncertain). For the most part we did not detect a difference in managerial styles between the two departments, so we combine responses, and highlight the exceptions to this rule of interdepartmental congruence.

THE MANAGEMENT CONTINUUM

The presumption guiding our work was that police legitimacy can be enhanced when measures of relevant performance are made available to managers. Of course, simply making the information available is insufficient; managers must believe they are accountable for managing performance and must take steps to communicate the chiefs' expectations and their own expectations to their subordinates. We identified three patterns that formed a management continuum. Supervisors who did nothing fell at one end of the spectrum, and those who seemed to routinely address the importance of customer service at the other; supervisors whose approach was best characterized as intermittently directing attention to customer service fell in the middle. See figure 11.

Supervisors' Responses

In both departments, very few respondents stated that either they or their commander were not communicating expectations about the importance of procedural justice as an outcome for which their subordinates were responsible. The few individuals who did not direct attention to customer service either ignored the departments' push to stress procedurally just policing or more actively spoke against it. For example, when asked what if anything they had told their subordinates about the importance of customer service, we heard responses such as: "I tell them officer safety is the goal, not customer service"; "It is kind of difficult. I can't go to every call and hold their hand."

Supervisors whose efforts were intermittent reported mentioning that patrol should do its best to "be respectful" or "watch your tone" when handling calls, or "try" to emphasize customer service "when possible." "It's hard to tell adults [patrol officers] what to do. But I say things like don't swear and treat people with respect. Even if you think it is ridiculous you need to listen and don't curse." Their efforts generally reflected a commonsense approach, because their own expectations were very straightforward. Most of them presumed that reinforcing these statements at roll call every so often was sufficient, with only a subset going on to hold officers accountable by reviewing the feedback we provided each month or observing officers on calls and using concrete examples to reinforce their directives.

Most respondents reported making a regular effort to direct attention to the importance of customer service. Generally, this included sharing the information that was disseminated at Compstat meetings and mentioning the importance of

Intermittent attention

- Occasional mention at roll call - the *what* but not *why*
  - "Watch your tone out there"
  - "Try" to think about customer service "if possible"
  - "Don't swear if you don't have to"

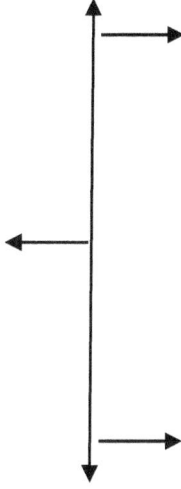

Regular attention/support

- Regular emphasis at roll call - the *what* and *why*
  - "Don't use jargon, explain what you are doing. It makes people feel better which makes your job easier."
- Shared monthly Compstat presentations
- Supervisors responded to calls and gave feedback on quality of the interaction/completed Service Quality Control Reports

No attention/resistance

- No mention made to subordinate officers
- Supervisors undermined command staff expectations
- "Officer safety is the goal, not customer service"

FIGURE 11. The Management Continuum.

customer service during line-up or roll call. In Schenectady, the importance of regularly completing Service Quality Control Reports (SQCR) was emphasized as a means to routinely direct attention to customer service. Among those who routinely stressed the importance of customer service at line-up or roll call, three basic messages were delivered. One was the message that customer service was important to command staff, so, like it or not, patrol needed to go along with it. While the supervisor did not personally support the emphasis—and made that clear—s/he was still going to monitor subordinates' performance in these terms because they recognized that their own performance turned on platoon-level measures of customer satisfaction. The second message communicated was that customer service was important, but without reference to *why* it was important. The final message delivered by managers was that customer service was a priority to command staff *and* to the field supervisor. In addition, these supervisors differed from others in that they seemed also to articulate to their subordinates *why* it was important:

> "The better you are with customer service the less frustrated you will be on the street."
>
> "I tell them it isn't a big change from what they do now. They just need to be clear with what they are doing, don't use jargon, and explain why you are doing what you are doing. It makes people feel better, which makes your job easier."
>
> "I've spoken to officers saying talk to people don't demand things. When you treat someone like an ass you'll end up fighting with them."

For the most part, the message communicated to officers by supervisors who regularly drew attention to the importance of customer service mirrored that of those who only intermittently addressed this dimension of police performance. Most managers explained that it is part of a supervisor's job to monitor officer behavior, so they routinely reminded their officers to "be courteous" or "explain what's happening." "Treat those you treat as if they were family." You "treat them like your mom should be treated." Supervisors who connected positive interactions with citizens and improved outcomes for officers were in the minority.

We detected one meaningful difference between the two sites in what supervisors emphasized when discussing customer service. Managers in Syracuse were more likely than Schenectady supervisors were to frame their discussion of customer service in terms of monitoring, responding to, and directing subordinates to avoid citizen complaints. This emphasis was also apparent in officers' descriptions of steps supervisors had taken to manage this dimension of police performance.

Among those who framed supervisory efforts to enhance customer service in terms of citizen complaints, supervisors either did so privately on an individual basis or they addressed the individual officer and also drew lessons from the incident-level to bring to the platoon. Some supervisors did express their view that citizens should be treated with dignity and respect, and that when they were not, the result would be a justified complaint. We contrast supervisors who acknowledged the appropriateness of citizens expecting quality treatment with those supervisors who did not focus on what citizens should rightfully expect. These supervisors focused on officers and managers and the value to them in avoiding the attention brought on by complaints.

The responses below characterize the responses of supervisors who focused on citizen complaints as the avenue for enhancing the quality of police interactions. When asked what, if anything, they had done to communicate their expectations of how subordinates should treat citizens to subordinates, we heard the following:

> "If people get complaints, we handle them and do what we should. We don't want young guys treating people poorly. We hold them accountable."
>
> "Even if the complaint is unfounded, follow up with officers on how they could have handled it better so there would not have been a complaint. A lot of complaints are that the officer was rude, etc., not polite."
>
> "Nothing per se. We have a system in place where at the sergeant-level, if a citizen has a complaint with an officer we address it."
>
> "We make sure individual complaints are taken care of."
>
> "When we have issues that we hear or see we'll bring them up at roll call and explain the issues related to the complaints."
>
> "Handle complaints if we get them . . . don't want anybody looking at the platoon poorly, so will get angry sometimes."

While the content of (valid) citizen complaints overlaps somewhat with procedurally *un*just policing, complaints represent only the tip of the proverbial customer disservice iceberg, and moreover, high-quality police service in the form of procedurally just performance is not equivalent to action that provides no grounds for complaint. In the typical U.S. city, complaints are filed in a small fraction of the incidents in which citizens believe that police have acted improperly, and even when valid complaints are filed and thoroughly investigated, evidentiary constraints often forestall administrative action in individual cases. Furthermore, and perhaps more important, procedurally just policing is more than taking no actions that are complaint-worthy. We return to this below.

Patrol Officers' Responses

We also asked patrol officers what, if anything, their field supervisors did to direct their attention to the importance of customer service. Their responses corroborated supervisors' descriptions. Patrol responses supported the three management styles described above and shown in figure 11. Managers whom we describe as taking no steps to direct attention to customer service were described by their subordinates as doing "nothing" or "nothing really." Intermittent efforts were described by officers in the following ways:

> "I've heard them say watch your attitudes with people. No swearing. Do what you have to, but don't lose your cool right away."

"Mention it occasionally. Just mention it to us on heated calls. Not all people are super nice all the time, and cops are people."

"He touches on it once in a while. He tells us not to yell and swear if you don't have to."

"Been times at line up, reminders to be courteous and watch language."

"Once in a while they might bring it up. No *lecture* every day."

"Every now and again they reinstate *[sic]* the fact they want us to figure out the call and 'leave everyone happy.'"

Officers whose descriptions of field supervisors' management style suggested routine efforts to direct attention to customer service made comments such as:

"Roll call training and [the supervisor] brings it up in general conversation to remain professional, regardless of other person's demeanor."

"Reminds us of how important it is to be courteous to people. Reminds us to act appropriately."

"Supervisors regularly go over calls, review calls. They show up on-site and afterwards they give us feedback. They are making sure we are being professional and getting back to people."

"We are made aware of the surveys. Supervisors regularly show up on calls and give us regular reviews."

"They tell us: 'We have an image to uphold, remember to follow the policy, and don't use excessive force. Remember, you are always being watched.' They [supervisors] are always reminding us. They do a good job of reminding us."

Again, in Syracuse in particular, monitoring performance in terms of customer service was perceived by many officers as a primarily reactive, initiated by management only in response to a civilian complaint. In officers' own words, it was:

"More reactive than proactive. But that is the nature of the beast."

"Always stress not to get civilian complaints."

"Address when there is a complaint and what you can do better."

"Hands-off attitude unless there is a complaint."

"Only when there is a complaint."

"I don't know. If there is a complaint they address it and explain how to properly handle the call if they don't like what they did."

In our observations and interviews, we did not sense strong efforts to actively undermine the administration's desire to inculcate a customer-service orientation within the departments. To be sure, some managers felt that the customer-service emphasis was inappropriate, and these individuals tended to frame the administration's emphasis as reflecting a deliberate choice to prioritize citizens' needs over officers'.

IMPACT OF MEASURING PERFORMANCE

Schenectady command staff first saw a report of the survey-based performance measures at the Compstat meeting of December 21, 2011. If we think of the initiation of procedural justice performance measurement as an intervention or treatment, then the first post-intervention contacts in Schenectady would have been in the latter half of December or perhaps the first half of January (survey wave 11 or 12). Since the corresponding meeting in Syracuse was on January 11, 2012, the first post-intervention contacts in Syracuse would have been in the latter half of January (wave 13).

Subjective Experience

Given the fairly weak connections between officers' procedural justice and citizens' subjective experience, we would expect little or no detectable change in the procedural justice index, based on the police services survey data, over time. We would therefore expect that even very effective efforts on the parts of platoon commanders and others would be manifested in only small and perhaps undetectable changes at the margins in citizens' subjective experience. The survey items each provide for a rough calibration of citizens' perceptions, with arguably greater differentiation when they are combined, but even so, the procedural justice index is limited in the differences that it can capture. Moreover, a sample size of fifty per wave or even a hundred per month limits our capacity to distinguish real (but small) change from sampling error.

Analyzed as monthly means over time, the procedural justice index fluctuated between 6 and 10, with few exceptions. The post-intervention mean was somewhat higher than the pre-intervention mean in Schenectady, though that reflected one spike that began prior to the intervention and another toward the end of surveying, and somewhat lower in Syracuse.

A simple comparison of pre- and post-intervention means takes no account of other factors that affect subjective experience, and whose effects would not necessarily even out over time. Using the same preliminary model of subjective experience that we presented in chapter 4, therefore, we estimated the difference in subjective experiences that followed the initiation of measuring performance in the context of a regression model. We add a linear trend variable and a nonlinear trend variable to the models to account for temporal variation other than that attributable to the initiation of measurement.

The regression results (details of which can be found in Worden and McLean 2016) by and large replicate what appeared as month-to-month fluctuation. Schenectady exhibits a modest (but statistically insignificant) increase in overall subjective experience in the post-intervention period, while a negligible difference can be seen in Syracuse. Across all three platoons together in each department, no improvement over time can be detected. Allowing the pre-/post-intervention difference to vary across the three platoons, there is some evidence that different platoons followed different trajectories, but only in one case (that of Syracuse's platoon 3) is the difference large enough to be statistically significant. The addition of the controls for the characteristics of individual incidents provides a similarly mixed set of estimated changes over time, none of which is statistically significant. Estimated changes in Syracuse are not all in the same direction, though none of them can be reliably differentiated from zero.

Observed Police Behavior

Observational measures of officers' procedural justice and injustice much more directly tap the outcomes that we might expect police managers could affect. The timing of the observations, which were done after the survey, meant that the measures based on observational data could not be incorporated into Compstat reporting of procedural justice performance measures. But insofar as managerial efforts were made to improve these outcomes, we might expect to find evidence of it in the observation-based measures of officers' procedural justice and injustice. The pre-intervention levels of procedural justice fluctuated between 6.4 and 7.5, with an overall mean of 7.0, while the post-intervention means fluctuate between 6.2 and 7.7, with an overall mean of 7.0. Procedural injustice varies between 0.3 and 1.3, with pre- and post-intervention means of slightly over or under 0.7.

When we take into account any possible trends over time and the other factors that we included in the models of procedural justice and injustice in chapter 7, we find only one meaningful difference in the post-intervention period on either measure: procedural justice improved on platoon 3 subsequent to the introduction of measuring citizens' subjective experience. No reliable difference can be detected on the other platoons or in the measure of procedural injustice. See Worden and McLean 2016.

From the interviews with patrol officers and supervisors on Schenectady's platoon 3, we gather that routine efforts were made to direct attention to the importance of procedurally just policing. Sergeants indicated that the platoon commander generally followed up with them to share the survey results after the monthly Compstat meeting. Following that, either they or the lieutenant would share this information at line-ups following the Compstat meeting, in addition to routinely issuing general reminders to officers to be mindful of the way they interacted with citizens. Officers' descriptions of their supervisors' efforts to manage police performance in these terms corroborated this management style. Some supervisors on the other platoons described themselves, and were described by their subordinates, as taking some of the same steps, but we did not detect as much platoon-level consistency in the management approach. And that is an important point: it would probably not be sufficient for the platoon commander to draw subordinates' attention to the virtues of procedural justice (or "customer service"); all or most of the first-line supervisors would also need to be on board, and it appears that in the case of Schenectady's platoon 3, they may have been on board.

SUMMARY

Measuring procedural justice performance did not generally result in detectable improvements over time. Despite the fact that the administration's push to make departments more customer-service-oriented was a top-down initiative, developed without input from rank and file, and included civilians in defining the latter's performance—two conditions often associated with thwarted efforts to promote change—we did not sense that overt resistance played a meaningful role in limiting improvements over time. Several factors may explain why broad improvements in performance were not detectable, none of which we presume to be confined to the study departments. First and most simply, both the study departments began with high baseline levels of subjective experience, leaving little room for improvement. Furthermore, monthly measures of police performance were injected into Compstat mechanisms that, as in other police departments, do not heavily emphasize accountability. And of utmost importance, even had managers directed more attention to this aspect of police performance than they previously had, our data suggest that what officers do and do not do is only weakly related to subjective experience. In the case of one of Schenectady's platoons, however, whose commander and supervisors all gave the quality of police-citizen interactions regular attention and also drew connections to valued outcomes, officers' procedural justice improved at the margin.

In addition, and despite our efforts to explain concepts, the idea of procedurally just policing was ambiguous for many officers and supervisors, and their efforts to make sense of the concept and the implications it represented for their daily work may have colored both the extent to which managers embraced more actively managing this aspect of police performance and the extent to which officers altered their behavior in meaningful ways. To this we turn in chapter 9.

9

Procedural Justice and Street-Level Sensemaking

We sought to understand whether, how, and with what consequences police managers would make use of information about the quality of officers' performance in managing their subordinates. To do so, we conducted semi-structured interviews with patrol officers and patrol supervisors that tapped their views with respect to the emphasis on customer service. The methodology is described in chapter 8. We analyzed their responses to understand their interpretations of the administrative priority, that is, the sense that they made of the push toward procedurally just policing. We begin with a discussion of sensemaking as an organizational phenomenon, and then turn to the qualitative data to extend the discussion to Syracuse and Schenectady in order to understand and interpret the complex reality behind efforts to translate into practice the top-down mandate of procedurally just policing.

SENSEMAKING AND STREET-LEVEL RECEPTIVITY

Police departments adopt new practices or programs such as community policing, Compstat, or democratic policing to meet instrumental goals. However, we know that the path from reform to implementation is far from straight. It is well documented in the policing literature that efforts to bring about change in policing often fall short of expectations (Rosenbaum and Lurigio 1994; Skogan 2008). Often, the "technical core"—in policing, the street-level work of patrol officers or detectives—is, in effect, buffered from the structures with which the work is not compatible. "[D]ecoupling enables organizations to maintain standardized, legitimating, formal structures while their activities vary in response to practical considerations," (Meyer and Rowan 1977, 357; also see Orton and Weick 1990).

Organizations are "inhabited" by people, as one body of literature on institutional theory reminds us, and those people translate structural demands into practice. Police officers are particularly resistant to initiatives that involve civilians in defining their work or evaluating their performance (Skogan 2008). Furthermore, initiatives and new programs are less likely to be adopted when department leaders neglect to solicit officers' views about major issues of policy and practice and are not transparent. Officer cynicism is also a key element that drives employee resistance to change, seriously thwarting innovation in policing (Wykoff and Skogan 1994; Lurigio and Skogan 1994). Another force that shapes employees' willingness to be responsive to directives is the extent to which they are committed to the organization and internalize its values. As Beth Bechky observes, "It is clear that the most direct line into practice and meaning is the people doing the work and interpretation" (2015, 1163).

Uncertainty characterizes police life. Situations officers are tasked with handling are dynamic and ill-defined, direct supervision is uncommon, and the exercise of discretion is the norm. Organizational rules and regulations are developed to decrease the uncertainty that is characteristic of policing (Manning 1989). But organization theory tells us that people do not simply implement policies. Rather, they respond to the situations they face and their interpretations of these situations (Blumer 1969). Moreover, many policies and reforms (e.g., community policing, democratic policing, procedurally just policing) are replete with ambiguity leaving the members of police organizations to "interpret, label, enact, or otherwise make sense of innovations and reforms in their environment (Maguire and Katz 2006, 506). In an uncertain organizational environment, actors have the leeway to form their own interpretations as they seek to impose order and routines in order to carry out their duties. Karl Weick (1995) describes this as a process of "sensemaking"— making sense of or "structuring the unknown" (Waterman 1990, 4). When a reform is introduced, organizations and actors within must first define what they understand the reform to mean at a broad level and also for their everyday work life. How an organization's leadership sets the stage for reform and communicates expectations downstream (Gioia and Chittipeddi 1991), and the extent to which employees are able to understand the nature and purpose of the change (Lurgio and Skogan 1994; Amburgey et al. 1993) influence the extent to which reforms are adopted.

Employee support or resistance to reform efforts turns, in part, on the meaning actors attribute to the change (George and Jones 2001; Bartunek et al. 2006), particularly to the implications of change for improving or reducing the quality of their work life (Bartunek and Moch 1987). Where there is ambiguity, people interpret and insert their own understanding in order to translate policy into practice. Wesley Skogan describes the impact ambiguity can have on change efforts in this way: "Sergeants interpret the operational meaning of official policies at the street level, so when roles and rules are up for grabs, they have to have a clear vision they can support if change is really going to occur there" (2008, 25).

Thus, we found it productive to apply two concepts from organization theory—sensemaking and loose coupling[1]—to frame our understanding and discussion of the extent to which a quality management strategy was enacted in the study police departments. Weick introduced the concept of loose coupling in the 1970s. His examination of educational systems led him to posit that organizations cannot be understood in terms of their formal structure, goals, and functions. The different components of an organization are typically not tightly connected, creating uncertainty in the organizational environment and the need for adaptations. Weick (1976) notes several features of a loosely coupled system, including several means to reach the same end, lack of coordination, and limited regulation. We turn now to the feedback gathered through interviews with patrol officers and frontline police supervisors.

Frontline Sensemaking

From our interviews with patrol officers and supervisors in Syracuse and Schenectady, it appears that uniformed personnel strongly resisted neither administration's efforts to make police more customer-service oriented. However, even where managers and officers seemed willing to accept that customer service was an appropriate consideration in assessing police performance, there was some slippage in taking the measures of performance that we provided and actively managing them. The interviews we conducted with field supervisors and officers are useful in unpacking the thought processes around deciding what customer service meant for them, how it might impact their daily routine, and whether this implied a positive or negative change to their daily work. We would suppose that the conclusions to which officers came influenced decisions about how to act on management directives and, similarly, the conclusions to which frontline supervisors came would influence their reactions to upper management and also whether and how they assessed subordinates' performance in terms of the quality of their interactions.

The interpretive process of sensemaking is influenced by the setting of expectations. In our examination, it began when command staff conveyed their expectations to mid-level managers. The latter in turn then conveyed both their own expectations and their understanding of command staff expectations to their subordinate officers. Dennis Gioia and Kumar Chittipeddi use the term "sensegiving" to describe such efforts "to influence the sensemaking and meaning construction of others" (1991, 442).

Field supervisors and officers in our study used similar logic in assessing or making sense of the appropriateness of emphasizing the quality of police-citizen interactions.

We turn now to a discussion of the factors involved in the interpretive process and that influenced resistance to or acceptance of the change. The two different ranks viewed the appropriateness of assessing police performance using nontraditional metrics, and made sense of "customer service" and "procedural justice," in similar ways. We detected little change in views between the two waves of interviews or across the two departments, so we combine interview responses from the two different time periods and departments, and note exceptions to these more general rules. We turn first to patrol officers' responses to a series of questions designed to understand how they interpreted and judged the administrations' efforts to assess their performance in terms of the quality of their interactions with the public.

Patrol Officers

Officers had mixed feelings about the appropriateness of the departments' emphasis on the importance of customer service: a number felt it was appropriate; others held that it was "appropriate but with a caveat"; and a third group believed the focus was not appropriate. These judgments shaped the extent to which officers resisted or accepted the departments' decision to measure and direct attention to the quality of the service they provide. They form a continuum of resistance, as shown in figure 12 below.

As respondents talked to us about the emphasis on the quality of their interactions with citizens, the starting point for many centered on the idea of conceiving of citizens in police encounters as customers or clients. Officers shared with us a range of reactions to the idea that a customer-service orientation should be applied to police work, and also to the appropriateness of making service quality the partial basis for assessing their performance. At one end of the continuum were those who expressed the view that their department's emphasis on service quality was appropriate. These officers did not find it troubling to think of the citizens with whom they interacted as consumers of a service the police provide. To them, the nature of the service police provide was compatible with a customer-service orientation, so the departments' emphasis was appropriate:

"We are there for the people and community. It would be unfair if we weren't treating people fairly or appropriately in accordance with the law."

"It [service quality] is very important. That is who we work for."

"Yeah, I think it is fair that they place an importance on it [service quality]. It's a service business."

"Yes, absolutely. . . . If I called the police what would I expect from them. Regardless of station in life, treat everyone the same."

"Part of my performance is to help people. Even when I'm arresting people I say to them, 'Is there anything I can do to help you when you get out?' . . . There are certain things I have to do, but if you explain that to them then sometimes they'll say, 'I understand, Sir.'"

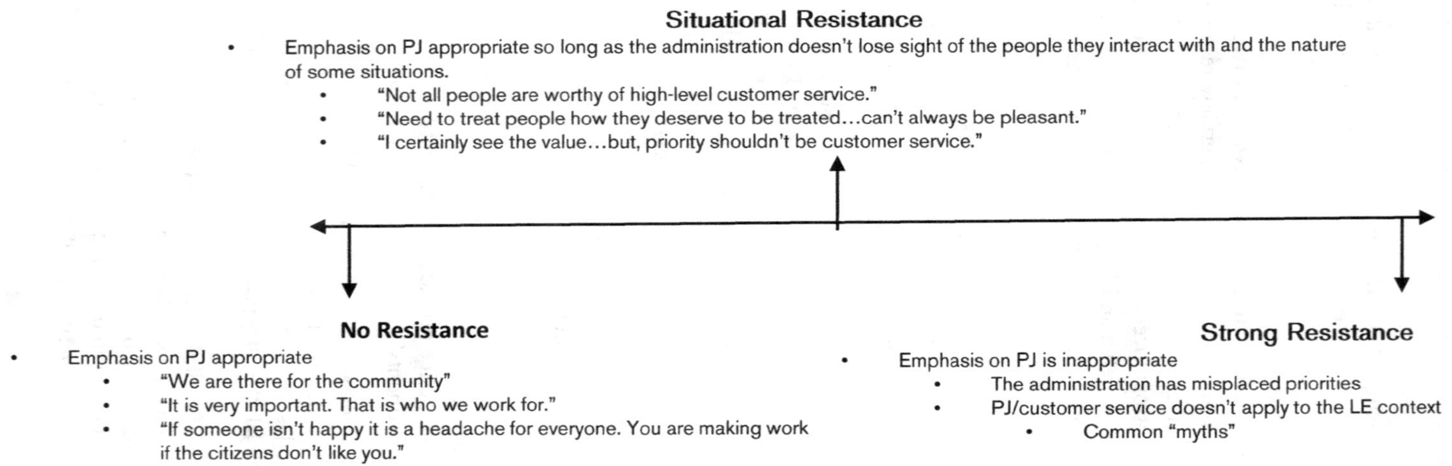

Situational Resistance

- Emphasis on PJ appropriate so long as the administration doesn't lose sight of the people they interact with and the nature of some situations.
  - "Not all people are worthy of high-level customer service."
  - "Need to treat people how they deserve to be treated...can't always be pleasant."
  - "I certainly see the value...but, priority shouldn't be customer service."

Strong Resistance

- Emphasis on PJ is inappropriate
  - The administration has misplaced priorities
  - PJ/customer service doesn't apply to the LE context
    - Common "myths"

No Resistance

- Emphasis on PJ appropriate
  - "We are there for the community"
  - "It is very important. That is who we work for."
  - "If someone isn't happy it is a headache for everyone. You are making work if the citizens don't like you."

FIGURE 12. The Resistance Continuum.

"We deal with everyone. All the victims and people with their cat in a tree, but you need to treat them all the same. Just because it is not an emergency to us, if they are calling us, it is to them."

Another set of officers expressed the same view that administrations' focus on customer service was appropriate but offered caveats. These officers are represented in the middle of the resistance continuum. Typically the caveat offered centered on the notion of citizens in police encounters being conceived of as customers and/or lumping citizens into a single group. Officers talked about the importance of administrators and supervisors not losing sight of either the "types" of people with whom police interact or the nature of the situations. These officers were accepting of the decision to measure their performance in terms of the quality of their interactions as long as supervisors understood it wasn't reasonable to expect "high-quality" service with all people or all situations. A theme that comes through here is the "we/they" mentality described as part of the police culture (Kaeppeler et al. 1998; Skolnick 1966):

"The emphasis is appropriate. You try to be as professional as you can, but at a point though you have to raise your voice. You try to be nice and polite, but some people don't get that."

"If you have decent people skills you won't have a large amount of complaints.... But, some individuals just aren't happy because they don't get what they want even if what they want isn't an option."

"Not all people are worthy of high-level customer service."

"Your action is dictated by their [citizens'] behavior."

On the far right of the resistance continuum were those officers who strongly opposed assessing their performance in these terms. The reasons they shared were similar to those described by officers who fell in the middle of the continuum. The difference between the two groupings of officers was that these officers saw no situations or circumstances under which to accept administrators' focus. Many believed that the concept of customer service was being inappropriately applied to policing. Disagreement was also rooted in the belief that the type of citizens with whom the police interact simply could not and would not ever be satisfied. These officers presumed that the nature or outcome of the encounter would be determinative of the citizen's subjective experience:

"We don't have customers so there is no customer service. It shouldn't apply. We aren't providers. The people we talk to don't want something. We [the police] need something. Who do we deal with? They don't call for no reason on a good day."

"I think the focus is overzealous. People call in complaints but some are not legitimate. Useless. Normally we deal with people on their worst day. We handle the call however we do. If I pulled you out of your home, how would you like it?"

"Administration has it as a high priority. They want to . . . mend relationships as it has had a rocky road. Do I care? No. We aren't there for a good reason. We just put them in jail and ruined their life. People try to get out from under charges by saying things happened."

"It think it is stressed too much. Everyone knows the level of people we deal with. Not a lot of pleasant people. It is hard to react with politeness when people are abrasive and cursing."

"No because we are stuck between a rock and a hard place. People don't like us to begin with."

Another reason for the avowed skepticism and resistance to the emphasis on customer service was that it was perceived to symbolize the relative importance of the police force and the community, respectively: some officers inferred that citizens' concerns and citizen satisfaction were more important to the administration than in-house levels of satisfaction and morale. This group was also concerned that the departments' priorities were out of balance, believing that concern with citizen satisfaction outweighed the emphasis on fighting crime and disorder, enforcing the law, meeting victims' needs, and, of great concern, that it even outweighed concern for officer safety. The perceived failure of the administration to direct attention in-house was seen as a stressor and as a contributing factor to low morale:

"Need to boost morale. Happy employees would boost what we do out there, and they would have better customer service in the end."

" It's the public opinion department. Policy dictated by opinion. But we don't deal with the best of people."

"I am not looking for a pat on the back but just respect and not to be treated like a 'kid.'"

"It is all about pleasing the people. Not about us. That is their [command staff's] main concern."

"Focus so much on the public, they [the administration] forget about us. Patrol is underappreciated and always told to do more. The feedback to us is always negative. We do small things that administration doesn't see. They rush to judgment without asking what happened. They just assume we're wrong, and it's very stressful to work in this type of environment."

"It is too much. But I guess it is about PR. . . . There is too much non-police work. We are too soft."

"We treat suspects as innocent until proven guilty, but the uniform guy is guilty until proven innocent. It's how the department treats you."

"Everyone here should be able to treat people with respect but not at the expense of officer safety. We could be right but management doesn't see it that way. Officers should come first."

"It should be . . . public safety, then my safety, then customer service. Not gonna [sic] compromise my safety for customer service."

"I certainly see the value . . . but, priority shouldn't be customer satisfaction. It should be a second priority. Safety of people and yourself is first."

"In some respects they [administration] put the emphasis in the wrong place. They need to worry more about the true victims and less about the people that don't deserve it. We need more emphasis on true victims than the perceptions of a wife beater. Who cares what he thinks?"

Research tells us that the sensemaking and sensegiving processes are iterative (Gioia and Chittipeddi 1991). Indeed, we found support for our hypothesis that as experience accumulated and allowed supervisors and officers to assess the actual impact that managing the elements of procedural justice had on their day-to-day work, their early perceptions might change. We had only some of the same respondents in the two waves of interviews, so we can only make cautious comparisons about the predominant themes that emerged in wave 1 interviews, compared to wave 2. The most meaningful difference we detected between the interviews conducted at the outset of the project compared to those at the conclusion of the project was in the prevalence of officers who seemed outright resistant to their department's emphasis on customer service and the appropriateness of assessing their own performance in these terms. Concerns appeared to diminish over time. It would seem that uniform personnel were girded to offer some resistance, but that resistance may have diminished as officers realized that the heightened emphasis amounted to no meaningful change in their everyday work life. It was loosely coupled. Moreover, it seemed that with the passage of time, officers were more at ease with supervisors' ability to be fair—to treat them in a procedurally just manner—when making decisions about the quality of the service officers delivered. In wave 2, some respondents who touched on the argument that you cannot expect all people to be "happy" went on to give command staff and supervisors credit for differentiating "real" complaints from "false" and giving officers the benefit of the doubt. Of course, the difference between waves might also simply be the result of interviewing different people in each wave.

> "Command staff understand who we are dealing with. Upset people that go to jail whether an officer has done them wrong or not. . . . They [command staff] accurately assess the situation and the citizen complaining."

Frontline Supervisors

Frontline supervisors can play a key role in efforts to bring about organizational change. Therefore, as we did with officers, we explored sergeants' views on the appropriateness of viewing the quality of police service delivery through a customer-service lens. Perhaps not surprisingly, since sergeants are only one step removed from officers, we found consistent themes when we compared officers and sergeants' responses.

A handful of frontline supervisors expressed the view that a customer-service orientation "fit" when applied to police work and stated they were receptive to assessing performance in those terms. Many supervisors went further and identified pragmatic reasons to support the administration's focus. This additional source of support was more common among sergeants compared to officers.

For examples: community support makes the job easier; it lowers the chances of getting a complaint filed against you or a subordinate; and it helps to build a supply of support from the community into which they may need to tap.

> "Part of why we are here is to help the public, and if we treat them with the respect they are due, they are more apt to help us with future investigations."
>
> "If someone isn't happy it is a headache for everyone. You are making work for the sergeant if the citizens don't like you."
>
> "With an enlightened department, such as us, it starts in the academy. I see more kids being taught that this is how you do things, as opposed to a run-and-gun show. Your job is harder if the citizen isn't satisfied. If you start out screaming and yelling, it is hard to go down. You can always escalate, but it is hard to go the other way."
>
> "Sure, bottom line here is service to the public. They are our employers. We are here to serve the public like any business. The fact that you can satisfy people is important. You need to maintain your role and enforce the law. Some won't be happy about it, but that's the way it is. Ten people at a call, and five are happy. I think that is a success."

Just as some officers were guarded in their willingness to embrace fully the decision to assess police performance in terms of service quality so, too, were frontline supervisors. A group of frontline supervisors said that they would support their commanding officers' directives to assess the quality of subordinates' interactions with the public in these terms, so long as the administration understood that not all people or situations would allow for equal service quality, and, in addition, they would also need to take into account factors they judged to influence citizens' perceptions, but that were outside the control of the officer in the immediate situation (e.g., response time, policy/law, global views about police):

> "Need to treat people how they deserve to be treated . . . can't always be pleasant and respectful."
>
> "Customer service is low because of call volume. . . . You try to address people's issues but they get lost because no one can get back to them."
>
> "Too much sometimes. A lot could be solved with manpower. They want to cut back money, but they want customer service, but officers are there on calls and have two or three more holding. People want and expect something, but the officers are overworked, and the people they deal with are belligerent half the time."
>
> "Yes, to an extent. You have to realize that people they [officers] interact with might not be happy with you."

Frontline supervisors offered rationales for resisting an emphasis on procedural justice that were very similar to those expressed by officers on the far right of the resistance continuum. Supervisors here indicated that they believed the idea of conceiving of a citizen in a police encounter as a customer was inappropriate, which in turn colored their view of their department's move to assess performance in terms of the quality of the police-citizen encounter. Others did not buy into this proposition because they recognized that the citizens with whom their subordinates interact bring to the encounter preconceived views about police that would color citizens' judgments of the officer in the immediate encounter, yet might have little connection with what the officer actually did. As we heard with officers, some sergeants portrayed the administration's decision to fold measures of citizen satisfaction into assessments of police performance as one that prioritized the views of external customers over internal customers and would result in negative outcomes:

> "No. We are not in a customer-service business. We have a job to do. We are meeting with people when something is wrong so they aren't happy anyway. . . . I think no one is happy with us anyway. . . . People don't like the police. . . . I feel you would get bad ratings no matter how you do your job."

> "Customer service? We don't charge for our service. I don't understand the question. This isn't a fair question. . . . No one calls the police to say hello. We only see them at their worst. We are in an uphill battle. All the smiles and service doesn't make people happy. . . . You can't compare law enforcement to anything else. It is not a counter at the mall."

> "There is a fine line between customer service and having the edge to do the job correctly. We are more customer-service-based here than a PD [should be]."

> "We aren't going to make everyone happy. We aren't doing our job if everyone is happy. We have to protect people's safety."

> "Do they worry about the guys? They need to worry about the guys. Patrol takes a beating. . . . We need less emphasis on customer service. I shouldn't be looking at my job saying I only have x more years to go. I love my job, but it has been a long x years."

> "They are very concerned with public views of the agency and don't seem to worry about combatting crime . . . It is important, but the core mission should be to police. We need to solve and reduce crime."

> "I don't think it is the most intelligent thing from a police or administration view. Don't focus on customer service because then safety becomes less important. Focus on the end product, which is us [patrol]. Whether people are safe. The humans that work for you are just as important as people [citizens]."

Officers' Perceptions of Supervisors Buy-In

We expected variation in the extent to which frontline supervisors agreed with the top-down directive to manage subordinates' performance in terms of procedural justice. And, indeed, that variation emerged in their descriptions of how they felt about the directive. This variation was further corroborated in themes that emerged in officers' discussion about the extent to which they detected differences in the message conveyed by different sergeants regarding the importance of customer service. We turn now to a discussion of how officers perceived sergeants to differ in terms of buy-in to the customer-service-oriented approach adopted by the departments.

Officers attributed some of the variation in the message supervisors delivered about the importance of customer service to individual supervisors' orientations up or down the chain of command. Some were tapping into a perception that alignment with officers versus mid-level management, or "the streets" versus "the administration," influenced supervisors' perceptions:

"Half and half [buy-in]. Direct supervisors understand our way of thinking and they separate us from the administrative side."

"Varies per shift. Some are in the back seat of the administration, so it's important, but as you get further from administration they don't care as much."

"They were in our shoes too, and they know it is tough. There is a lot of situational customer service."

"It trickles all the way down. Sergeants see more of what we go through, so they are more sensitive than their higher-ups."

"Different by old school policing versus new school policing. The old school still pushes that you do what you want to, what you know, and you are in charge. New school is that you listen more. You see this across supervisors."

"Patrol supervisors are still on the road 'obviously the shit rolls downhill. So they are in a hard position.' They need to keep it as real as possible, 'but the street is the street.'"

Others did not detect much variation across supervisors, nor did they expect that what supervisors really thought would matter. They presumed that if command staff ordered frontline supervisors to focus on this aspect of performance, the latter would fall in line, given the nature of police organizations.

SUMMARY

Our intention was to understand officers' and frontline supervisors' views on the appropriateness of their administration's emphasis on procedurally just policing and assessing police performance in these terms. Our findings are consistent with the research that suggests that the fairness officers attribute to their organizational environment influences their own willingness to embrace service-oriented policing (Myhill and Bradford 2012). Consideration of internal procedural justice emerged as a factor for officers. They expressed resistance to the external focus on fairness and satisfaction because they felt the administration failed to take account of internal satisfaction. Others believed the external orientation would come at an expense; it would detract, for example, from community safety, officer safety, and concern and care for victims. Our findings are consistent with research that has found connections between officers' sense of "organizational justice"—that is, officers' perceptions of the procedural justice with which their superiors treat them—and officers' acceptance of and compliance with organizational rules and regulations (Tyler 2011; Skogan et al. 2014; Wolfe and Piquero 2011; Trinker et al.

2014). Employees who believe that they are treated in a procedurally just manner are more likely to identify with and support the organization and its values (Tyler and Blader 2003; Bradford and Quinton 2014). How strongly officers' perceptions of organizational justice are rooted in the actual practices of their organizations is an open question, but since their perceptions are real in their consequences even if they are ill-founded, their perceptions are important.

Judgments made by uniformed personnel about the soundness of assessing police performance in terms of citizens' subjective experiences also turned to a large degree on the nature of the citizens with whom officers interacted and the types of events that brought them together. For some, this did not preclude them from finding some value in measuring police performance in these terms, so long as managers and the highest levels of administration did not lose sight of "the streets." For others, however, citizen satisfaction and customer service were viewed as ill-fitting in the law-enforcement context, given the police task and the nature of their "clientele." It was clear from these comments that the underlying presumption was that citizen satisfaction had to compete with other departmental priorities. Most respondents indicated no awareness that research tells us that citizen satisfaction could assist in achieving goals of crime control, citizen cooperation, and citizen compliance—and thus officer safety.

The themes of this chapter reflect the sensemaking process. Both internal and external factors emerged as influential in either thwarting or supporting efforts to bring about change. We turn next to a review of the principal findings of our research and their implications.

10
—

Reflections on Police Reform

In this concluding chapter we first summarize the principal findings of our research and the contributions to knowledge that the findings represent. We then consider the implications of the findings for: (1) understanding procedural justice and police legitimacy; (2) police efforts to promote public trust and confidence; (3) police reform more generally; and (4) future research on procedural justice.

WHAT WE FOUND

Our analysis of Schenectady rests on a broader foundation of data, including not only the survey data on citizens' satisfaction and their judgments about the procedural justice of the police in their contact, and the interviews with commanders, patrol supervisors, and patrol officers, but also the observations of police-citizen encounters and the direct comparison of subjective experience and officer behavior. So we begin with what we take to be the principal findings from Schenectady, and then we consider the respects in which those findings are corroborated (or contradicted) by the findings from Syracuse.

In Schenectady, we observed moderate levels of procedural justice and low levels of procedural injustice in officers' behavior. These findings are not directly comparable to those of Jonathan-Zamir, Mastrofski, and Moyal, who constructed a single measure of procedural justice/injustice, and whose research was conducted in a suburban jurisdiction that they describe as a "professional, well-trained police agency, with leaders committed to several of the currently popular progressive police reforms, such as community and problem-oriented policing" (2015, 865). Insofar as comparisons can be drawn, officers in both Schenectady and "Everdene" exhibited procedural justice that varied across the procedural justice domains, and which was overall moderate. In Schenectady, we found low levels of procedural injustice.

We found that officers' patterns of procedural justice and procedural injustice are shaped in important ways by elements of the situations in which officers become involved and the behavior of citizens with whom officers interact. Procedural justice was greater in incidents that involved violent crime or interpersonal conflict, greater when the citizen was black, lower when the citizen was a suspect or third party rather than a victim or complainant, and lower when the citizen resisted the officer's authority. Procedural injustice was greater when the citizen was male, a suspect, intoxicated, resisted police authority, or disrespected police; injustice was lower when the citizen was black. As Jonathan-Zamir, Mastrofski, and Moyal did in Everdene, we can see room for improvement in the level of procedural justice in Schenectady, but such improvement might not be instrumental in improving either citizens' subjective experience or, through that experience, public trust and police legitimacy.

Citizens' subjective experiences are rather weakly related to the forms of officers' overt behavior that comprise procedural justice. Officers' procedural justice and injustice together explained no more than 12 percent of the variation in citizens' subjective experience in Schenectady. Procedural injustice had the greater effect on subjective experience, by far, such that we found asymmetry in the effects of justice and injustice that parallel previous findings based only on survey data. However, the Schenectady data suggest that this asymmetry stems not from the relatively strong effects of negative experiences but rather from citizens' tendency to overestimate the procedural justice with which police act in their encounters. The relationship between officers' procedural justice and citizens' subjective experience is weak partly because citizens tend to be fairly positive in their ratings of police performance, even when the procedural justice that we observed was fairly low. This pattern probably reflects the impact of citizens' more general attitudes toward the police on their perceptions of police actions in individual encounters with police.[1]

Citizens' judgments about procedural justice are also affected by whether (if not so much *how*) officers exercise forms of police authority: conducting searches or using physical force. Searches of citizens have strong effects on their assessments of procedural justice, unless citizens accede to them, while the use of physical force (but not verbal force) has a substantively notable effect as well. We have treated these forms of behavior as distinct from procedural justice as such. We believe that this treatment is consistent with the best judgments in previous research (which displays no consensus on these matters) and with the procedural justice model, which correctly holds that tough enforcement can nevertheless be fair (Schulhofer et al. 2011). We did not make a distinction between legal and illegal searches, nor did we make a distinction between reasonable and unreasonable force, but extant evidence suggests that citizens' judgments about the propriety of police action turns on their *perceptions* of procedural justice and not on the legality of officers' behavior, per se (Meares et al. 2012).

In this connection, we would note that unfavorable subjective experiences are more prevalent in police-initiated contacts but certainly not confined to those contacts. In fact, given the volume of citizen-initiated contacts through calls for service, in a fraction (about 15 percent) of which citizens judge procedural justice unfavorably, negative subjective experiences are more numerous, in absolute terms, in citizen-initiated contacts.

Neither indicator of police performance—a survey-based indicator or an observation-based indicator—revealed consistent changes that ensued from the survey-based measurement of performance. Overall, the month-to-month changes in measures of citizens' subjective experience were by and large within a range of sampling fluctuation, and with no change that could be attributed to the introduction of performance measures to monthly Compstat meetings. Given the weak connections between what officers do (and do not do) and what citizens later think about it, we might well see little or no change in survey-based measures of performance with good faith—even herculean—efforts by platoon commanders and field supervisors to manage their officers' behavior in police-citizen encounters. But neither did we see consistent changes in the observation-based measures of officers' procedural justice.

However, platoon commanders and especially first-line supervisors approached the management of this police outcome in different ways, which we characterized as forming a continuum. Some gave regular attention to the quality of police-citizen interaction during line-ups, and in that context shared survey results that had been delivered at the monthly Compstat meeting. They explained both what procedural justice means and why it is important. On one platoon, this appeared to affect officers' performance. On others, however, commanders and supervisors either attended to the issue only intermittently, alluding to what it means for officers' conduct but not its rationale, or were skeptical or even dismissive of the importance of "customer service."

This continuum reflects "sensemaking" by Schenectady's sergeants—that is, interpretation of what customer service or procedural justice represents and the appropriate emphasis to be placed on the quality of police-citizen interactions in the context of the demands of street-level police work. Based on their interpretations, some were receptive to the administration's emphasis on "customer service," finding it quite appropriate, while others were more guarded in their willingness to embrace the idea, or flatly opposed to it. This same process of sensemaking played out among patrol officers.

In Syracuse, we found patterns very similar to those in Schenectady on every score that we were able to measure. Citizens' subjective experiences were of a generally comparable nature, and they tended to bear the same relationships to other factors, including legitimacy, even though legitimacy was somewhat higher in Syracuse than in Schenectady. We also found similar patterns of variation in the management of procedural justice, and similarly mixed receptivity to a customer-service emphasis among patrol officers and supervisors.

No one study can be definitive on any question of social cause-and-effect, and no pair of police departments can be taken as representative of American police organizations, so firm conclusions will await replication of this study, but we can address some issues concerning the generalizability of these findings. We would observe, first, that if mid-level managers and frontline supervisors in mid-sized departments like Schenectady and Syracuse exhibit diversity in their interpretations of and support for a procedural justice model, we can safely anticipate that in larger agencies, mid-level managers and frontline supervisors will also diverge in the extent to which they embrace and actively manage the procedural justice with which their subordinates act, even when this outcome is measured on a regular basis.

Second, insofar as the more complete story could be told about the Schenectady police, whose officers' behavior we could observe through its video and audio recordings, we should be cautious in generalizing in view of the department's recent history and efforts to escape that history. The misbehavior of some Schenectady police officers was well publicized in local media, and a DOJ investigation suggested that the department suffered not only from its inability to terminate some sworn miscreants but also from systemic administrative deficiencies; the city's mayor openly considered disbanding the department. Be that as it may, scores on the trust index among Schenectady survey respondents were not very much different from those for the presumptively more typical Syracuse Police Department, and patterns of subjective experience were not much different across the two study departments.

Might the performance of Schenectady police have been elevated by the introduction of in-car cameras? The adoption of in-car cameras could be expected to improve the department's legitimacy, if only as a visible organizational reform and even if the operation of cameras was only loosely coupled with day-to-day police work. We cannot say whether and, if so, how much the introduction of cameras altered the routine performance of Schenectady police. Cameras were a matter of procedure that applied to all patrol units, day-in and day-out, and to which we believe (but cannot demonstrate) officers had become accustomed. In any case, we found only moderate levels of procedural justice and low levels of procedural injustice by officers as cameras rolled. Only their (infrequent) injustice had detectable effects on citizens' subjective experience. We would not suppose that procedural justice would be better managed in the absence of cameras, or that it would have greater effects on citizens' subjective experiences. Whether procedural justice could be better managed by making more extensive use of camera recordings is a question that we consider below.

An Institutional Perspective

Institutional theory is useful in understanding how the administrative emphasis on customer service in Schenectady and Syracuse was—and was not—translated into policing on the street, and more generally how the procedural justice model is likely to fare in police departments. This perspective directs our attention, first, to the fact that police work is comprised of a variety of functions, all or many of which are performed in a task environment that is heterogeneous, ambiguous, uncertain, and dangerous. The situations in which police intervene are complex. The goals of policing, and the information on the basis of which officers must make decisions, are ambiguous. The outcomes of alternative courses of action that officers might choose are uncertain. And in even the more seemingly mundane matters to which police attend a deadly risk is a part of the background. The technology of policing—that is, how the raw materials of citizens and their problems or behaviors are transformed into organizational outputs—is inevitably "intensive" (Thompson 1967), requiring that officers assess the many contingencies in a situation, choose a course of action on that basis, assess the immediate consequences of that choice, and potentially make additional and different choices as required. The tasks and technology of policing call, then, for the kind of discretion and judgment that society vests in occupations that are professions in every sense of the word – such as medicine or law. Indeed, the analogy between policing and medicine has frequently been drawn: both call for diagnostic skills and for prescription in order to remedy a problem.

The professionalization of police produced not true professionals, however, but rather police bureaucracies (partially) insulated from their political environments (Brown 1981). A Weberian bureaucracy is well suited for industrial settings that apply an assembly-line ("long-linked") technology to standardized raw materials, and where the task environment is homogeneous, the procedures for transforming raw materials into work products are well understood and can be specified in advance. But the same bureaucratic form is not so well suited for policing. Insofar as the bureaucratic structure conflicts with the nature of the work—the "technical core"—it is loosely coupled with what officers do. Michael Brown argues that the bureaucracy has actually made matters worse, in that a punitive system of supervision has amplified the uncertainties with which officers must cope. Notwithstanding these contradictions, however, the bureaucratic form has remained, as constituencies inside and outside policing take for granted that it is appropriate.

Recent reforms—community policing, public accountability mechanisms, and Compstat—have been superimposed on the existing structures, in spite of the fact that they are themselves not entirely compatible with the technical core, with the existing bureaucratic organization, and/or with one another. Community policing is in fact compatible with the work that police do, though not with the crime-fighting emphasis that was incorporated into the professional model, and even as community policing advocates sought to expand the police role, such that its success would not turn on its effect on crime, we are consistently drawn like a moth to flame to ask whether community policing reduces crime. Partly as a consequence, community policing has been a tough sell with the rank-and-file. Insofar as the profound structural changes that community policing requires have not been made, implementation has been shallow.

Public accountability through citizen oversight has left complainants unhappy and its advocates disappointed, and it appears that it has left officers largely unaffected in how they go about police work. More recent efforts to promote police accountability turn largely on administrative rule-making, which is compatible with the facets of police work that are also most compatible with the bureaucratic model: wherever police administrators can specify the circumstances under which police authority should or may not be exercised (e.g., arresting spouse abusers and not shooting at fleeing felons, respectively) *and* administrators can enforce compliance with the rules (i.e., sanction noncompliance). Many of the routine choices that police must make are beyond the reach of administrative rules, though it is possible that policies governing the use of less-lethal force *could* be coupled with police practice to the benefit of police and citizens alike, a possibility that we consider below.

In the New York City Police Department, Compstat appears to have achieved a level of managerial accountability that stimulated greater attention to the ends, and not merely the means, of police work. Compstat-like mechanisms introduced in other agencies have not, however, emphasized accountability or led to innovative problem-solving.

Superimposed on existing structures, the procedural justice model is likely to be similarly loosely coupled with police practice. If procedural justice is not measured reliably (or at all), no one would need to confront the fact that procedurally just policing has not become routine practice. A procedural justice model, we learned in our interviews with patrol officers and supervisors, is incompatible with police work as some officers experience it. We doubt very much that this is simply a manifestation of generational or personality differences among officers. It is more likely, we believe, attributable to the nature of the work that police perform and the cultural norms that grow out of that work. It is still appropriate to observe, as Brown did more than three decades ago, that "if there is a lesson to be learned from the experiences of the most recent generation of reformers, it is that simply enveloping policemen in a maze of institutional controls without grappling with the grimy realities of police work does not necessarily promote accountability and may only exacerbate matters" (1981, 303). Moreover, there is good reason to doubt that the practice of procedural justice by police in citizen encounters will substantially affect citizens' subjective experiences and, consequently, improve police legitimacy.

We should add, in this connection, that if a key element of the procedural justice model is the "organizational justice" with which police departments treat officers, it implies internal structures that depart from current structures in some important respects, and whose effects on officers' perceptions and behavior are open questions. Some empirical evidence suggests that the procedural justice with which a police agency is perceived by its officers to operate affects officers' views of the agency's legitimacy, and legitimacy in turn shapes officers' conformity to organizational regulations (Tyler, Callahan, and Frost 2007; Wolfe and Piquero 2011). This evidence is consistent with a claim made long ago that police officers' treatment of citizens is influenced by the police department's treatment of its officers (Guyot 1991). However, we have to allow for the possibility that officers' perceptions of organizational justice are as weakly connected to the actual administrative practices of police departments as citizens' perceptions of procedural justice are to the behaviors of police officers that comprise procedural justice. Altering the internal structures of police departments to better conform with principles of procedural justice may well have many benefits, but improvements in legitimacy and officer performance might not be among them.

We might also add—though our point is based on only casual observation—that police executives' interest in private-sector management prescriptions should be tempered by a careful consideration of the respects in which those prescriptions apply to police organizations. We have, for example, heard police chiefs talk enthusiastically about the Oz Principle (Connors et al. 2004), the three laws of performance (Zaffron and Logan 2011), and the Six Sigma methodology. (With the assistance of General Electric, Schenectady police command staff were trained in Six Sigma.) The analysis and advice that managers find in these sources might well be helpful, but they should not presume that what works effectively in manufacturing or other private-sector organizations will work equally well in the police environment.

IMPLICATIONS

Understanding Public Attitudes and Procedural Justice

One implication of the findings reported here for understanding public trust in police and procedural justice is that it is imperative to draw a sharp distinction between procedural justice as citizens' subjective experience and procedural justice as officers' overt behavior. They are different phenomena, even if we can use the same conceptual framework to define and operationalize them. Most previous research has relied on surveys of citizens to measure procedural justice, and most previous research on police behavior has not measured procedural justice. Using survey and observational methods to measure both citizens' perceptions and officers' behavior, respectively, we find the former are not straightforward reflections of the latter.

We already knew that citizens' judgments about procedural justice, and their satisfaction, in police-citizen encounters are very much subjective. But we may have underappreciated the degree to which they are subjective. Most survey research is cross-sectional; panel surveys are difficult and expensive to execute. But the handful of panel surveys show not only that subjective experience affects global attitudes toward the police, including trust and confidence, but also and especially that global attitudes have a large bearing on subjective experience. These reciprocal effects are far from balanced. What citizens take away from their encounters with the police in the form of their attitudes toward the police is shaped by what they brought to their encounters much more than by what police do. Citizens' subjective experience with the police is also influenced by broader contextual frames, such as the reputation of the police department and (for blacks) a history of discrimination, and by citizens' related interactions with personnel from other agencies, such as 911 center dispatchers or jail staff in booking facilities. Only a small fraction of the variation in subjective experience is attributable to how officers at the scene actually act. From the relationships between citizens' perceptions of procedural justice and citizens' satisfaction or beliefs about police legitimacy, it is safe to draw only inferences about the connections among these outlooks and not inferences about how these outlooks are shaped by what police do.

In order to describe, analyze, and understand procedural justice as it is enacted by police, it is necessary to observe it directly (in person or through recordings). We cannot rely on citizens' responses to surveys. Systematic social observation is a well-established method for measuring police behavior, and it can certainly be adapted to the measurement of procedural justice by police. Doing so potentially opens an analytic door to answering a wide range of questions about the levels of procedural justice that prevail in police-citizen encounters and the forces that influence procedural justice by police—all of the situational, individual, organizational, and community factors that have been examined in extant research on the use of police authority (see Worden and McLean 2014b).

Creating Police Legitimacy

If future research replicates our findings from Schenectady concerning the relationship of citizens' subjective experience to officers' procedural justice, then our interpretation of survey-based measures of the quality of police performance in citizen encounters must be more circumspect. From this analysis it appears that subjective assessments do not reflect officers' performance very well. The survey-based procedural justice index varied with the nature of the contact (a call for service or a police-initiated contact) and the forms of authority that police exercised, but it varied with procedural justice mainly insofar as officers behaved in procedurally unjust ways, and overall procedural justice and injustice together accounted for little of the variation in citizens' judgments. Encounters in which officers performed very well in terms of conforming to principles of procedural justice—such as explaining their actions or listening to citizens—were not much more likely to yield positive assessments by citizens than encounters in which officers did not exhibit procedural justice. As a source of information about how well officers perform in procedural justice terms, it appears that citizen surveys—even surveys of people involved in recent contacts documented in police records—are of very limited utility.

That citizens' responses to surveys do not reflect officers' behavior very accurately does not mean that the measures derived from citizen surveys are useless. Whether they are firmly or only weakly rooted in officers' actions, citizens' perceptions are real, and their consequences are real too. Public trust is important for police. We think it likely that police departments benefit from higher levels of public trust and confidence. Police officers may benefit when their departments enjoy higher levels of public trust, insofar as citizens are more likely to be compliant in individual police-citizen encounters, and more likely to be cooperative in providing information and otherwise "coproducing" community safety by working with police. Efforts by a police department to build its stock of public trust can be expected to redound to the department's advantage and its community's benefit.

But it does not appear that police can do much to "create" legitimacy through the procedural justice of their day-to-day interactions with citizens. Officers can detract from public trust at the margin by acting with procedural injustice. But they add if at all only imperceptibly to public trust by acting with greater procedural justice. For example, and more particularly, when police conduct a stop, and when they conduct a frisk or search during that stop, the citizen's subjective experience is unlikely to be affected for the better when the officer takes affirmative steps to be procedurally just. In general, police may be able to influence, but they do not *control,* any of the outcomes that really matter—crime, disorder, citizen satisfaction—because these are also influenced by many other social forces. Successful efforts to influence public trust will consist mainly of measures other than managing the procedural justice of street-level behavior.

That public trust does not turn to a meaningful degree on managing street-level procedural justice might be good news, insofar as what gets measured does not always get managed, at least not in an institutionalized organization. In a bureaucracy—even a paramilitary bureaucracy—in which the task environment is ambiguous and uncertain, mid-level managers and frontline workers must interpret agency mandates against the imperatives of the work as they understand them. This can result in loose coupling between the practices that management espouses and the practices that are applied on the street and that represent, in the aggregate, the service delivered by the agency. In an agency that publicly espouses an approach that highlights the value of procedural justice, but in the absence of reliable measures of actual performance in those terms, there might well be a wide divergence between the public pronouncements by the agency and its day-to-day performance on the street. But it would be a divergence about which agency managers could remain blissfully ignorant. The public pronouncements might add to the department's legitimacy, in that they signal an appreciation by department leaders that it is important. But the decoupled technical core would continue unaffected.

We hasten to add that we do not mean to imply that the adoption of structures that serve institutional purposes therefore do not and cannot serve more conventional technical-rational purposes in an organization, and even if the structures serve only more symbolic purposes, it does not follow that their adoption was an act of administrative duplicity. We do not doubt that when police executives adopt community policing, or early intervention systems, or Compstat, for example, they do so in good faith to achieve the instrumental benefits they promise, but structural features of policing and police organizations undermine these measures.

Officers' views on how they should do their jobs, particularly how they should interact with citizens, mediate the implementation of a procedural justice model of policing, and many officers in the study departments did not embrace procedural justice concepts, even though our observations indicated that Schenectady police performed fairly well in procedural justice terms. Officer safety is an overriding consideration, and given the structural forces that understandably make safety a high priority, it is likely to remain so; managerial efforts to alter this feature of police culture have not been promising.

Like street-level personnel, managers must also interpret agency mandates and whether and how to manage the things that get measured. Crime has been measured as a part of the Uniform Crime Reporting system for decades, and yet as the newly appointed commissioner of the NYPD, William Bratton found it necessary in 1994 to reengineer the department to prompt police managers to embrace (or "own") crime-fighting as a responsibility. Measuring valued outcomes is almost certainly necessary, but it is not sufficient.

It might be possible for police administrators to exercise more control over officers' procedural justice, in spite of the shortcomings of citizen surveys as a performance indicator, by making use of in-car and body-worn cameras to extend the capacity of the bureaucracy to monitor officers' performance. Just as police-recorded video (and especially audio) enabled us to conduct armchair observation of police-citizen encounters, in-car and perhaps especially body-worn cameras enable police supervisors to monitor their subordinates' performance as never before. We know of only anecdotal evidence, but it is likely that the availability of video has already improved the capacity of internal affairs investigators to sustain or unfound complaints about discourtesy (though discourtesy is ambiguous). Field supervisors in urban departments have always been able to observe officers' behavior directly, but they had to be strategic about it, since the number of subordinates for whom a supervisor is responsible and their dispersion across the precinct's landscape requires supervisors to pick and choose whom they observe and when. Police video introduces a whole new supervisory calculus.

But the obstacles to direct supervision have not been merely logistical. In many departments a strong norm of autonomy holds. Once rookie status is shed, officers expect to be treated like professionals, with a measure of deference to their competence and judgment. It is one thing to review recordings of police-citizen encounters to investigate allegations of misconduct, or to more proactively scan for major violations of departmental procedure, but it is another to micromanage officers' interactions with citizens. As Brown observes, "the animosity that some patrolmen display toward a supervisor who attempts to monitor closely their actions and the reluctance of many supervisors to interfere with patrolmen stem largely from the force [of the norm prohibiting such second-guessing]" (1981, 90). Technology is adapted to organizational settings more than organizational settings are adapted to technology (though typewriter manufacturers may disagree with us), and so we doubt that body-worn cameras are about to usher in a new era of scientific police management based on the procedural justice analogs to Frederick Taylor's time-and-motion studies.

Consider another street-level bureaucracy, schools. School administrators are much better able to observe teachers' classroom performance directly than police supervisors have been able in the past to observe officers' performance, Nevertheless, teachers have enjoyed a great deal of autonomy, and administrators display what educational researchers have characterized as a logic of confidence: an assumption that teachers are doing what they should be doing and that the organization is functioning as it should be (Eden 2001; Elmore 1999; Meyer and Rowan 1978).

If police departments choose to use cameras to monitor the procedural justice with which officers act, they have several options. They could actively monitor officers' behavior, sanctioning officers who violate department procedures when they engage in some forms of procedurally unjust behavior (whether or not a citizen complains about it), and coaching officers whose performance leaves room for improvement with respect to procedural justice. They could even try to establish and apply a standard of workmanship (Bittner 1983) that incorporates procedural justice, though they probably could not require that officers meet that standard. Alternatively, departments could more passively monitor officers' behavior, reviewing camera recordings only when officers' behavior is called into question; this would leave the cameras more loosely coupled with routine police practices. Based on our findings, we think it likely that merely providing for cameras would contribute as much to police legitimacy as active monitoring, since any improvement in officers' procedural justice is unlikely to yield corresponding improvements in citizens' subjective experience and police legitimacy.

More generally, it appears that organizational reform is a more promising approach to building police legitimacy than managing procedural justice in police-citizen encounters.[2] The reforms that we reviewed in chapter 2—community policing, early intervention systems, Compstat—have probably done more than street-level procedural justice could to increase the legitimacy of the agencies that adopted them, even if the reforms were weakly implemented and loosely coupled to the technical core of policing. Other reforms that might be expected to improve police legitimacy include personnel practices that are designed to provide for greater congruence between the composition of police departments and the communities they serve (National Research Council 2004, 312–14), educational requirements and training (Gau 2014, 3364), and proactively disseminating information to the public and managing media relations (Gau 2014, 3365). Let us take a closer look at some of these possibilities.

Implications for Police Reform

Piecing together the findings of our inquiry, extant research on policing, and clues about successful police reforms, we can cautiously trace some implications for contemporary reform. Let us begin this exercise by considering the case of reform in Cincinnati, where rioting followed the fatal shooting of an unarmed black teenager by police in 2001, after fourteen black men—but no whites—had died in police deadly force incidents since 1995 (Fisher 2014). Cincinnati's mayor requested a federal investigation of the Cincinnati Police Department's use of force, an investigation that culminated in a memorandum of agreement (MOA) that stipulated a number of reforms (Schatmeier 2013). Among other changes, the MOA required that CPD revise its policies governing the use of force to provide for a force continuum, to require documentation of every use of force, and to require on-scene investigation of uses of force by a supervisor (Memorandum of Agreement 2002). The MOA also established a Citizen Complaint Authority and required measures designed to facilitate the filing of citizen complaints against the police and to better ensure the participation of civilians in their review. It further mandated the establishment of a risk-management system (i.e., an early intervention system). In these respects, the MOA resembled the public accountability reforms described in chapter 2 as features of the institutional environment of police departments. The implementation of the reforms—achieving "substantial compliance"—was overseen by a court-appointed monitor from 2002 until 2007.

But in addition, Cincinnati police also entered into a "collaborative agreement" with parties to a lawsuit that had been filed in federal court prior to the DOJ investigation, including the American Civil Liberties Union, the Fraternal Order of

Police, and the Cincinnati Black United Front (Schatmeier 2013). The collaborative agreement, as an alternative resolution of the suit's claims, provided for CPD's adoption of community- and problem-oriented policing (CPOP). In particular, for example:

> The Parties, and especially the CPD, understand that fully engaging the community is a fundamental key to effective law enforcement. The CPD will continue to implement policies and procedures that are guided by the principles of community problem-oriented policing. In accordance with these principles, the CPD continues to work in partnership with the community to solve problems that impact the community. (In re Cincinnati Policing 2003, 7)

Both agreements were overseen by the same court-appointed monitor, though the collaborative agreement also provided for the selection of an independent evaluator. The RAND Corporation was selected and, among other things, conducted two surveys of the community—one in 2005 and a second in 2008—and also analyzed police-citizen interactions in annual samples of traffic stops across four years by coding the audio and video recordings captured by CPD's in-car cameras (Ridgeway et al. 2009; also see Dixon et al. 2008).

The surveys of the community—surveys of the general population and not of people with police contact—showed modest improvement in the public's assessments of "police professionalism," that is, judgments about whether police treat people with dignity and respect, are polite, apply the law fairly, consider people's views when making decisions, and so forth. On a scale that combined eight such survey items, the mean for blacks in 2005 was about 2.4, 0.6 lower than that for others, but still above 2.0, which signified generally favorable judgments. By 2008, the mean for blacks had increased 0.15 along this four-point scale, a small (but statistically reliable) increase, while the mean for others was unchanged.

RAND's analysis of interactions in traffic stops found a number of racial disparities in the invasiveness of traffic stops—in the likelihood of a search and the duration of stops, for example. It also examined the quality of communications, finding that "the best predictor for good officer communication was good driver communication, and vice versa" (Ridgeway et al. 2009, 83). RAND found some evidence of change over time in the quality of officers' communication: "the observers rate them as better at listening to what the drivers say, as well as showing more patience and helpfulness in 2007 than in 2005" (2009, 86), though the magnitude of the improvement is not specified.

Moreover, as recent studies have shown, the use of force by Cincinnati declined, not only for the duration of the federal monitoring but thereafter. Joshua Chanin shows that the use of force by Cincinnati police dropped 46 percent between 2002 and 2012, even as crime remained stable, and officer injuries dropped by more than half; in addition, citizen complaints declined. Thus, as Chanin points out, "six years removed from DOJ and monitor oversight, the Department has experienced little or no backsliding, a finding supported by consistent reductions in undesirable outcomes, including use of force incidence and allegations of abusive or unlawful behavior. In short, the reform effort in Cincinnati appears to have transformed the CPD" (2015, 179–80).

Indeed, a *Washington Post* article, written in the aftermath of the death of Michael Brown in Ferguson, Missouri, identified the CPD as a department whose practices might be worthy of emulation (Fisher 2014). No one claims that all is well in Cincinnati. RAND's surveys documented a persistent—albeit somewhat narrower—racial gap in public trust. And in 2014, the *Post* journalist observed that "mistrust of police in Cincinnati—even after full-scale retraining and a 120-point catalogue of altered procedures—remains palpable in black neighborhoods." But he also said that "thirteen years after riots that threatened to wreck Cincinnati's reputation and economy, many here say the police have become gentler, smarter, more transparent and more targeted in how they go after bad guys."

Pinpointing the specific reform(s) that deserve credit for these changes is impossible, but based on extant theory and evidence about police behavior, management, and community relations, we suspect that a lot of credit should be given to use-of-force policies and procedures that would seem to have been at least moderately coupled with street-level practice, and to the adoption of community and problem-oriented policing. The decline in the incidence of physical force is stunning, and it is surely not due to commensurate declines in citizen resistance. Cincinnati police became more restrained in their use of force. Certainly this could be partly attributable to training that CPD delivered to its officers, including training for a cadre of volunteer officers who were to handle incidents involving the mentally ill. But a change of this magnitude seems unlikely to stem from only formal training; we think it more likely that more restrictive policies that were executed by supervisors made a very substantial difference. We interviewed a small nonrandom sample of CPD supervisors in early 2016, and while we certainly heard about a mix of supervisory approaches, we were impressed by those who took quite seriously their responsibility, not only for assessing their subordinates' compliance with CPD force policies, but especially for ensuring that their officers were using sound tactics that minimized the risk of resistance, force, and injury. We would not infer that the coupling of policy and practice was uniformly tight, but it appears to us to have been sufficiently tight to have some very beneficial impacts on police use of force.

That such coupling does not follow the adoption of such policies is evident from DOJ's investigation of the Ferguson police. Ferguson's policies resemble those of the CPD:

> Under FPD General Order 410.00, when an officer uses or attempts to use any force, a supervisor must respond to the scene to investigate. The supervisor must complete a two-page use-of-force report assessing whether the use of force complied with

FPD's force policy. Additional forms are required for ECW uses and vehicle pursuits. According to policy and our interviews with Chief Jackson, a use-of-force packet is assembled—which should include the use-of-force report and supplemental forms, all police reports, any photographs, and any other supporting materials—and forwarded up the chain of command to the Chief. (U.S. Department of Justice 2015, 38).

But in Ferguson, "supervisors do little to no investigation; either do not understand or choose not to follow FPD's use-of-force policy in analyzing officer conduct; rarely correct officer misconduct when they find it; and do not see the patterns of abuse that are evident when viewing these incidents in the aggregate" (38). Coupling use of force policy with street-level practice requires managerial commitment and effort, but the CPD's experience suggests that it is feasible.

The use of physical force by police is often a contentious issue. Reasonable force is to some extent a matter of interpreting ambiguous circumstances, and police and public interpretations tend to diverge. Few citizens who are subjected to the application of physical force by police consider it proper. Among our Schenectady respondents, we found evidence that suggests that the use of physical force by police detracts from citizens' judgments of procedural justice; the effect was not of sufficient magnitude to achieve statistical significance at conventional levels, perhaps because the use of physical force was very infrequent. Reductions in the use of force by police, these results imply, could do more to "create" legitimacy on the street than increases in the procedural justice with which officers act.

Further extrapolating from our findings, other research, and Cincinnati's experience with the use of force, we would speculate that similar benefits in public trust could follow from policies and supervisory oversight and instruction in conducting searches. The case law of search and seizure is complex. Jon Gould and Stephen Mastrofski (2004) examined the frequency with which officers conducted discretionary searches (beyond "plain view") and how often the searches were unconstitutional (based on a matrix of Fourth Amendment court rulings); they found that nearly one-third of the searches were assessed as unconstitutional. If we can generalize from Gould and Mastrofski's findings, it seems safe to project that close adherence to the law would reduce the frequency with which police search citizens. If we can generalize from the findings from Schenectady and Syracuse, fewer searches would yield an improvement in citizens' subjective experiences, again creating more legitimacy. If policies governing searches were as tightly coupled to police practice as use of force policies appear to be coupled to practice in Cincinnati, then the formulation and implementation of such policies would be a useful step in police reform.

Community and problem-oriented policing was another major component in Cincinnati's reform agenda. We discussed the appeal of community policing in the institutional environment, and surely this was no less true in Cincinnati than elsewhere. Community policing is procedurally just on a community scale: it gives the community voice in identifying the public safety problems about which it is most concerned, and signifies the commitment of the police to addressing the matters that would contribute most to community improvement, as the community sees it. Moreover, community policing need not be tightly coupled to day-to-day patrol and investigative practice in order to achieve these outcomes; even specialized community policing units can serve as a bridge between the police and the public, and mount problem-solving initiatives to address community concerns. That is, even loosely coupled community policing is not (necessarily) window-dressing.

In addition, we should recognize that public attitudes are likely to change only very slowly, if at all. Despite the advances that have been made in Cincinnati, public attitudes have been largely stable. That the change in blacks' attitudes toward the Cincinnati police that RAND detected in its survey results was greater than zero is unlikely the product of sampling artifacts. But the improvement was small—0.15 on a four-point scale of police professionalism. Street-level practice, particularly with respect to the use of force, changed far more dramatically than public attitudes did.

Future Research

Whether these findings—some from one police department and others from two departments—are generalizable to other settings is an open question, to be answered by future research. One research question that we would nominate as a high priority for future research is the hypothesized relationship between officers' procedural justice and citizens' subjective experience. Clues that the relationship is fairly weak can be seen in previous research that has involved panel surveys, with estimates of the effects of prior attitudes toward police on satisfaction and/or procedural justice with individual contacts with police. But empirical evidence on this relationship that rests on measures of the two constructs—officers' procedural justice and citizens' subjective experience—drawn from independent data sources would be far preferable.

Research on officers' procedural justice need not extend to citizens' perceptions in order to be valuable, for much remains to be learned about patterns of procedurally just (and unjust) behavior. We might suppose that, like other forms of police behavior, procedurally just policing varies with the characteristics and behaviors of citizens and other characteristics of the situations in which police and citizens interact; the backgrounds and outlooks of individual police officers; the nature and intensity of the cues that officers receive from police administrators and supervisors about how they may and should treat citizens; and the community or neighborhood context for police-citizen encounters.

Extant research on police behavior sensitizes us to the ways in which officers' behavior is influenced by the features of the situations in which they interact with citizens. The use of police authority is shaped by both legal factors, such as the seriousness of the offense and the strength of evidence, and by extralegal factors, such as citizens' sex, demeanor, and (sometimes) race. We might especially expect that procedural justice—*how* police use their authority—would also be affected (but not determined) by the degree of respect and cooperation that citizens offer to police. Our examination of situational variables confirmed the hypothesized relationship of procedural injustice to citizen disrespect and resistance, though questions about causal order remained. Moreover, these variables accounted for only one-third or less of the variation in procedural justice or injustice.

Research on several forms of police officers' behavior—arrests, use of force, stops, and several forms of misconduct—all suggests that behavior varies among individual officers. For example, Samuel Walker (2005, 100) summarized several investigations that suggest that small numbers of officers account for disproportionately large fractions of citizen complaints and use-of-force reports. Steven Brandl et al. (2001) found that less experienced officers are disproportionately represented among officers with multiple complaints about the use of excessive force. Many years ago, Hans Toch (1980; also see Toch 1996) found that violence-prone officers are especially sensitive to citizens' challenges to their authority. Ellen Scrivner (1994) discovered five groups of officers among those referred to police psychologists due to their use of excessive force, including: officers with personality disorders; officers whose job-related experiences—for example, traumatic incidents such as police shootings—put them at risk for abusing force; young and inexperienced officers who were also "highly impressionable and impulsive"; officers who develop inappropriate patrol styles; and officers with personal problems. Christopher Harris (2010) showed that officers differ in their career "trajectories" of misconduct. Research persuasively confirms what many police officers and administrators have observed for themselves: that "operational styles" (Brown, 1981) and police dysfunctions vary across individual officers.

Recent research indicates that the traits, outlooks, and cognitive schema of officers may be important in understanding and explaining these individual variations. William Terrill et al. (2003) reported that officers whose occupational attitudes conform more closely to the tenets of the traditional police culture are more prone to the use of their coercive authority.[3] Similarly, Eugene Paoline and William Terrill (2005) found that such officers are more likely to conduct searches during traffic stops. Matthew Hickman (2008) found that cynicism predicts "problem police behavior," while Michael Cuttler and Paul Muchinsky (2006) found that personality traits and work history predict "dysfunctional job performance." Other characteristics of officers—their race, sex, and educational background—have all been hypothesized to affect how officers do their jobs, though the evidence on these hypotheses is mixed and inconclusive (National Research Council 2004). In view of the findings that officers' choices about the application (and misapplication) of their authority in making stops, using force, and invoking the law are all shaped to a degree by individual factors, there is good reason to believe that many of these same factors may help to account for the procedural justice with which police authority is exercised. In particular, we might expect that the officers whose outlooks most resemble those of the traditional police culture, and those who are more cynical, would be those least receptive to a procedural justice emphasis. If so, then the contours of rank-and-file resistance to procedurally just policing would resemble those of resistance to community policing (cf. Herbert 2009).

Previous research shows not only that individual officers' *behavior* varies, but also that their *performance* varies: some officers perform *better* than others. This should come as no surprise, as it is surely true of any occupational group, but it is especially difficult to demonstrate empirically in policing because positive police performance is so difficult to conceive and measure. David Bayley and James Garofalo (1987, 1989) asked officers themselves to identify peers who they considered to be especially skilled in handling conflict; in the three NYPD precincts they studied, Bayley and Garofalo thereby identified a set of exceptionally skilled officers on whom they conducted systematic observations. They found that these officers exhibited somewhat distinctive patterns of interaction with citizens, particularly in situations that were potentially conflictual: they "tended to be more concerned to get the fullest possible picture [of the incident] and to find a long-run solution, especially one that satisfied the complainant, while [comparison officers] showed less sympathy for complainants' problems, and were quicker to say that the police couldn't do anything" (1987, 13). They added that the more skilled officers "offered more information about ways to resolve problems, while [comparison officers] lectured citizens about how to act in the future and threatened a stern response if they were called back" (13). While Bayley and Garofalo did not frame their analysis in the terms of procedural justice, we might retrospectively observe that the skilled officers acted in ways that independent observers would be likely to interpret as showing concern for citizens' needs and concerns, and affording citizens an opportunity to explain their situations.

In general, based on extant research, we might reasonably speculate that some officers perform consistently well in terms of procedural justice, either preventing citizen disrespect and resistance or responding to it with equanimity and professionalism, and otherwise exhibiting a high quality of decision-making; we need to learn from these officers what they do (and do not do) and why, which implies that we need to understand how officers perceive and interpret their encounters with citizens—the perceptual and cognitive processes that yield different reactions to similar stimuli—including how officers see the different clientele they serve, and whether/why some are more or less deserving of procedural justice. We might further suppose that typical or average officers sometimes perform poorly in procedural justice terms, and we also need to learn from these officers what they do (and do not do) and why.

As Stephen Mastrofski et al. (2002, 542) suggest, the quality of police-citizen interactions might be influenced by administrators in one or both of two ways: obtrusive (or "bureaucratic") controls, such as rules, regulations, and sanctions for rule violations; and unobtrusive (or "professional") controls, such as training and socialization. As a practical matter, and for reasons that we explained in chapters 2 and 8, the establishment of such practices is likely to progress unevenly across organizational units, managers, supervisors, and officers, such that we are likely to find variation not only in behavioral conformity with procedural justice but also in awareness, recognition, understanding, and acceptance of procedural justice concepts and principles.

Therein lies a key question: what accounts for the tighter coupling of policy and practice in some agencies—such as Cincinnati, perhaps—than in others—such as Ferguson? The question has been recently posed, but not answered, in connection with sustaining reforms wrought by consent decrees and settlement agreements, which coercively "unfreeze" an organization for change. But after the cessation of court-appointed monitoring, and the leverage that the court brings to bear to ensure that reforms are implemented is withdrawn, the coupling of the reforms may loosen, and the practices in which they are intended to result may lapse. How, if at all, can such reforms be installed in such a way that they will survive not only the discontinuation of court supervision but also administrative turnover?

Finally, while we believe that steps to better prepare officers to exercise their authority—including especially searches and the use of force—are the most promising avenues of police reform, extant research offers little evidence about how police organizations can effectively perform these functions. Training and supervision are frequently mentioned. Such prescriptions rest largely on logic and wishful thinking, and certainly not on social scientific evidence. Academics and practitioners alike frequently comment on the crucial role that frontline supervisors play, but studies of how they play it, and how well they play it, are rarely conducted. There are no simple, easy answers, to be sure, but there is no credit for asking the right questions either.

METHODOLOGICAL APPENDIX

Our research in Schenectady and Syracuse employed multiple methods, including both interviews and observation. An overview of each method was provided in the pertinent chapter; here we provide additional details concerning their execution. We begin with the police services survey, which formed the basis for the measures of citizens' subjective experience that were incorporated into the department's management accountability meetings each month. Then we describe the survey of key informants—leaders of neighborhood organizations—in each city. We turn then to a description of interviews with patrol officers and supervisors (i.e., sergeants), and interviews with police commanders. Finally, we further describe the observations of police-citizen encounters in Schenectady, which were accomplished by watching and listening to recordings drawn from the in-car video and audio that has been a routine procedure in that department for some time.

THE POLICE SERVICES SURVEY

The police services survey sampled records of calls for service, stops, and arrests. Recorded contacts were assessed for their eligibility for inclusion in the survey sample. Officer-initiated incidents were removed from CAD records, as were records that lacked a recognizable first *or* last name, such that records with only, for example, "unknown," "passerby," "neighbor," or "security" in the name fields were eliminated. Arrests that had been sealed by the courts and included no name were removed, though with the limited time delay between the end of a sampling period (one half of a month) and the extraction of data, this was rare. Stop or field interview records that listed neither a phone number nor an address (or recorded the address as "homeless") were eliminated. In Syracuse, stop records do not include a phone number, and so efforts were made to "append" a telephone number given a name and address. Finally, if the same person appeared more than once in the same subpopulation in a single sampling period, only the most recent incident was sampled.

TABLE 7 Survey Sampling and Disposition Summary

	Schenectady			Syracuse		
	Arrests	Field interviews	Calls for service	Arrests	Stops	Calls for service
Eligible	6,745	3,127	33,880	8,779	12,472	117,031
Sampled	6,745	3,127	10,782	8,779	12,472	10,800
Called	5,377	2,192	9,965	7,168	1,809	9,914
Contacted	622	138	2,061	535	205	2,108
Of those contacted:						
Completed	62.7%	58.0%	64.5%	61.9%	49.8%	65.0%
Incomplete	7.7%	7.2%	5.1%	9.5%	5.9%	5.1%
Refused	26.7%	30.4%	25.4%	22.4%	33.7%	22.8%
Screened out	0.2%	0.7%	2.2%	0.9%	0.5%	2.3%
Language barrier	2.7%	3.6%	2.7%	5.2%	10.2%	4.8%

During each sampling period we randomly sampled three hundred calls for service, and we included all arrests and stops/field interviews in the sample of contacts. We over-represented arrests and stops/field interviews in order to better capture for separate analysis a number of incidents in which procedural justice would presumably be more challenging for officers. Surveying extended over approximately two weeks, until new semi-monthly samples were drawn, and so respondents were interviewed within one to five weeks of their contact. Table 7 summarizes the sampling and survey dispositions for each subpopulation in each site across the eighteen months of surveying. All of the eligible arrests and stops/field interviews were sampled, as were more than 30 percent of the calls for service in Schenectady and nearly 10 percent of the calls for service in Syracuse. Most of those who were sampled were called, excepting the stops in Syracuse, for which the process of appending telephone numbers to names and addresses was only partially successful. Substantial fractions—nearly 20 percent in each city—of the people who had called for service were contacted, and of those who were contacted, nearly two-thirds completed the interview. People who were arrested or stopped/field interviewed were much more difficult to contact; 6 to 12 percent of those who were called were contacted by interviewers.[1] Of those who were contacted, however, completion rates were generally around 60 percent, excepting Syracuse stops. About one-quarter of those contacted declined to participate; small proportions were screened out (people who were under eighteen years of age and who had called for service could not be removed from the sample as ineligible because no information about their age was in the CAD record) or were unable to complete the interview in English.

Table 8 below summarizes the sampling and sample attrition in terms of the characteristics of the populations from which the samples were drawn. In each of five columns—the eligible population, the sample, those who were sampled and called, those who were contacted, and those who completed the interview—the table displays a percentage breakdown by each characteristic. The first three rows show a breakdown by the type of contact, and they show the margins by which arrests and stops were overrepresented in the samples (e.g., in Schenectady, arrests were 15.4 percent of the eligible population of contacts, but 32.7 percent of the sample), and they also show the sources of attrition from that sample.

TABLE 8 Sampling and Disposition Details

Schenectady	Eligible for interview (N = 43,752)	Sampled (20,654)	Called (17,539)	Contacted (2,824)	Interviewed (1,800)
Contact type					
Arrests	15.4%	32.7%	30.7%	22.2%	21.7%
Calls for service	77.4%	52.2%	56.8%	72.9%	73.9%
Field interviews	7.1%	15.1%	12.5%	4.9%	4.4%
Wave					
Baseline + (1–12)	33.9%	32.3%	31.3%	32.5%	33.3%
1st quarter (13–18)	16.2%	17.1%	17.3%	16.2%	16.8%
2nd quarter (19–24)	19.4%	17.8%	17.9%	16.4%	16.6%
3rd quarter (25–30)	16.1%	17.2%	17.3%	17.7%	16.7%
4th quarter (31–36)	14.3%	15.7%	16.2%	17.3%	16.7%
Platoon					
Midnight: 8 a.m.	21.3%	24.1%	23.5%	20.0%	18.6%
8 a.m.–4 p.m.	35.5%	34.6%	35.4%	37.0%	39.3%
4 p.m.–midnight	43.2%	41.3%	41.1%	43.0%	42.1%
Calls: Problem type	N = 33,880	10,782	9,965	2,061	1,330
Violent crime	4.8%	4.8%	4.6%	4.1%	4.1%
Interpersonal conflict	18.1%	18.3%	17.8%	16.4%	14.8%
Nonviolent crime	26.6%	27.0%	27.3%	28.5%	30.5%
Suspicious circumstance	5.3%	5.0%	5.1%	5.0%	5.0%
Dependent person	7.7%	7.7%	7.7%	6.9%	7.2%
Traffic	10.0%	9.5%	9.7%	11.5%	12.9%
Public nuisance	13.7%	13.7%	13.7%	14.8%	14.2%
Medical	0.4%	0.3%	0.3%	0.1%	0.1%
Other assistance	7.6%	8.1%	8.1%	7.9%	7.8%
Other	3.0%	2.8%	2.8%	2.6%	1.6%
Unknown	2.8%	2.8%	2.8%	2.1%	1.8%
Arrests: top charge	N = 6,745	6,745	5,377	626	390
Felony	16.5%	16.5%	16.3%	10.2%	11.0%
Misdemeanor	61.0%	61.0%	61.9%	67.3%	67.7%
Violation	10.0%	10.0%	9.3%	11.7%	12.8%
Infraction/other	12.5%	12.5%	12.4%	10.9%	8.5%
Arrests: type					
Crime in progress	25.9%	25.9%	24.1%	24.0%	24.4%
Complaint	26.9%	26.9%	26.2%	24.3%	24.6%
Arrest warrant	20.0%	20.0%	21.3%	24.1%	25.9%
Bench warrant	14.7%	14.7%	15.5%	14.4%	12.3%
Summons	11.5%	11.5%	11.9%	13.1%	12.8%
Other	1.0%	1.0%	0.9%	0.2%	0
Arrests: disposition					
Held	62.2%	62.2%	61.4%	58.1%	56.2%

TABLE 8 *(continued)*

Schenectady	Eligible for interview (N = 43,752)	Sampled (20,654)	Called (17,539)	Contacted (2,824)	Interviewed (1,800)
Released	4.3%	4.3%	4.4%	5.1%	4.9%
Appearance ticket	33.1%	33.1%	33.8%	36.3%	38.7%
Other	0.4%	0.4%	0.4%	0.5%	0.3%
Arrests: race/ethnicity					
White	41.1%	41.1%	42.3%	53.7%	55.1%
Black	43.4%	43.4%	41.9%	31.8%	28.5%
Hispanic	8.9%	8.9%	8.7%	6.2%	7.4%
Other	6.6%	6.6%	7.1%	8.3%	9.0%
Arrests: sex					
Male	72.4%	72.4%	70.5%	67.7%	66.2%
Female	27.6%	27.6%	29.4%	33.3%	33.8%
Field interviews: race/ethnicity	N = 3,127	3,127	2,192	138	80
White	35.0%	35.0%	37.0%	34.8%	36.2%
Black	44.8%	44.8%	46.0%	40.6%	45.0%
Hispanic	6.2%	6.2%	4.8%	5.8%	5.0%
Other/missing	14.0%	14.0%	12.2%	18.8%	13.8%
Field interviews: sex					
Male	80.5%	80.5%	80.2%	76.8%	72.5%
Female	18.6%	18.6%	19.3%	23.2%	27.5%

Syracuse	Eligible for interview (N = 138,568)	Sampled (32,337)	Called (18,899)	Contacted (2,853)	Interviewed (1,803)
Contact type					
Arrests	6.5%	28.0%	30.7%	18.8%	18.4%
Calls for service	84.5%	33.4%	56.8%	74.0%	76.0%
Stops	9.0%	38.6%	12.5%	7.2%	5.6%
Wave					
Baseline + (1–12)	31.9%	32.2%	32.0%	30.4%	33.3%
1st quarter (13–18)	15.7%	17.8%	17.2%	16.4%	16.6%
2nd quarter (19–24)	18.7%	16.2%	17.4%	18.2%	16.7%
3rd quarter (25–30)	18.5%	17.8%	17.3%	17.5%	16.2%
4th quarter (31–36)	15.2%	16.0%	16.2%	17.5%	17.1%
Platoon					
10 p.m.–6 a.m.	27.3%	33.0%	29.0%	27.4%	25.6%
6 a.m.–2 p.m.	25.6%	23.2%	27.1%	25.9%	27.6%
2 p.m.–10 p.m.	47.1%	43.8%	43.9%	46.7%	46.8%
Calls: Problem type	N = 117,031	10,800	9,914	2,108	1,370
Violent crime	15.3%	15.8%	15.3%	12.6%	12.4%
Interpersonal conflict	11.6%	11.8%	11.8%	11.7%	12.6%
Nonviolent crime	10.7%	10.4%	10.4%	10.2%	11.3%

TABLE 8 *(continued)*

Syracuse	Eligible for interview (N = 138,568)	Sampled (32,337)	Called (18,899)	Contacted (2,853)	Interviewed (1,803)
Suspicious circumstance	5.7%	5.5%	5.5%	5.8%	6.3%
Dependent person	6.5%	6.6%	6.5%	5.2%	4.9%
Traffic	12.5%	12.7%	13.0%	13.7%	14.7%
Public nuisance	14.0%	13.6%	13.9%	16.6%	18.0%
Medical	10.0%	9.7%	9.9%	9.7%	7.4%
Other assistance	6.3%	6.6%	6.4%	6.7%	5.7%
Other	1.4%	1.4%	1.3%	1.5%	1.7%
Unknown	6.1%	5.9%	6.0%	6.3%	4.9%
Arrests: top charge	N = 8,779	8,779	7,168	536	331
Felony	31.6%	31.6%	32.4%	26.3%	23.9%
Misdemeanor	45.0%	45.0%	46.1%	50.2%	51.1%
Violation	17.8%	17.8%	16.8%	19.8%	21.5%
Infraction/other	5.6%	5.6%	4.7%	3.7%	3.6%
Arrests: type					
Crime in progress	47.7%	47.7%	46.6%	47.9%	45.3%
Complaint	28.0%	28.0%	28.4%	28.4%	30.2%
Arrest warrant	15.8%	15.8%	16.5%	17.0%	17.2%
Bench warrant	3.3%	3.3%	3.2%	2.8%	3.3%
Summons	0	0	0	0	0
Other	5.2%	5.2%	5.2%	3.9%	3.9%
Arrests: disposition					
Held	96.1%	96.1%	96.2%	96.1%	96.1%
Released	0.3%	0.3%	0.3%	0.9%	0.9%
Appearance ticket	0.3%	0.3%	0.3%	0.2%	0.3%
Other	3.3%	3.3%	3.2%	2.8%	2.7%
Arrests: race/ethnicity					
White	31.9%	31.9%	32.1%	36.2%	38.7%
Black	58.7%	58.7%	59.1%	54.7%	53.5%
Hispanic	7.4%	7.4%	6.8%	7.1%	6.3%
Other	2.0%	2.0%	2.0%	2.0%	1.5%
Arrests: sex					
Male	76.7%	76.7%	76.3%	71.1%	70.4%
Female	23.3%	23.3%	23.7%	28.9%	29.6%
Stops: race/ethnicity	N = 12,472	12,472	1,809	205	102
White	37.0%	37.0%	53.3%	61.5%	54.9%
Black	52.4%	52.4%	40.1%	29.3%	40.2%
Hispanic	7.2%	7.2%	2.7%	3.4%	3.9%
Other	3.4%	3.4%	3.9%	5.8%	1.0%
Stops: sex					
Male	73.2%	73.2%	72.7%	70.7%	66.7%
Female	26.0%	26.0%	26.7%	28.8%	33.3%

An assessment of the representativeness of the interviewed sample can be made by comparing the percentages in the column furthest right with those in the second column for the eligible population. In Schenectady, for example, interviewed arrestees comprise 21.7 percent of the sample, compared with 15.4 percent of the eligible population. Field interviews in that site were underrepresented, however, given the low rate at which interviewers were able to contact them. Similar patterns hold for arrests and stops in Syracuse. In both sites, contacts during the day shift were slightly overrepresented.

The table also displays a breakdown of call types among eligible calls for service, classified into a common set of problem type categories based on the CAD field.[2] In general, the interviewed sample resembles the eligible population in each site fairly closely.

The interviewed samples of arrestees bear a close resemblance to the eligible populations in terms of the top charge (though felony arrestees are slightly underrepresented), the basis for or "type" of arrest, and the immediate disposition of the arrest (though arrestees who were held—placed in a lock-up—were somewhat underrepresented). White arrestees were overrepresented relative to black arrestees, especially in Schenectady, and male arrestees were overrepresented relative to females. Among stops, males were somewhat underrepresented in both sites, and in Syracuse, whites were overrepresented relative to blacks.

Since the samples are stratified, with different probabilities of sample selection across the different subpopulations, and since the response rates varied across subpopulations, we weight the cases for most analyses of the survey data in order to represent the entire contact population in each site. We apply weights that reproduce the original population proportion that each subpopulation represents, though these weights are very nearly the same as those that are based only on the probabilities of sample selection (with correlations over 0.90).

We conducted a review of 154 selected cases to ensure as much as possible that we analyze only cases in which the respondent described his/her experience in the sampled incident and not some other event.[3] This review indicated that seventy-five cases were certainly a mismatch: that the respondent described a contact with the police other than the sampled contact. Two-thirds (51) of those were in Syracuse, and about 80 percent were calls for service. All seventy-five of these cases were dropped from the analyses reported in chapters 4 and 7. We also compiled information on the number of calls placed by each respondent not only during the sampling period but during the preceding and succeeding sampling periods, and we found sixty-eight additional cases (forty-six of them in Syracuse) in which the same phone number appeared four or more times in that broader time period around the sampled contact; we treat these cases as of questionable reliability, on the assumption that the respondent would be hard-pressed to distinguish the sampled contact from others at about the same time, and we tested the sensitivity of our results to the inclusion of these cases.

We also note that our sampling frames were not mutually exclusive; while it does not occur often, some people who called for assistance were arrested. Furthermore, if it involves multiple persons, the same event can be the subject of multiple interviews, each concerning the experience of a different person. On nine occasions, two different people were interviewed about the same incident: six times when one person called for assistance and the other person was arrested; twice when two people were arrested in connection with the same incident; and once when two people were stopped at the same time.

In addition, we note that across eighteen months of surveying, any one person might well appear in the sample multiple times, and in fact, 101 people were each interviewed more than once about different incidents; all but seven of the 101 were interviewed twice, and one was interviewed four times, together accounting for 210 of the 3,603 contacts with police. Finally, a nontrivial proportion of those who called for service reported that they did not have a face-to-face interaction with an officer, and these respondents are not included in the analyses of procedural justice, inasmuch as we are interested in citizens' direct encounters with the police.

KEY INFORMANT SURVEY

We contacted thirty-seven prospective Syracuse respondents in wave 1, followed by thirty-six in wave 2, and thirty-five in the final wave.[4] Syracuse final response rates in waves 1 through 3 were as follows: 67 percent (N = 25); 44.4 percent (N = 16); and 28.5 percent (N = 10), respectively. We contacted twenty-nine prospective respondents in Schenectady in wave 1, twenty-seven in wave 2, and twenty-six in wave 3.[5] Schenectady final response rates for waves 1 through 3 were as follows: 48.2 percent (N = 14); 44.4 percent (N = 12); and 50.0 percent (N = 13), respectively. The response rate in Syracuse declined substantially between waves 1 and 3. While the initial response rate in Schenectady (48.2 percent) was somewhat lower than initial rate in Syracuse, it remained more stable over the subsequent survey waves. We did not add new e-mail addresses for respondents after wave 1. The responses are based on a true panel.

PATROL INTERVIEWS

We conducted interviews with patrol sergeants and patrol officers in order to assess the views of the rank and file regarding the emphasis on customer service, how (if at all) administrative expectations were reverberating down through the ranks, and any sources of resistance to a customer-service orientation.

We followed a similar process in both sites. During line-up or roll call, a supervising officer announced that an interviewer would be available during the first several hours of the shift to speak with officers about customer service. In Schenectady, interviewers were given access to a private office adjacent to the roll call room in which to conduct the interviews. Interviews in Syracuse were slightly less private in that no separate room was designated for conducting interviews. They were held in a common area outside several private offices. Interviewers stayed several hours into each shift, leaving only after they determined they had exhausted the willing interviewee pool.

Wave 1 yielded thirty-one completed interviews in Syracuse and sixteen in Schenectady. Respondents in both sites were fairly well distributed between patrol officers and sergeants: 61 and 62 percent patrol officers in Syracuse and Schenectady, respectively. We completed fourteen wave 2 interviews in Syracuse and twenty-six in Schenectady. Despite the fact that we used the same process in each wave to recruit subjects, the breakdown of officers and sergeants was very different in wave 2, compared to wave 1; the wave 2 sample was predominantly comprised of patrol officers (86 percent and 81 percent in Syracuse and Schenectady, respectively).

COMMANDER INTERVIEWS

In Schenectady we interviewed the three lieutenants who commanded the department's patrol platoons, as well as the three lieutenants who commanded the Investigative Services Bureau. In Syracuse we interviewed each of the three platoon captains and the lieutenant in charge of the department's Crime Reduction Team. The semi-structured instrument included items on performance expectations for subordinates, perspective on their department's Compstat process and their own role in it, their understanding and opinion of the department's effort to systematically measure and incorporate information on citizens' assessments of police performance into the Compstat process, and what steps they had taken to direct attention to customer service.

SCHENECTADY OBSERVATIONS

Our observers coded 539 encounters from among those that we sampled and obtained recordings from the Schenectady police. Table 9 below charts the similarities and differences among the population of incidents we sampled for observation, the sample, the set of incidents for which we obtained recordings, and the set of incidents that were coded by both observers.

In chapter 6, we discussed some of the advantages and disadvantages of observing police-citizen encounters after-the-fact through audio and video recordings. Here we assess our observers' capacity to detect what transpires in the sampled police-citizen encounters.

Table 10 shows the frequencies with which observers were able to see and identify the primary citizens and the primary officers. Each of 539 coded incidents appear twice in the table, once for each observer. Primary officers were identifiable most (94 percent) of the time, whether they were visible on camera or not. Primary citizens were also identifiable most (83 percent) of the time, though not quite so often as primary officers. Across all 539 incidents, both observers were able to identify the primary citizen in 417, while in 63 neither observer was able to identify the primary citizen; in the remaining 59 incidents, one but not the other observer judged that s/he was able to identify the primary citizen.

Table 11 shows the estimated proportions of the audio that was unintelligible, for incidents in which both observers could identify the primary citizen, in which neither could do so, and in which only one could do so. In the median encounter 20 percent of the audio was unintelligible, and in less than 15 percent of the encounters, two-thirds or more of the incident's audio was unintelligible. Poor audio quality seems not to have seriously impaired observers' capacity to identify primary citizens, however; even with one-third or less of the audio, both observers identified the primary citizen in two-thirds of the encounters.

We prompted each observer to estimate the level of his/her confidence in the coding of each encounter, using the categories that form the columns of table 12.[6] Overall, observers had a great deal of confidence in their coding: in 47 percent of the encounters the observer had complete confidence in the coding, and in 35 percent the observer was "mostly" confident. But as table 12 shows, the observers' confidence falls as the proportion of the audio that is unintelligible rises. Table 12 also cross-tabulates observers' confidence in their coding by whether the primary officer and primary citizen, respectively, is visible and/or identifiable. When the primary officer and primary citizen are identifiable, confidence is fairly high

TABLE 9 Characteristics of the Observation Population and Sample

	Survey population* (N = 1,800)	Observation sample (N = 1,049)	Incidents received (N = 648)	Incidents coded (N = 539)
Contact type				
Arrests	21.7%	34.8%	26.4%	27.1%
Calls	73.9%	57.6%	65.4%	64.2%
Field interviews	4.4%	7.6%	8.2%	8.7%
Wave				
Baseline + (1–12)	33.3%	32.0%	34.9%	33.8%
1st quarter (13–18)	16.8%	17.2%	18.1%	19.1%
2nd quarter (19–24)	16.6%	18.4%	15.9%	16.0%
3rd quarter (25–30)	16.7%	15.8%	16.4%	17.1%
4th quarter (31–36)	16.7%	16.6%	14.8%	14.1%
Patrol area**				
1	18.0%	18.3%	9.9%	7.7%
2	6.9%	6.7%	7.1%	6.7%
3	16.0%	16.3%	17.3%	17.1%
4	13.0%	12.8%	13.9%	14.4%
5	16.1%	16.7%	17.9%	19.2%
6	5.0%	4.1%	4.9%	5.0%
7	15.9%	15.4%	18.7%	18.8%
8	9.0%	9.4%	10.2%	11.2%
Platoon				
Midnight–8 a.m.	18.6%	21.9%	21.3%	20.6%
8 a.m.–4 p.m.	39.3%	34.0%	32.7%	31.5%
4 p.m.–midnight	42.1%	44.0%	46.0%	47.9%
Calls: Problem type				
Violent crime	2.5%	1.8%	1.9%	2.0%
Other personal crime	2.7%	2.3%	1.2%	0.9%
Public nuisance	14.7%	13.7%	13.0%	12.1%
Other assistance	11.1%	9.9%	8.5%	7.2%
Traffic	16.2%	16.9%	16.7%	17.1%
Nonviolent crime	29.3%	29.3%	31.1%	31.8%
Dependent person	3.7%	3.8%	5.0%	5.2%
Interpersonal conflict	14.3%	15.2%	16.7%	17.9%
Suspicious circumstance	3.8%	3.3%	2.8%	2.9%
Unknown	1.6%	3.5%	2.8%	2.6%
Medical	0.1%	0.1%	0.2%	0.2%
Arrests: charge level				
Felony	11.0%	10.4%	7.6%	6.8%
Misdemeanor	67.7%	67.9%	71.9%	76.0%

TABLE 9 *(Continued)*

	Survey population* (N = 1,800)	Observation sample (N = 1,049)	Incidents received (N = 648)	Incidents coded (N = 539)
Violation	12.8%	13.4%	14.0%	12.3%
Infraction/other	8.5%	8.2%	6.4%	4.8%
Arrests: type				
Complaint	24.6%	23.6%	29.2%	30.8%
Crime in progress	24.4%	26.0%	34.5%	35.6%
Arrest warrant	25.9%	24.7%	9.4%	6.8%
Bench warrant	12.3%	12.1%	8.2%	5.5%
Summons	12.8%	13.7%	18.7%	21.2%
Arrests: disposition				
Held	56.2%	54.5%	50.3%	48.6%
Released	4.9%	5.2%	6.4%	7.5%
Appearance ticket	38.7%	40.0%	43.3%	43.8%
Other	0.3%	0.3%	0%	0%
Arrests: race/ethnicity				
White	55.1%	56.2%	52.6%	52.7%
Black	28.5%	27.1%	28.7%	26.7%
Hispanic	7.4%	7.4%	9.4%	10.3%
Other	9.0%	9.3%	9.4%	10.3%
Arrests: sex				
Male	66.2%	66.6%	68.4%	69.9%
Female	33.8%	33.4%	31.6%	30.1%
Field interviews: race/ethnicity				
White	36.2%	36.2%	35.8%	36.2%
Black	45.0%	45.0%	41.5%	40.4%
Hispanic	5.0%	5.0%	3.8%	4.3%
Other	13.8%	13.8%	18.9%	19.1%
Field interviews: sex				
Male	72.5%	72.5%	75.5%	74.5%
Female	27.5%	27.5%	24.5%	25.5%

* Four cases were inadvertently excluded from the sampling
** Excludes 133 cases in the survey population with missing data

whether the primary officer or citizen is visible or not; confidence declines substantially when one or both cannot be identified. It appears that the recorded audio is more important for these purposes than the video.[7]

Overall, observers were completely or mostly confident in their coding when the police-citizen interaction was audible and, mainly as a consequence, they could identify the primary citizen and also determine what transpired. In general the audio was fairly good,

TABLE 10 Visibility and Identifiability of Primary Citizen and Primary Officer

Primary Officer	Primary Citizen			
	Visible and identifiable	Not visible/NA but identifiable	Not visible/NA and not identifiable	Totals
Visible and identifiable	333	200	103	636
Not visible but identifiable	38	279	55	372
Visible but not identifiable	7	14	13	34
Not visible and not identifiable	10	12	14	36
Totals	388	505	185	1,078

TABLE 11 Identification of Primary Citizen and Unintelligible Audio

Percentage of audio unintelligible	Observers Who Could Identify the Primary Citizen			
	Neither	One	Both	Totals
0–10	26 (26%)	33 (34.4%)	228 (37.3%)	287 (35.5%)
11–25	16 (16%)	17 (17.7%)	144 (23.5%)	177 (21.9%)
26–49	13 (13%)	15 (15.6%)	85 (13.9%)	113 (14.0%)
50–67	22 (22%)	15 (15.6%)	80 (13.1%)	117 (14.5%)
68–89	17 (17%)	10 (10.4%)	54 (8.8%)	81 (10.0%)
90–99	6 (6%)	6 (6.2%)	21 (3.4%)	33 (4.1%)

TABLE 12 Observers' Confidence in Coding

	Level of Confidence in Coding					
	Completely	Mostly	Fairly	A little	Not at all	Total N
Percentage of audio unintelligible						
0–10	70.6%	26.3%	2.4%	0.4%	0.4%	255
11–25	45.6%	41.9%	9.4%	2.5%	0.6%	160
26–49	27.4%	51.6%	18.9%	2.1%	0.0%	95
50–67	6.9%	45.1%	36.3%	10.8%	1.0%	102
68–89	7.5%	32.8%	34.3%	23.9%	1.5%	67
90–99	9.1%	18.2%	54.5%	9.1%	9.1%	22
Primary Officer Visible and/or Identifiable						
Visible and identifiable	51.2%	32.2%	11.8%	3.9%	0.9%	543
Not visible but identifiable	44.9%	40.9%	10.2%	3.7%	0.3%	323
Visible but not identifiable	18.5%	29.6%	48.1%	0	3.7%	27
Not visible and not identifiable	20.8%	41.7%	25.0%	12.5%	0	24
Primary Citizen Visible and/or Identifiable						
Visible and identifiable	55.5%	28.7%	11.8%	3.4%	0.6%	321
Not visible but identifiable	46.8%	39.8%	9.5%	3.7%	0.2%	432
Not visible/NA and not identifiable	32.3%	37.2%	22.6%	5.5%	2.4%	164

TABLE 13 Items Coded "Not Determinable"

Number of items	Total	Percentage of audio unintelligible					
		0–10	11–25	26–49	50–67	68–89	90–99
0	47.1%	45.3%	45.2%	37.2%	33.3%	40.7%	36.4%
1	18.4%	24.4%	17.5%	11.5%	17.1%	7.4%	6.1%
2	12.7%	15.7%	15.3%	21.2%	11.1%	3.7%	3.0%
3–5	11.9%	10.5%	14.7%	21.2%	20.5%	9.9%	3.0%
6–10	5.1%	3.1%	4.0%	8.0%	9.4%	9.8%	9.1%
11–20	2.9%	1.0%	2.3%	0.9%	6.0%	12.3%	18.2%
21–30	1.3%	0	0.6%	0	2.6%	4.9%	15.2%
>30	0.6%	0	0.6%	0	0	1.2%	9.1%
Total N	1,078	287	177	113	117	81	33

with 80 percent of the typical incident audible. There is no doubt that information about the interaction—about what citizens and officers said to one another—is lost as a result of observers' inability to hear portions of that interaction, and that appears to be more important than the visual information that is sacrificed by relying on in-car cameras. That loss of information can be expected to bias our measures of procedural justice downward, and to that degree, this truncated variation will attenuate our estimates of the strength of relationships at the margin.

Another perspective on the effectiveness with which observers could detect the features of police-citizen interaction is the number of items on the protocol that they deemed "not determinable," which was a listed option for most of the items. In nearly half of the incidents, none of the eighty-eight items concerning the interaction of the primary citizen with the primary officer was characterized as not determinable, and in more than three-quarters of the incidents, only two or fewer items were not determinable; see table 13. Observers' ability to make determinations turned to a large degree on the quality of the audio. As table 13 shows, the number of not-determinable items rises with the proportion of the audio that is unintelligible.[8]

Our analysis was confined to encounters in which both observers identified the primary citizen, and which were not discarded because our review showed that the respondent told us about an incident other than the sampled incident. The first of those two criteria excludes 122 encounters and the second excludes six. The 411 encounters that meet these criteria are the encounters in the validity and reliability of whose measures we can place the greatest confidence. Among these encounters (822 sets of codes), the observer was mostly or completely confident in the coding in nearly three-quarters, and in more than 85 percent they used a not determinable code fewer than four times.

NOTES

1 THE PROCEDURAL JUSTICE MODEL AS REFORM

1. State of Missouri v. Darren Wilson, Transcript of Grand Jury, 5: 197ff.

2. Ibid., 4: 17ff.

3. Four decades of research on the public's attitudes toward the police has yielded several consistent findings, though much remains a mystery. See, e.g., Brandl et al. 1994; Dean 1980; Dunham and Alpert 1988; Frank et al. 1996; Furstenberg and Wellford 1973; Jacob 1971; Miller et al. 2004; Parks 1984; Reisig and Parks 2000; Rosenbaum et al. 2005; Sampson and Bartusch 1998; Scaglion and Condon 1980; Skogan 2005; Smith and Hawkins 1973; Weitzer 1999, 2000a, 2000b; Weitzer and Tuch 1999, 2005.

4. See, e.g., Lind and Tyler 1988; Tyler 1987, 1988, 1990, 2005; Tyler and Folger 1980; Tyler and Huo 2002; Tyler et al. 1985.

2 POLICE DEPARTMENTS AS INSTITUTIONALIZED ORGANIZATIONS

1. See, in general, Meyer and Rowan 1977, Scott 2014. On police particularly, see Crank 1994, 2003, Crank and Langworthy 1992, Mastrofski and Uchida 1993.

2. Personnel levels are dynamic, of course, and by 2011, fiscal pressures had reduced staffing somewhat. We use the 2007 numbers because they allow us to place the study departments in the national context, using the LEMAS data.

3. Syracuse Citizen Review Board by-laws, p. 2; www.syrgov.net/uploadedFiles/City_Hall/CRB/CRB%20by-laws%202012.pdf, accessed November 14, 2016.

4. Compstat-like mechanisms have gone by different names in departments that have adopted them. With due respect for the Syracuse Police Department, we will use the more generic "Compstat" to refer to the management accountability structure in that department.

5. See, e.g., Jim Bueermann's comments on the procedures for traffic stops in Redlands in Tyler 2009.

3 POLICE LEGITIMACY

1. www.electionstudies.org/nesguide/toptable/tab5a_1.htm, accessed November 15, 2016.

2. www.electionstudies.org/nesguide/toptable/tab5a_5.htm, accessed November 15, 2016.

3. www.gallup.com/poll/163055/confidence-institutions-2013-pdf.aspx, accessed November 15, 2016.

4. One of us once heard a police chief remark on the likely effects on the attitudes of children when they see the police take their father away in handcuffs.

5. Some research suggests that parental influences on political attitudes may be partly genetic. See Alford et al. 2005; Hatemi et al. 2009; Smith et al. 2012.

6. We include here even respondents to the police services survey who did not have direct contact with officers—that is, whose calls for assistance were handled over the phone.

7. As Michael Lipsky (1980) points out, even calls for service are nonvoluntary in the sense that citizens do not have alternatives from which to choose: if they want police assistance, the agency that serves their jurisdiction is a monopoly provider.

8. Most (79 percent) of the respondents who were sampled from among arrests, and who were taken into custody, reported to interviewers that they had been arrested. But of those who were released in the field, on their own recognizance or with an appearance ticket, only 39 percent reported that they had been arrested; much of the disparity we would attribute to the respondents' misunderstanding.

9. Factor analyses of the key informant survey data also yield a trust factor comprised of the trust items and one identification item: I am proud of the work of the S__ police. The other identification items, however, formed a second factor. The public accountability items (listed in table 5) also loaded on the trust factor.

10. All four of the obligation items on the survey loaded on a single factor, but the inclusion of the fourth in a scale degraded the reliability of the scale. That fourth item was the statement "There are times when it is okay to ignore what the police tell you to do."

4 PROCEDURAL JUSTICE IN CITIZENS' SUBJECTIVE EXPERIENCES

1. Unless otherwise indicated, the denominators for percentages include "don't know" responses and refusals, which comprise the balance of the percentages not shown in the tables in this chapter. All of the results for procedural justice reported in this chapter exclude respondents whose requests for assistance were handled over the phone or who otherwise had no face-to-face contact with police.

2. Differences in the sampling strategies across these surveys make us very cautious in drawing comparisons, and they are offered only to place the Schenectady and Syracuse results in a broader context. Chicago residents were surveyed in 2003; those who reportedly had a contact with Chicago police in the preceding twelve months were asked a series of questions about that contact (see Skogan 2006). Residents of five New York City precincts

were surveyed in 2001–2; those who reportedly had a contact with NYPD were asked questions about that contact (see Miller et al. 2003). The National Police Research Platform conducted surveys of people who had one of three kinds of contacts with any of three agencies: the Oak Park (IL) police; the River Forest (IL) police; and the Boston police. The three kinds of contacts included reported crimes, reported traffic accidents, and traffic stops. See Rosenbaum et al. 2011.

3. We exclude from this analysis respondents who reportedly did not interact directly with officers.

4. A factor analysis of these nine items yields a single factor with an eigenvalue (6.00) greater than 1. With one exception (explained actions), the factor coefficients are all above 0.80.

5. 2 = very favorable; 1 = somewhat favorable; -1 = somewhat unfavorable; and -2 = very unfavorable. Don't know and not applicable responses were coded 0. This simple, additive index correlates at 0.99 with the scale formed by weighting the items in proportion with their factor coefficients, and so we use the more readily interpreted additive scale. The scale has a high level of reliability, with an alpha of 0.93.

6. See Whitaker 1982.

7. This difference does not hold when the analysis focuses on only those who were arrested. That it does not could be an artifact of the survey design, which posed questions about searches only of respondents who were reportedly stopped by the police. But in 40 percent of the arrest cases, the respondent indicated neither that police stopped him/her nor that s/he contacted police, but rather that police contacted him/her for some reason (mainly when a third party called police). For these latter cases we lack survey data on searches, and so the survey data understate the prevalence of searches among all police-citizen contacts.

6 PROCEDURAL JUSTICE IN POLICE ACTION

1. The same challenges arise even when only two rather than four elements of procedural justice—quality of decision-making and quality of treatment—are differentiated.

2. For further discussion of the technique of systematic social observation, see Mastrofski et al. 1998; Mastrofski, Parks, and McCluskey 2010; Worden and McLean 2014a; Worden, McLean, and Bonner 2015.

3. Previous instruments provided for measures of police "manner," but to our knowledge no one has analyzed this construct.

4. Nearly 90 percent of the police disrespect "involved at least one act of commission (a statement or gesture) as opposed to one of omission (ignoring a query)." Other factors that affected police disrespect included: the citizen's lack of self-control (in the form of intoxication, emotional distress, or mental disorder), and the citizen's social status (sex, age, class).

5. Unfortunately for us, their study was published after our observation instruments had been finalized and observations were more than half-completed.

6. They subsequently conducted similar observations in a second research site; see Mastrofski et al. 2016.

7. Six observers performed this work. We began with four, two of whom were undergraduate students, one white male and one white female, both of them majoring in psychology. The other two of the original four observers were graduate students, one (a Hispanic

female) at the dissertation stage of a Ph.D. in criminal justice, and one (a white female) at the dissertation stage of a Ph.D. in sociology. When they returned to school at the end of the summer, the two undergraduates were replaced by a graduate student (a white female) who was finishing a master's degree in criminal justice, and an undergraduate (a white male) majoring in criminal justice. Incidents were assigned randomly to observers such that each observer was paired with others across his/her caseload. Ultimately, the individual observers each coded 123 to 243 encounters.

8. We adapted existing CATI software, originally developed under BJS auspices, to this data-entry application.

9. Four of the 1,800 incidents were inadvertently omitted from the sampling frame for drawing the observation sample.

10. Five of these were the original arrests in the field that eventuated, following the issuance of a bench warrant, in the citizen later turning himself in at the desk; both events are assigned the same incident number in the record management system, but it was the latter included in our sample.

11. The only study of which we are aware that has compared observational data to another type of data on the same incidents is Parks 1984, which analyzed the degree to which observers and citizens agreed about the actions of the police.

12. One recent study, in Rialto, CA, found that when officers were randomly assigned to wear body cameras, they were less likely to use force, which was interpreted as a social desirability effect of the video surveillance; see Farrar 2014 and Ariel et al. 2014. In Schenectady, however, officers are as a daily matter of course recorded.

13. The department's general order concerning the in-car video system provides that "platoon commanders *may* request to review a recording" (emphasis added); it also provides that the supervisor of the Office of Professional Standards "shall" periodically review recordings. One rough gauge of the extent to which cameras have altered officers' behavior is the incidence of secondary arrests, i.e., arrests that include charges for resisting arrest, assault on a police officer, or obstructing governmental administration. These are the kinds of charges that are associated with the (proper or improper) use of force by police. In calendar year 2002, 147 arrests involved one or more such charges. In 2004, the year after cameras were installed, 183 arrests involved one or more such charges, and the corresponding counts for 2005 and 2006 are 218 and 196, respectively—more, not fewer, than the year preceding cameras. During the eighteen months of the police services survey, there were 381 arrests with one or more such charges, a rate of 254 annually. Another rough gauge of changes in officer behavior is the frequency with which arrest reports indicate that the arrestee was injured. In 2002, 23 arrestees were injured at the time of arrest; in 2003, 56 were injured, and in 2004 and 2005, 66 and 59 were injured, respectively.

14. This interpretation of officers' use of police authority differs from some. For example, Paternoster et al. 1997 treated both handcuffing and other uses of physical force as reverse indicators of procedural justice, on the assumption that they amount to information about the status of the citizen against whom these actions were taken. Yet the same logic was not extended to the act of taking a citizen into custody—arrest. By treating the use of police authority, in its various forms, as distinct variables rather than incorporating them into the measure of procedural justice (or injustice), we can isolate the factors about which there is theoretical ambiguity.

15. We also exclude six cases in which both observers identified the primary citizen, but our review of the details of these cases showed that the citizen referenced a different incident in responding to the survey. We considered including in the analysis the cases in which only one observer identified the primary citizen, but insofar as the behavioral scales are less reliable for these cases, their inclusion would tend to deflate the estimated empirical relationships; the scale scores in these cases were systematically lower than those of cases in which both observers identified the primary citizen.

16. The intra-class correlation (ICC) is commonly used as a measure of inter-rater reliability; see Hallgren 2012. We estimated ICCs for scale scores averaged across the two observers.

17. Most of the procedural justice that we detected on this dimension was in officers asking what happened, listening, and paying attention, and seldom in requesting/suggesting/persuading the citizen to do anything other than provide information.

18. We resolved the ambiguity of explanation as a component of procedural justice—it could be treated as a manifestation of neutrality or trustworthy motives—somewhat arbitrarily. The measure of neutrality is comprised only of explanation, so on that subscale explanation cannot be confused with other actions.

19. Sometimes no explanation is necessary. When no explanation was offered, whether or not anything called for explanation, no addition to the scales is made. Instead we account for the inapplicability of explanation, from the citizen's perspective, in an analysis of subjective experience (see chapter 7).

20. Derogatory comments were defined in the coding instructions as "words, expressions or gestures that are socially interpreted as insulting, rude, vulgar, obscene, disparaging or belittling." Disrespect " . . . can include a variety of verbal statements: calling the officer names, making derogatory statements about the officer or his family, making disparaging or belittling remarks, slurs (racial, sexual, lifestyle). Ignoring the officer's commands or questions also constitutes disrespect. If the citizen is argumentative, the citizen may or may not be disrespectful, depending on how it was done. If the citizen disagrees with the officer or questions/objects to his actions but does so in a polite tone-then do NOT code this citizen as disrespectful. However, if the citizen speaks loudly or interrupts the officer, then code this as disrespectful. Certain gestures and actions are to be coded as disrespectful. 'Flipping the bird' (displaying the 2nd finger in the direction of the police), obscene gestures, spitting in the presence of an officer (even if not in the direction of the officer)."

21. The inclusion of a control for incidents in which no explanation was necessary had no bearing on the results, and the coefficient was substantively and statistically insignificant. It is not shown in the tabular results.

7 CITIZENS' SUBJECTIVE EXPERIENCE AND POLICE ACTION

1. Among the observed arrests, we have too few felonies, violations, and appearance tickets to estimate separate effects for each, so felonies and misdemeanors were combined in a single dummy variable, appearance tickets and releases were combined in a single variable, and violations together with infractions form the reference category for charge seriousness. In addition, a small handful of calls classified as other or unknown were included with the much more numerous nuisance calls to form the reference category.

2. We operationalized searches in terms of observational and survey data; if either source indicated that a search was conducted, we treated it as a search.

3. We reestimated the parameters of these models after excluding any case in which (a) both coders were either "not at all confident" in their coding or only "a little confident," or (b) one coder was "fairly confident" and the other coder was "a little confident" or less confident. We thus excluded just six cases. All of the results were similar to those reported in the table. We also added a control for instances in which no explanation for the officers' actions was considered necessary, which had no substantively or statistically significant effect and whose inclusion did not alter the estimated effects of other variables.

4. Additional analysis that distinguishes among forms of resistance suggests that it is passive resistance that accounts for most of this relationship.

5. Call for service codes, based on the information that call-takers elicit from callers, often differ from classifications of incidents based on more complete information. See Klinger and Bridges 1997.

8 PROCEDURAL JUSTICE AND MANAGEMENT ACCOUNTABILITY

1. Some officers, we discovered, are vaguely aware of research that reported (or is widely thought to have found) that a "friendly" demeanor puts officers at risk of getting killed (U.S. Federal Bureau of Investigation 1992), which was widely disseminated through training/workshops across the United States.

9 PROCEDURAL JUSTICE AND STREET-LEVEL SENSEMAKING

1. Maguire and Katz (2002) applied this same approach to the community policing movement in the United States.

10 REFLECTIONS ON POLICE REFORM

1. The effects of prior attitudes do not appear to be mediated very much by forms of citizen behavior—i.e., resistance or disrespect—that elicit behavior by police that citizens experience as procedurally unjust.

2. These approaches are described in National Research Council 2004, chapter 8.

3. That is, these officers emphasize law enforcement as their occupational role and espouse an aggressive approach that also allows for occasional violations of civil liberties; they also hold negative attitudes toward both the citizenry and police supervisors.

METHODOLOGICAL APPENDIX

1. For some of those whom interviewers were unable to contact, we had what proved to be a number that was not in service. But for most (82 percent), interviewers' inability to make contact was a result of unanswered calls.

2. We caution readers against comparing the departments with one another, since the call type codes and communications practices differ across the departments.

3. The main indications that we may have a mismatched event stem from a comparison of the respondent's description of how the contact began against the contact subpopulation from which the incident was sampled (calls for service, arrests, stops/field interviews). We identified three types of potential errors: (1) incidents that were sampled from (presumptive) stops, but the respondent said that the contact began when s/he contacted the police; (2) incidents sampled from arrest records, but the respondent said that the contact began when s/he contacted the police; (3) incidents sampled from CAD records, but the respondent said that the contact began because the respondent was stopped—while in a car or on foot—by the police.

4. Respondents fell out between waves 1 and 2 when one nonrespondent contacted in wave 1 asked to be removed from the mailing, and one additional prospective respondent fell out between waves 2 and 3 when an e-mail bounced back.

5. One key informant whom we contacted in wave 1 asked to be removed from the e-mail distribution list, and the remainder fell out due to bad e-mail addresses.

6. This item was added to the coding protocol after coding got under way and so it is missing for 161 of the 1,078 cases.

7. Needless to say, both video and audio would be preferred to one or the other. But these results suggest that the lack of video in some cases is not a crucial factor.

8. The item about unintelligible audio was added to the coding protocol partway into the coding, and so it is missing for 270 of the 1,078 coded incidents.

REFERENCES

Alford, John R., Carolyn L. Funk, and John R. Hibbing. "Are Political Orientations Genetically Transmitted?" *American Political Science Review* 99 (2005): 153–68.

Alpert, Geoffrey. 2015. Personal correspondence with Robert E. Worden, May 31.

Amburgey, Terry L., Dawn Kelly, and William P. Barnett. 1993. "Resetting the Clock: The Dynamics of Organizational Change and Failure." *Administrative Science Quarterly* 38 (1): 51–73.

Anderson, Eugene W., and Claes Fornell. 2000. "Foundations of the American Customer Satisfaction Index." *Total Quality Management* 11: S869–S882.

Anderson, Eugene W., Claes Fornell, and Roland T. Rust. 1997. "Customer Satisfaction, Productivity, and Profitability: Differences between Goods and Services." *Marketing Science* 16: 129–45.

Ariel, Barak, William A. Farrar, and Alex Sutherland. 2014. "The Effect of Police Body-Worn Cameras on Use of Force and Citizens' Complaints Against the Police: A Randomized Controlled Trial." *Journal of Quantitative Criminology.* Advance on-line publication.

Augustyn, Megan Bears. 2015. "Updating Perceptions of (In)Justice." *Journal of Research in Crime and Delinquency* 53: 255–86.

Barry, Dan. 2001. "The Electric City Sees Its Police in a Harsh Light; Officers' Pranks and Crimes Hit Home in Schenectady." *New York Times,* August 17. www.nytimes.com/2001/08/17/nyregion/electric-city-sees-its-police-harsh-light-officers-pranks-crimes-hit-home.html?module = Search&mabReward = relbias%3Ar%2C{%221%22%3A%22RI%3A7%22}.

Bartunek, Jean M., and Michael K. Moch. 1987. "First-Order, Second-Order, and Third-Order Change and Organization Development Interventions: A Cognitive Approach." *Journal of Applied Behavioral Science* 23 (4): 483–500.

Bartunek, Jean M., Denise M. Rosseau, Jenny W. Rudolph, and Judith A. DePalma. 2006. "On the Receiving End: Sensemaking, Emotion, and Assessments of an Organizational Change Initiated by Others." *Journal of Applied Behavioral Science* 42 (2): 182–206.

Bayley, David H., and James Garofalo. 1987. *Patrol Officer Effectiveness in Managing Conflict during Police-Citizen Encounters.* Albany, NY: Hindelang Criminal Justice Research Center.

———. 1989. "The Management of Violence by Police Patrol Officers." *Criminology* 27: 1–25.

Behn, Robert D. 2008. "The Seven Big Errors of PerformanceStat." Rappaport Institute/Taubman Center Policy Brief. Cambridge, MA: Kennedy School of Government.

Bechky, Beth A. 2011. "Making Organizational Theory Work: Institutions, Occupations, and Negotiated Orders." *Organization Science* 22: 1157–67.

Bittner, Egon. 1974. "Florence Nightingale in Pursuit of Willie Sutton: A Theory of the Police." In *The Potential for Reform of Criminal Justice,* ed. Herbert Jacob. Beverly Hills, CA: Sage.

———. 1983. "Legality and Workmanship: Introduction to Control in the Police Organization." In *Control in the Police Organization,* ed. Maurice Punch. Cambridge, MA: MIT Press.

Blumer, Herbert. 1969. *Symbolic Interactionism: Perspectives and Methods.* Englewood Cliffs, NJ: Prentice Hall.

Bobb, Merrick J., and staff. 2009. *Los Angeles County Sheriff's Department: 27th Semiannual Report.* Los Angeles: Police Assessment Resource Center.

Boydstun, John E. 1975. *San Diego Field Interrogation: Final Report.* Washington, DC: Police Foundation.

Bradford, Ben, and Jonathan Jackson. 2009. "Public Trust in Criminal Justice: A Review of the Research Literature in the United States." MS. http://ssrn.com/abstract = 1369704.

Bradford, Ben, and Paul Quinton. 2014. "Self-Legitimacy, Police Culture and Support for Democratic Policing in and English Constabulary." *British Journal of Criminology* 54: 2013–46.

Braga, Anthony A., Christopher Winship, Tom R. Tyler, Jeffrey Fagan, and Tracey L. Meares. 2014. "The Salience of Social Contextual Factors in Appraisals of Police Interactions with Citizens: A Randomized Factorial Experiment." *Journal of Quantitative Criminology* 30 (4): 599–627.

Brandl, Steven G., James Frank, Robert E. Worden, and Timothy S. Bynum. 1994. "Global and Specific Attitudes toward the Police: Disentangling the Relationship." *Justice Quarterly* 11 (1): 119–34.

Brandl, Steven G., Meghan S. Stroshine, and James Frank. 2001. "Who Are the Complaint-Prone Officers? An Examination of the Relationship between Police Officers' Attributes, Arrest Activity, Assignment, and Citizens' Complaints about Excessive Force." *Journal of Criminal Justice* 29: 521–29.

Bratton, William. 1998. *Turnaround: How America's Top Cop Reversed the Crime Epidemic.* New York: Random House.

Brick, Bradley T., Terrance J. Taylor, and Finn-Aage Esbenson. 2009. "Juvenile Attitudes towards the Police: The Importance of Subcultural Involvement and Community Ties." *Journal of Criminal Justice* 37: 488–95.

Brown, Michael K. 1981. *Working the Street: Police Discretion and the Dilemmas of Reform.* New York: Russell Sage.

Capowich, George E., Janice A. Roehl, and C. Andrews. 1994. *Evaluating Problem-Oriented Policing: Assessing Process and Outcomes in Tulsa and San Diego.* Report to NIJ. Washington, DC: Institute for Social Analysis.

Cavanagh, Caitlin, and Elizabeth Cauffman, "Viewing Law and Order: Mothers' and Sons' Justice System Legitimacy Attitudes and Juvenile Recidivism." *Psychology, Public Policy, and Law* 21 (2015): 432–41.

Chanin, Joshua M. 2015. "Examining the Sustainability of Pattern or Practice Police Misconduct Reform," *Police Quarterly* 18: 163–92.

Christopher Commission. 1991. Report of the Independent Commission on the Los Angeles Police Department. Los Angeles: The Commission.

Cintron, Justina R. 2003. "The New York Experience: Existing Models of Citizen Oversight." *Government, Law and Policy Journal* 5: 11–26.

Clarke, Ronald V. 1998. "Defining Police Strategies: Problem Solving, Problem-Oriented Policing and Community-Oriented Policing." In *Problem-Oriented Policing: Crime-Specific Problems, Critical Issues and Making POP Work,* ed. Tara O'Connor Shelley and Anne C. Grant. Washington, DC: Police Executive Research Forum.

Cohen, Jacqueline, and Jens Ludwig. 2003. "Policing Crime Guns." In *Evaluating Gun Policy,* ed. Jens Ludwig and Phillip J. Cook. Washington, DC: Brookings Institution.

Connors, Roger, Tom Smith, and Craig Hickman. 2004. *The Oz Principle: Getting Results through Individual and Organizational Accountability.* Portfolio.

Cordner, Gary, and Elizabeth Perkins Biebel. 2005. "Problem-Oriented Policing in Practice." *Criminology & Public Policy* 4 (2): 155–80.

Crank, John P. 1994. "Watchman and Community: Myth and Institutionalization in Policing." *Law & Society Review* 28 (2): 325–51.

———. 2003. "Institutional Theory of Police: A Review of the State of the Art." *Policing: An International Journal of Police Strategies & Management* 26: 186–207.

Crank, John P., and Robert Langworthy. 1992. "An Institutional Perspective of Policing." *Journal of Criminal Law and Criminology* 83 (2): 338–63.

Cross, Jenny, and Greg Newbold. 2010. "Presumptive Arrest in Partner Assault: Use of Discretion and Problems of Compliance in the New Zealand Police." *Australian & New Zealand Journal of Criminology* 43: 51–75.

Cutlar, Shanetta Y. Brown. 2003. Correspondence with Michael T. Brockbank re: Investigation of the Schenectady Police Department. U.S. Department of Justice, Civil Rights Division, March 19. www.justice.gov/crt/about/spl/documents/schenectady_ta.pdf.

Cuttler, Michael J., and Paul M. Muchinsky. 2006. "Prediction of Law Enforcement Training Performance and Dysfunctional Job Performance with General Mental Ability, Personality, and Life History Variables." *Criminal Justice and Behavior* 33: 3–25.

Dai, Mengyan, James Frank, and Ivan Sun. 2011. "Procedural Justice during Police-Citizen Encounters: The Effects of Process-Based Policing on Citizen Compliance and Demeanor." *Journal of Criminal Justice* 39 (2): 159–68.

Davis, Robert C., Nicole J. Henderson, Janet Mandelstam, Christopher W. Ortiz, and Joel Miller. 2005. *Federal Intervention in Local Policing: Pittsburgh's Experience with a Consent Decree.* Washington, DC: Office of Community Oriented Policing Services.

Day, Elizabeth, 2015. "#BlackLivesMatter: The Birth of a New Civil Rights Movement." *Guardian,* July 19. www.theguardian.com/world/2015/jul/19/blacklivesmatter-birth-civil-rights-movement.

Dean, Deby. 1980. "Citizen Ratings of the Police: The Difference Contact Makes." *Law & Policy Quarterly* 2 (4): 445–71.

DeAngelis, Joseph. 2009. "Assessing the Impact of Oversight and Procedural Justice on the Attitudes of Individuals Who File Police Complaints." *Police Quarterly* 12 (2): 214–36.

DiMaggio, Paul J., and Walter W. Powell. 1983. "The Iron Cage Revisited: Institutional Isomorphism and Collective Rationality in Organizational Fields." *American Sociological Review* 48: 147–60.

Dixon, Travis L., Terry L. Schell, Howard Giles, and Kristin L. Drogos. 2008. "The Influence of Race in Police-Civilian Interactions: A Content Analysis of Videotaped Interactions Taken During Cincinnati Police Traffic Stops." *Journal of Communication* 58 (3): 530–49.

Dunham, Roger G., and Geoffrey P. Alpert. 1988. "Neighborhood Differences in Attitudes toward Policing: Evidence for a Mixed-Strategy Model of Policing in a Multi-Ethnic Setting." *Journal of Criminal Law & Criminology* 79 (2): 504–23.

Eck, John, and William Spelman. 1987. *Problem Solving: Problem-Oriented Policing in Newport News.* Washington, DC: Police Executive Research Forum.

Eckholm, Erik, 2014. "Witnesses Told Grand Jury That Michael Brown Charged at Darren Wilson, Prosecutor Says." *New York Times,* November 24.

Eden, Devorah. 2001. "Who Controls the Teachers? Overt and Covert Control in Schools." *Educational Management Administration & Leadership* 29: 97–111.

Edvardsson, Bo, Michael D. Johnson, Anders Gustafsson, and Tore Strandvik, 2000. "The Effects of Satisfaction and Loyalty on Profits and Growth: Products versus Services." *Total Quality Management* 11: S917–S927.

Eisenstadt, Marnie. 2012. "Black Police Officers Sue Syracuse, Claiming Race Discrimination in Hiring and Promotion." *Post-Standard* (Syracuse, NY), March 28.

Eith, Christine A., and Matthew R. Durose. 2011. *Contacts between Police and the Public, 2008.* Special Report. Washington, DC: U.S. Dept. of Justice, Office of Justice Programs, Bureau of Justice Statistics.

Eitle, David. 2005. "The Influence of Mandatory Arrest Policies, Police Organizational Characteristics, and Situational Variables on the Probability of Arrest in Domestic Violence Cases." *Crime & Delinquency* 51 (3): 573–597.

Elmore, Richard F. 1999. "Building a New Structure for School Leadership." *American Educator* 21: 6–13.

Engel, Robin S. 2002. "Patrol Officer Supervision in the Community Policing Era." *Journal of Criminal Justice* 30: 51–64.

———. 2001. "Supervisory Styles of Patrol Sergeants and Lieutenants." *Journal of Criminal Justice* 29: 341–55.

Engel, Robin Shepard, and Robert E. Worden. 2003. "Police Officers' Attitudes, Behavior, and Supervisory Influences: An Analysis of Problem-Solving." *Criminology* 41: 131–66.

Fagan, Jeffrey, and Tom R. Tyler. 2005. "Legal Socialization of Children and Adolescents." *Social Justice Research* 18 (3): 217–41.

Farrar, William. 2014. "Operation Candid Camera: Rialto Police Department's Body-Worn Camera Experiment." *Police Chief,* January.

Ferraro, Kathleen J. 1989. "Policing Woman Battering." *Social Problems* 36: 61–74.

Fischer, Craig, ed. 2014a. *Legitimacy and Procedural Justice: A New Element of Police Leadership*. Washington, DC: Police Executive Research Forum.

———, ed. 2014b. *Legitimacy and Procedural Justice: The New Orleans Case Study*. Washington, DC: Police Executive Research Forum.

Fisher, Marc. 2014. "Cincinnati Still Healing from Its Riots, and Has Lessons to Share with Ferguson," *Washington Post,* September 5. https://www.washingtonpost.com/politics/cincinnati-still-healing-from-its-riots-and-has-lessons-to-share-with-ferguson/2014/09/05/2ff8b944-34a1-11e4-9e92-0899b306bbea_story.html.

Fornell, Claes, Michael D. Johnson, Eugene W. Anderson, Jaesung Cha, and Barbara Everitt Bryant. 1996. "The American Customer Satisfaction Index: Nature, Purpose, and Findings." *Journal of Marketing* 60: 7–18.

Frank, James, Steven G. Brandl, Francis T. Cullen, and Amy Stichman. 1996. "Reassessing the Impact of Race on Citizens' Attitudes toward the Police: A Research Note." *Justice Quarterly* 13 (2): 321–34.

Frank, James, Brad W. Smith, and Kenneth J. Novak. 2005. "Exploring the Basis of Citizens' Attitudes toward the Police." *Police Quarterly* 8 (2): 206–28.

Furstenberg, Frank F., and Charles F. Wellford. 1973. "Calling the Police: The Evaluation of Police Service." *Law and Society Review* 7 (3): 393–406.

Fyfe, James J. 1979. "Administrative Interventions on Police Shooting Discretion." *Journal of Criminal Justice* 7 (4): 309–23.

———. 1988. "Police Use of Deadly Force: Research and Reform." *Justice Quarterly* 5: 165–205.

Gau, Jacinta M. 2011. "The Convergent and Discriminant Validity of Procedural Justice and Police Legitimacy: An Empirical Test of Core Theoretical Propositions." *Journal of Criminal Justice* 39 (6): 489–98.

———. 2014. "Organizational Change and Police Legitimacy." In *Encyclopedia of Criminology and Criminal Justice,* ed. Gerben Bruinsma and David Weisburd. New York: Springer.

George, Jennifer M. and Gareth R. Jones. 2001. "Towards a Process Model of Individual Change in Organizations." *Human Relations* 54 (4): 419–44.

Gerstenson, Joseph, and Dennis L. Plane. 2007. "Trust in Government: 2006 American National Election Studies Pilot Report." MS. www.electionstudies.org/resources/papers/Pilot2006/nes011890.pdf

Gioia, Dennis A., and Kumar Chittipeddi. 1991. "Sensemaking and Sensegiving in Strategic Change Initiation." *Strategic Management Journal* 12: 433–48.

Goldstein, Joseph. 1960. "Police Discretion Not to Invoke the Criminal Process: Low-Visibility Decisions in the Administration of Justice." *Yale Law Journal* 69: 542–94.

Gould, Jon B., and Stephen D. Mastrofski. 2004. "Suspect Searches: Assessing Police Behavior under the U.S. Constitution." *Criminology & Public Policy* 3: 315–61.

Guyot, Dorothy. 1991. *Policing as though People Matter.* Philadelphia: Temple University Press.

Haarr, Robin N. 2001. "The Making of a Community Policing Officer: The Impact of Basic Training and Occupational Socialization on Police Recruits." *Police Quarterly* 4 (4): 402–33.

Hallet, Tim. 2010. "The Myth Incarnate: Recoupling Processes, Turmoil, and Inhabited Institutions in an Urban Elementary School." *American Sociological Review* 75: 52–74.

Hallet, Tim, and Marc J. Ventresca. 2006. "Inhabited Institutions: Social Interactions and Organizational Forms in Gouldner's *Patterns of Industrial Bureaucracy*." *Theory and Society* 35: 213–36.

Hallgren, Kevin A. 2012. "Computing Inter-Rater Reliability for Observational Data: An Overview and Tutorial." *Tutorials in Quantitative Methods in Psychology* 8 (1): 23–34.

Harmon, Rachel. 2009. "Promoting Civil Rights through Proactive Policing Reform." *Stanford Law Review* 62:1–68.

Harris, Christopher J. 2010. *Pathways of Police Misconduct: Problem Behavior Patterns and Trajectories from Two Cohorts*. Durham, NC: Carolina Academic Press.

Hart, Timothy C., and Callie Rennison. 2003. *Reporting Crime to the Police, 1992–2000*. NCJ Publication No. 195710. Washington, DC: U.S. Department of Justice, Bureau of Justice Statistics.

Hatemi, Peter, Carolyn Funk, Hermine Maes, Judy Silberg, Sarah Medland, Nicholas Martin, and Lindon Eaves. "Genetic Influences on Political Attitudes over the Life Course." *Journal of Politics* 71 (2009): 1141–58.

Hawdon, James. 2008. "Legitimacy, Trust, Social Capital, and Policing Styles: A Theoretical Statement." *Police Quarterly* 11 (2): 182–201.

Hay, Carter, "Parenting, Self-Control, and Delinquency: A Test of Self-Control Theory." *Criminology* 39 (2001): 707–36.

Herbert, Steve. 1998. "Police Subculture Reconsidered." *Criminology* 36 (2): 343–69.

———. 2009. *Citizens, Cops, and Power: Recognizing the Limits of Community*. Chicago: University of Chicago Press.

Hickman, Matthew. 2008. "On the Context of Police Cynicism and Problem Behavior." *Applied Psychology in Criminal Justice* 4: 1–44.

Hirschel, David, Eve Buzawa, April Pattavina, and Don Faggiani. 2007. "Domestic Violence and Mandatory Arrest Laws: To What Extent Do They Influence Police Arrest Decisions?" *Journal of Criminal Law and Criminology* 98 (1): 255–98.

Hurwitz, Jon, and Mark Peffley. 2005. "Explaining the Great Racial Divide: Perceptions of Fairness in the U.S. Criminal Justice System." *Journal of Politics* 67 (3): 762–83.

In re Cincinnati Policing. 2003. United States District Court, S.D. Ohio, Western Division. Case No. C-1-99-3170. https://casetext.com/case/in-re-cincinnati-policing.

Jacob, Herbert. 1971. "Black and White Perceptions of Justice in the City." *Law and Society Review* 6 (1): 69–90.

Jennings, M. Kent, and Richard Niemi, "The Transmission of Political Values from Parent to Child." *American Political Science Review* 62 (1968): 169–83.

Jennings, M. Kent, and Richard Niemi. "Continuity and Change in Political Orientations: A Longitudinal Study of Two Generations." *American Political Science Review* 69 (1975): 1316–35.

Jennings, M. Kent, Laura Stoker, and Jake Bowers. "Politics across Generations: Family Transmission Reexamined." *Journal of Politics* 71 (2009): 782–99.

Johnson, Michael D., and Claes Fornell, 1991. "A Framework for Comparing Customer Satisfaction across Individuals and Product Categories." *Journal of Economic Psychology* 12: 267–86.

Jonathan-Zamir, Tal, Stephen D. Mastrofski, and Shomron Moyal. 2015. "Measuring Procedural Justice in Police-Citizen Encounters." *Justice Quarterly* 32 (2015): 845–71.

Jones, Dana A., and Joanne Belknap. 1999. "Police Responses to Battering in a Progressive Pro-Arrest Jurisdiction." *Justice Quarterly* 16: 249–73.

Jones, Jeffrey M. 2015. "In U.S., Confidence in Police Lowest in 22 Years." www.gallup.com/poll/183704/confidence-police-lowest-years.aspx, June 19.

Kappeler, Victor, Richard Sluder and Geoffrey Alpert. 1998. *Forces of Deviance: Understanding the Dark Side of Policing.* 2nd ed. Prospect Heights, IL.: Waveland Press.

Katz, Charles M. 2001. "The Establishment of a Police Gang Unit: An Examination of Organizational and Environmental Factors." *Criminology* 39 (1): 37–75.

Kelly, Kimbriell. 2016. "Can Big Data Stop Bad Cops?" *Washington Post,* August 21.

Kerstetter, Wayne A., and Kenneth A. Rasinski. 1994. "Opening a Window into Police Internal Affairs: Impact of Procedural Justice Reform on Third-Party Attitudes." *Social Justice Research* 7 (2): 107–27.

Klinger, David A., 1994. "Demeanor or Crime? Why 'Hostile' Citizens Are More Likely to Be Arrested." *Criminology* 32: 475–93.

———. 1995. "The Micro-Structure of Nonlethal Force: Baseline Data from an Observational Study." *Criminal Justice Review* 20: 169–86.

———. 1996. "More on Demeanor and Arrest in Dade County." *Criminology* 34: 61–82.

———. 1997. "Negotiating Order in Patrol Work: An Ecological Theory of Police Response to Deviance." *Criminology* 35: 277–306.

Klinger, David A., and George S. Bridges, 1997. "Measurement Error in Calls-for-Service as an Indicator of Crime." *Criminology* 35: 705–26.

Knauss, Tim. 2012. "Syracuse Has a New Citizen Review Board Administrator." *Post-Standard* (Syracuse, NY), April 10.

Leiber, Michael J., Mahesh K. Nalla, and Margaret Farnworth. 1998. "Explaining Juveniles' Attitudes toward the Police." *Justice Quarterly* 15: 151–74.

Lersch, Kim Michelle, Tom Bazley, and Tom Mieczkowski. 2006. "Early Intervention Programs: An Effective Police Accountability Tool, or Punishment of the Productive?" *Policing* 29 (1): 58–76.

Lieske, Joel A. 1978. "The Conditions of Racial Violence in American Cities: A Developmental Synthesis." *American Political Science Review* 72: 1324–40.

Lind, E. Allan, and Tom R. Tyler. 1988. *The Social Psychology of Procedural Justice.* New York: Plenum Press.

Lindblom, Charles E., and David K. Cohen. 1979. *Usable Knowledge: Social Science and Social Problem Solving.* New Haven, CT: Yale University Press.

Lipsky, Michael. 1980. *Street-Level Bureaucracy: Dilemmas of the Individual in Public Services.* New York: Russell Sage Foundation.

Livingston, Debra. 2004. "The Unfulfilled Promise of Citizen Review." *Ohio State Journal of Criminal Law* 1:653–69.

Luibrand, Shannon, 2015. "How a Death in Ferguson Sparked a Movement in America," CBS News, August 7. www.cbsnews.com/news/how-the-black-lives-matter-movement-changed-america-one-year-later.

Lundman, Richard J. 1994. "Demeanor or Crime? The Midwest City Police-Citizen Encounters Study," *Criminology* 32: 631–56.

Lundman, Richard J. 1996. "Demeanor and Arrest: Additional Evidence from Unpublished Data," *Journal of Research in Crime and Delinquency* 33: 306–23.

Lurigio, Arthur J., and Wesley G. Skogan. 1994. "Winning the Hearts and Minds of Police Officers: An Assessment of Staff Perceptions of Community Policing in Chicago." *Crime and Delinquency* 40 (3): 315–30.

MacQueen, Sarah, and Ben Bradford. 2015. "Enhancing Public Trust and Police Legitimacy during Road Traffic Encounters: Results from a Randomised Controlled Trial in Scotland." *Journal of Experimental Criminology* 11: 419–43.

Maguire, Edward R., and Charles M. Katz. 2002. "Community Policing, Loose Coupling, and Sensemaking in American Police Agencies." *Justice Quarterly* 19 (3): 501–34.

Manning, Peter K. 1977. *Police Work: The Social Organization of Policing.* Cambridge, MA: MIT Press.

———. 1989. "Occupational Culture." In *Encyclopedia of Police Science,* ed. William Bailey. New York: Garland.

Mastrofski, Stephen D., Tal Jonathan-Zamir, Shomron Moyal, and James J. Willis. 2016. "Predicting Procedural Justice in Police-Citizen Encounters," *Criminal Justice and Behavior* 43: 119–39.

Mastrofski, Stephen D., Roger B. Parks, and John D. McCluskey. 2010. "Systematic Social Observation in Criminology." In *Handbook of Quantitative Criminology,* ed. Alex R. Piquero and David Weisburd. New York: Springer.

Mastrofski, Stephen D., Roger B. Parks, Albert J. Reiss Jr., Robert E. Worden, Christina De-Jong, Jeffrey B. Snipes, and William Terrill. 1998. *Systematic Observation of Public Police: Applying Field Research Methods to Policy Issues.* National Institute of Justice Research Report No. 172859. Washington, DC: National Institute of Justice.

Mastrofski, Stephen D., Michael D. Reisig, and John D. McCluskey. 2002. "Police Disrespect toward the Public: An Encounter-Based Analysis." *Criminology* 40 (3): 519–51.

Mastrofski, Stephen D., and R. Richard Ritti. 1996. "Police Training and the Effects of Organization on Drunk Driving Enforcement." *Justice Quarterly* 13 (2): 291–20.

Mastrofski, Stephen D., R. Richard Ritti, and Debra Hoffmaster. 1987. "Organizational Determinants of Police Discretion: The Case of Drinking-Driving." *Journal of Criminal Justice* 15 (5): 387–402.

Mastrofski, Stephen D., Jeffrey B. Snipes, and Anne E. Supina. 1996. "Compliance on Demand: The Public's Response to Specific Police Requests." *Journal of Research in Crime & Delinquency* 33 (3): 269–305.

Mastrofski, Stephen D. and Craig D. Uchida. 1993. "Transforming the Police." *Journal of Research in Crime & Delinquency* 30 (3): 330–58.

Mastrofski, Stephen D. and James J. Willis. 2010. "Police Organization Continuity and Change: Into the Twenty-first Century." *Crime and Justice* 39 (1): 55–144.

Mastrofski, Stephen D., Robert E. Worden, and Jeffrey B. Snipes. 1995. "Law Enforcement in a Time of Community Policing." *Criminology* 33 (4): 539–63.

Mazerolle, Lorraine, Emma Antrobus, Sarah Bennett, and Tom R. Tyler. 2013. "Shaping Citizen Perceptions of Police Legitimacy: A Randomized Field Trial of Procedural Justice." *Criminology* 51 (1): 33–63.

McCluskey, John D. 2003. *Police Requests for Compliance: Coercive and Procedurally Just Tactics.* New York: LFB Scholarly Publishing LLC.

McCluskey, John D., Stephen D. Mastrofski, and Roger B. Parks. 1999. "To Acquiesce or Rebel: Predicting Citizen Compliance with Police Requests." *Police Quarterly* 2 (4): 389–416.

McGarrell, Edmund F., Steven Chermak, Alexander Weiss, and Jeremy Wilson. 2001. "Reducing Firearms Violence through Directed Police Patrol." *Criminology & Public Policy* 1 (1): 119–48.

Meares, Tracey. 2009. "The Legitimacy of the Police among Young African-American Men." *Marquette Law Review* 92 (4): 651–66.

Meares, Tracey L., Tom R. Tyler, and Jacob Gardener. 2012. "Lawful or Fair? How Cops and Laypeople Perceive Good Policing." Yale Law School, Public Law Working Paper No. 255. http://papers.ssrn.com/sol3/papers.cfm?abstract_id = 2116645.

Memorandum of Agreement between the United States Department of Justice and the City of Cincinnati, Ohio, and the Cincinnati Police Department. 2002. www.cincinnati-oh. gov/police/linkservid/EA1A2C00-DCB5-4212-8628197B6C923141/showMeta/0.

Meyer, John W., and Brian Rowan. 1977. "Institutionalized Organizations: Formal Structure as Myth and Ceremony." *American Journal of Sociology* 83 (2): 340–63.

Meyer, John W., and Brian Rowan. 1978. "The Structure of Educational Organizations." In *Environments and Organizations,* ed. Marshall W. Meyer. San Francisco: Jossey-Bass.

Miller, Joel, Robert C. Davis, Nicole J. Henderson, John Markovic, and Christopher W. Ortiz. 2003. *Public Opinions of the Police: The Influence of Friends, Family, and News Media.* Report to the National Institute of Justice. New York: Vera Institute of Justice.

Moore, Mark H. 2002. *Recognizing Value in Policing: The Challenge of Measuring Police Performance.* Washington, DC: Police Executive Research Forum.

Muir, William Ker, Jr. 1977. *The Police: Streetcorner Politicians.* Chicago: University of Chicago Press.

Murphy, Kristina, and Adrian Cherney. 2012. "Understanding Cooperation with Police in a Diverse Society." *British Journal of Criminology* 52 (1): 181–201.

Murphy, Kristina, Lyn Hinds, and Jenny Fleming. 2008. "Encouraging Public Cooperation and Support for Police." *Policing & Society: An International Journal of Research and Policy* 18 (2): 136–55.

Myhill, Andy, and Ben Bradford. 2012. "Can Police Enhance Public Confidence by Improving Quality of Service? Results from Two Surveys in England and Wales." *Policing & Society: An International Journal of Research and Policy* 22 (4): 397–425.

National Research Council. 2004. *Fairness and Effectiveness in Policing: The Evidence.* Edited by Wesley Skogan and Kathleen Frydl, Committee to Review Research on Police Policy and Practices. Committee on Law and Justice. Washington, DC: National Academies Press.

Nelson, Paul. 2009. "Tarnishing the Badge: A Decade of Trouble for Schenectady Police." *Albany Times-Union,* February 19.

———. 2010. "Imprisoned Ex-Police Leader to Go Free Friday." *Albany Times-Union,* October 14.

———. 2013. "Probe Clears Police, At Last." *Albany Times-Union,* January 4. www.timesunion. com/local/article/Probe-clears-police-at-last-4164914.php.

Nilsson, Lars, Michael D. Johnson, and Anders Gustafsson, 2001. "The Impact of Quality Practices on Customer Satisfaction and Business Results: Product versus Service Organizations." *Journal of Quality Management* 6: 5–27.

Nivette, Amy E., Manuel Eisner, Tina Malti, and Denis Ribeaud. 2014. "The Social and Developmental Antecedents of Legal Cynicism." *Journal of Research in Crime and Delinquency.* Advance on-line publication.

O'Brien, John. 2010a. "Syracuse Police Officer to Receive $400K in Sexual Discrimination Suit." *Post-Standard* (Syracuse, NY), March 23.

———. 2010b. "Syracuse Mayor Blocks Award for Police Officer Because He Used Excessive Force Against a Suspect." *Post-Standard* (Syracuse, NY), June 23.

O'Brien, John, and Jim O'Hara. 2013. "Onondaga County DA: Syracuse Police Violations of Suspects' Rights 'Shocking.'" *Post-Standard* (Syracuse, NY), January 11. www.syracuse.com/news/index.ssf/2013/01/onondaga_county_da_syracuse_po.html.

Olzak, Susan, Suzanne Shanahan, and Elizabeth H. McEneaney. 1996. "Poverty, Segregation, and Race Riots: 1960 to 1993." *American Sociological Review* 61: 590–613.

Orren, Gary, 1997. "Fall from Grace: The Public's Loss of Faith in Government." In *Why People Don't Trust Government,* ed. Joseph S. Nye Jr., Philip D. Zelikow, and David C. King. Cambridge, MA: Harvard University Press.

Orton, J. Douglas, and Karl E. Weick. 1990. "Loosely Coupled Systems: A Reconceptualization." *Academy of Management Review* 15: 203–23.

Paoline, Eugene A., III. 2004. "Shedding Light on Police Culture: An Examination of Officers' Occupational Attitudes." *Police Quarterly* 7 (2): 205–36.

Paoline, Eugene A., III, Stephanie M. Myers, and Robert E. Worden. 2000. "Police Culture, Individualism, and Community Policing: Evidence from Two Police Departments." *Justice Quarterly* 17 (3): 575–605.

Paoline, Eugene A., III, and William Terrill. 2005. "The Impact of Police Culture on Traffic Stop Searches: An Analysis of Attitudes and Behavior." *Policing: An International Journal of Police Strategies and Management* 28: 455–72.

———. 2014. *Police Culture: Adapting to the Strains of the Job.* Durham, NC: Carolina Academic Press.

Parks, Roger B. 1984. "Linking Objective and Subjective Measures of Performance." *Public Administration Review* 44 (2): 118–27.

Parks, Roger B., Stephen D. Mastrofski, Christina DeJong, and M. Kevin Gray. 1999. "How Officers Spend Their Time with the Community." *Justice Quarterly* 16 (3): 483–518.

Paternoster, Raymond, Robert Brame, Ronet Bachman, and Lawrence W. Sherman. 1997. "Do Fair Procedures Matter? The Effect of Procedural Justice on Spouse Assault." *Law & Society Review* 31 (1): 163–204.

Perez, Douglas W. 1994. *Common Sense about Police Review.* Philadelphia: Temple University Press.

Piquero, Alex R., Jeffrey Fagan, Edward P. Mulvey, Laurence Steinberg, and Candice Odgers. "Developmental Trajectories of Legal Socialization among Serious Adolescent Offenders." *Journal of Criminal Law and Criminology* 96 (2005): 267–98.

Police Executive Research Forum. 2000. *National Evaluation of the Problem-Solving Partnerships (PSP) Project for the Office of Community Oriented Policing Services (COPS).* Washington, DC: U.S. Department of Justice, Police Executive Research Forum.

Pratt, Travis C., Michael G. Turner, and Alex R. Piquero. "Parental Socialization and Community Context: A Longitudinal Analysis of the Structural Sources of Low Self-Control." *Journal of Research in Crime and Delinquency* 41 (2004): 219–43.

President's Task Force on 21st Century Policing. 2015. *Final Report of the President's Task Force on 21st Century Policing.* Washington, DC: Department of Justice, Office of Community Oriented Policing Services.

Prottas, Jeffrey Manditch. 1978. "The Power of the Street-Level Bureaucrat in Public Service Bureaucracies." *Urban Affairs Review* 13: 285–312.

Reiner, Jake. 2012. "Citizen Review Board Gets a Second Chance: More Structure This Time." *DemocracyWise,* March 8.Syracuse, NY: S. I. Newhouse School of Public Communications, Syracuse University.

Reisig, Michael D., Jason Bratton, and Marc G. Gertz. 2007. "The Construct Validity and Refinement of Process-Based Policing Measures." *Criminal Justice & Behavior* 34 (8): 1005–28.

Reisig, Michael D., and Roger B. Parks. 2000. "Experience, Quality of Life, and Neighborhood Context: A Hierarchical Analysis of Satisfaction with Police." *Justice Quarterly* 17 (3): 607–30.

Reisig, Michael D., Scott E. Wolfe, and Kristy Holtfreter. 2011. "Legal Cynicism, Legitimacy, and Criminal Offending: The Nonconfounding Effect of Low Self-Control." *Criminal Justice and Behavior* 38: 1265–79.

Reiss, Albert J., Jr. 1971. *The Police and the Public.* New Haven, CT: Yale University Press.

Reuss-Ianni, Elizabeth. 1983. *Two Cultures of Policing: Street Cops and Management Cops.* New Brunswick, NJ: Transaction Publishers.

Ridgeway, Greg, Terry L. Schell, Brian Gifford, Jessica Saunders, Susan Turner, K. Jack Riley, and Travis L. Dixon. 2009. *Police-Community Relations in Cincinnati.* Santa Monica, CA: RAND Corporation.

Rosenbaum, Dennis P., and Daniel S. Lawrence. N.d. *Teaching Respectful Police-Citizen Encounters and Good Decision Making: Results of a Randomized Control Trial with Police Recruits.* Chicago: National Police Research Platform.

Rosenbaum, Dennis P. and Arthur J. Lurigio. 1994. "An Inside Look at Community Policing Reform: Definitions, Organizational Changes, and Evaluation Findings." *Crime and Delinquency* 40 (3): 299–314.

Rosenbaum, Dennis P., Amie M. Schuck, Sandra K. Costello, Darnell F. Hawkins, and Marianne K. Ring. 2005. "Attitudes toward the Police: The Effects of Direct and Vicarious Experience." *Police Quarterly* 8 (3): 343–65.

Rosenbaum, Dennis P., Amie M. Schuck, Daniel Lawrence, and Susan Hartnett. 2011. *Community-Based Indicators of Police Performance: Introducing the Platform's Public Satisfaction Survey.* Chicago: National Police Research Platform.

Rosenfeld, Richard, Michael J. Deckard, and Emily Blackburn. 2014. "The Effects of Directed Patrol and Self-Initiated Enforcement on Firearm Violence: A Randomized Controlled Study of Hot Spot Policing." *Criminology.* Advance on-line publication.

Roth, Jeffrey A. 2000. *National Evaluation of the COPS Program—Title I of the 1994 Crime Act.* Washington, DC: National Institute of Justice.

Roth, Jeffrey A., Jan Roehl, and Calvin C. Johnson. 2004. "Trends in the Adoption of Community Policing." In *Community Policing: Can It Work?* ed. Wesley G. Skogan. Belmont, CA: Wadsworth/Thomson Learning.

Saad, Lydia. 2015. "American's Faith in Honesty, Ethics of Police Rebounds." December 21. www.gallup.com/poll/187874/americans-faith-honesty-ethics-police-rebounds.aspx.

Sahin, Nusret M. 2014. "Legitimacy, Procedural Justice, and Police-Citizen Encounters." Ph.D. diss., Rutgers University.

Sampson, Rana, and Michael S. Scott, 2000. *Tackling Crime and Other Public Safety Problems*. Washington, DC: United States Department of Justice, Office of Community Oriented Policing Services.

Sampson, Robert J., and Dawn Jeglum Bartusch. 1998. "Legal Cynicism and (Subcultural?) Tolerance of Deviance: The Neighborhood Context of Racial Differences." *Law and Society Review* 32 (4): 777–804.

Sampson, Robert J., and Jacqueline Cohen. 1988. "Deterrent Effects of the Police on Crime: A Replication and Theoretical Extension." *Law & Society Review* 22: 163–89.

Sargeant, Elise, and Christine E. W. Bond. 2015. "Keeping It in the Family: Parental Influences on Young People's Attitudes to Police." *Journal of Sociology* 51: 917–32.

Scaglion, Richard, and Richard G. Condon. 1980. "Determinants of Attitudes toward City Police." *Criminology* 17 (4): 485–94.

Schatmeier, Elliot Harvey. 2013. "Reforming Police Use-of-Force Practices: A Case Study of the Cincinnati Police Department." *Columbia Journal of Law and Social Problems* 46: 539–86.

Schenectady. Office of Mayor. 2007. "Stratton Names Wayne Bennett Public Safety Commissioner." Press release, April 27. www.cityofschenectady.com/press%20releases/BennettReleaseLetterhead.pdf.

Schuck, Amie M. 2013. "A Life-Course Perspective on Adolescents' Attitudes to Police: DARE, Delinquency, and Residential Segregation." *Journal of Research in Crime and Delinquency* 50: 579–607.

Schuck, Amie M., and Dennis P. Rosenbaum. 2011. *The Chicago Quality Interaction Training Program: A Randomized Control Trial of Police Innovation*. Washington, DC: National Institute of Justice, National Police Research Platform.

Schulhofer, Stephen J., Tom R. Tyler, and Aziz Z. Huq. 2011. "American Policing at a Crossroads: Unsustainable Policies and the Procedural Justice Alternative." *Journal of Criminal Law* and *Criminology* 101 (2): 335–74.

Scott, W. Richard. 2014. *Institutions and Organizations: Ideas, Interests, and Identities*. 4th ed. Thousand Oaks, CA: Sage Publications.

Scrivner, Ellen M. 1994. *Controlling Police Use of Excessive Force: The Role of the Police Psychologist*. Research in Brief. Washington, DC: National Institute of Justice.

Searing, Donald, Gerald Wright, and George Rabinowitz. 1976. "The Primacy Principle: Attitude Change and Political Socialization." *British Journal of Political Science* 6: 83–113.

Sharma, Garima, and Darren Good. 2013. "The Work of Middle Managers: Sensemaking and Sensegiving for Creating Positive Social Change." *Journal of Applied Behavioral Science* 49: 95–122.

Sherman, Lawrence W. 2002. "Trust and Confidence in Criminal Justice." *National Institute of Justice Journal* 248: 22–31.

Sherman, Lawrence W., and Ellen G. Cohn, 1989. "The Impact of Research on Legal Policy: The Minneapolis Domestic Violence Experiment." *Law & Society Review* 23: 117–44.

Sherman, Lawrence W., and Dennis P. Rogan. 1995. "The Effects of Gun Seizures on Gun Violence: 'Hot Spots' Patrol in Kansas City." *Justice Quarterly* 12 (4): 673–93.

Silverman, Eli B. 2006. "Compstat's Innovation." In *Police Innovation: Contrasting Perspectives*, ed. David Weisburd and Anthony A. Braga. Cambridge: Cambridge University Press.

Skogan, Wesley G. 2005. "Citizen Satisfaction with Police Encounters." *Police Quarterly* 8 (3): 298–321.

———. 2006. "Asymmetry in the Impact of Encounters with Police." *Policing & Society: An International Journal of Research and Policy* 16 (2): 99–126.

———. 2008. "Why Reforms Fail." *Policing & Society: An International Journal of Research and Policy* 18 (1): 23–34.

Skogan, Wesley G., Maarten Van Craen, and Cari Hennessy. 2014. "Training Police for Procedural Justice." Working paper, Northwestern University.

Skolnick, Jerome H. 1966. *Justice without Trial: Law Enforcement in Democratic Society.* New York: Wiley, 1966.

Skolnick, Jerome H., and James J. Fyfe. 1993. *Above the Law: Police and the Excessive Use of Force.* New York: Free Press.

Smith, Kevin, John R. Alford, Peter K. Hatemi, Lindon Eaves, Carolyn Funk, and John R. Hibbing. "Biology, Ideology, and Epistemology: How Do We Know Political Attitudes Are Inherited and Why Should We Care?" *American Journal of Political Science* 56 (2012): 17–33.

Smith, Paul E., and Richard O. Hawkins. 1973. "Victimization, Types of Citizen-Police Contacts, and Attitudes toward the Police." *Law and Society Review* 8 (1): 135–52.

Smith, Tom W. 2008. *Trends in Confidence in Institutions, 1973–2006.* GSS Social Change Report No. 54. Chicago: NORC/University of Chicago.

Sneed, Tiemy, 2014. "Ferguson's Problems Are Not Ferguson's Alone." *U.S. News & World Report,* August 22.

Sparrow, Malcolm K., Mark H. Moore, and David M. Kennedy. 1990. *Beyond 911: A New Era for Policing.* New York: Basic Books.

Suchman, Mark. 1995. "Managing Legitimacy: Strategic and Institutional Approaches." *Academy of Management Review* 20: 571–610.

Sunshine, Jason, and Tom R. Tyler. 2003. "The Role of Procedural Justice and Legitimacy in Shaping Public Support for Policing." *Law & Society Review* 37 (3): 513–48.

Sviridoff, Michele, and Jerome E. McElroy. 1989. *Processing Complaints against Police in New York City: The Complainant's Perspective.* New York: Vera Institute.

Szymanski, David M., and David H. Herard, 2001. "Customer Satisfaction: A Meta-Analysis of the Empirical Evidence." *Journal of the Academy of Marketing Science* 29: 16–35.

Tankebe, Justice. 2009. "Public Cooperation with the Police in Ghana: Does Procedural Fairness Matter?" *Criminology* 47 (4): 1265–93.

Tankebe, Justice. 2013. "Viewing Things Differently: The Dimensions of Public Perceptions of Police Legitimacy." *Criminology* 51 (1): 103–35.

Tankebe, Justice. 2014. "Police Legitimacy." In *Oxford Handbook on Police and Policing,* ed. Michael D. Reisig and Robert J. Kane. New York: Oxford University Press.

Terrill, William, and Eugene A. Paoline III, 2016. "Police Use of Less Lethal Force: Does Administrative Policy Matter?" *Justice Quarterly,* advance on-line publication.

Terrill, William, Eugene A. Paoline, III, and Jason Ingram. 2012. *Assessing Police Use of Force Policy and Outcomes.* Report to the National Institute of Justice. East Lansing: Michigan State University.

Terrill, William, Eugene A. Paoline III, and Peter K. Manning. 2003. "Police Culture and Coercion." *Criminology* 41: 1003–34.

Thompson, James D. 1967. *Organizations in Action: Social Science Bases of Administrative Theory*. New York: McGraw-Hill.

Tilley, Nick. 2003. "Community Policing, Problem-Oriented Policing, and Intelligence-Led Policing." In *Handbook of Policing*, ed. Tim Newman. Portland, OR: Willan.

Toch, Hans. 1980. *Violent Men*. Rev. ed. Cambridge, MA: Schenkmen.

———. 1996. "The Violence-Prone Police Officer." In *Police Violence: Understanding and Controlling Police Abuse of Force*. Edited by William A. Geller and Hans Toch. New Haven, CT: Yale University Press.

Trinkner, Rick, Tom R. Tyler, and Phillip Atiba Goff. 2014. "Justice from Within: The Relations between a Procedurally Just Organizational Climate and Police Organizational Efficiency, Endorsement of Democratic Policing, and Officer Well-Being." Working Paper.

Tyler, Tom R. 1987. "Conditions Leading to Value-Expressive Effects in Judgments of Procedural Justice: A Test of Four Models." *Journal of Personality and Social Psychology* 52 (2): 333–44.

———. 1988. "What is Procedural Justice? Criteria Used by Citizens to Assess the Fairness of Legal Procedures." *Law & Society Review* 22 (1): 103–35.

———. 1990. *Why People Obey the Law*. New Haven, CT: Yale University Press.

———. 2003. "Procedural Justice, Legitimacy, and the Effective Rule of Law." *Crime and Justice* 30: 431–505.

———. 2004. "Enhancing Police Legitimacy." *Annals of the American Academy of Political and Social Science* 593 (1): 84–99.

———. 2005. "Policing in Black and White: Ethnic Group Differences in Trust and Confidence in the Police." *Police Quarterly* 8 (3): 322–41.

———. 2009. "Race, Police Legitimacy and Cooperation with the Police." NIJ *Research for the Real World Seminar*. www.nij.gov/multimedia/Pages/welcome.aspx.

———. 2011. "Race, Police Legitimacy and Cooperation with the Police." National Institute of Justice, *Research for the Real World Seminar*. Transcript accessed at www.nij.gov/multimedia/presenter/presenter-tyler/Pages/presenter-tyler-transcript.aspx.

Tyler, Tom R., and Steven L. Blader. 2003. "The Group Engagement Model: Procedural Justice, Social Identity, and Cooperative Behavior." *Personality and Social Psychological Review* 7: 349–61.

Tyler, Tom R., Patrick E. Callahan, and Jeffrey Frost. 2007. "Armed and Dangerous (?): Motivating Rule Adherence among Agents of Social Control." *Law & Society Review* 41 (2): 457–92.

Tyler, Tom R., and Jeffrey Fagan. 2008. "Legitimacy and Cooperation: Why Do People Help the Police Fight Crime in Their Communities?" *Ohio State Journal of Criminal Law* 6: 231–75.

Tyler, Tom R., and Robert Folger. 1980. "Distributional and Procedural Aspects of Satisfaction with Citizen-Police Encounters." *Basic and Applied Social Psychology* 1 (4): 281–292.

Tyler, Tom R., Phillip Atiba Goff, and Robert J. McCoun. 2015. "The Impact of Psychological Science on Policing in the United States: Procedural Justice, Legitimacy, and Effective Law Enforcement." *Psychological Science in the Public Interest* 16: 75–109.

Tyler, Tom R., and Yuen J. Huo. 2002. *Trust in the Law: Encouraging Public Cooperation with the Police and Courts*. New York, NY: Russell Sage.

Tyler, Tom R., Kenneth A. Rasinski, and Nancy Spodick. 1985. "Influence of Voice on Satisfaction with Leaders: Exploring the Meaning of Process Control." *Journal of Personality and Social Psychology* 48 (1): 72–81.

Tyler, Tom R., Stephen Schulhofer, and Aziz Z. Huq. 2010. "Legitimacy and Deterrence Effects in Counterterrorism Policing: A Study of Muslim Americans." *Law & Society Review* 44 (2): 365–402.

United States [cited as U.S.]. Department of Justice. 2015. *Investigation of the Ferguson Police Department.* Washington, DC: Department of Justice, Civil Rights Division.

———. Federal Bureau of Investigation. 1992. *Killed in the Line of Duty: A Study of Selected Felonious Killings of Law Enforcement Officers.* Washington, DC: U.S. Department of Justice.

———. National Advisory Commission on Civil Disorders. 1968. Report of the National Advisory Commission on Civil Disorders. Washington, DC: The Commission.

Walker, Samuel. 1993. *Taming the System: The Control of Discretion in Criminal Justice, 1950–1990.* New York: Oxford University Press.

———. 2001. *Police Accountability: The Role of Citizen Oversight.* Belmont, CA: Wadsworth.

———. 2003. "The New Paradigm of Police Accountability: The U.S. Justice Department 'Pattern or Practice' Suits in Context." *St. Louis University Public Law Review* 22: 3–52.

———. 2005. *The New World of Police Accountability.* Thousand Oaks, CA: Sage.

Waterman, Robert H., Jr. 1990. *Adhocracy: The Power to Change.* Memphis, TN: Whittle Books.

Weick, Karl E. 1976. "Educational Organizations as Loosely Coupled Systems." *Administrative Science Quarterly* 21 (1): 1–19.

———. 1995. *Sensemaking in Organizations.* Thousand Oaks, CA: Sage Publications.

Weick, Karl E., Kathleen M. Sutcliffe, and David Obstfeld. 2005. "Organizing and the Process of Sensemaking." *Organization Science* 16 (4): 409–21.

Weisburd, David, Stephen D. Mastrofski, Ann Marie McNally, Rosann Greenspan, and James J. Willis. 2003. "Reforming to Preserve: Compstat and Strategic Problem Solving in American Policing." *Criminology & Public Policy* 2 (3): 421–455.

Weisburd, David, Stephen D. Mastrofski, James J. Willis, and Rosann Greenspan. 2006. "Changing Everything so That Everything Can Remain the Same: Compstat and American Policing." In *Police Innovation: Contrasting Perspectives.* Edited by David Weisburd and Anthony A. Braga. Cambridge: Cambridge University Press.

Weitzer, Ronald. 1999. "Citizens' Perceptions of Police Misconduct: Race and Neighborhood Context." *Justice Quarterly* 16 (4): 819–46.

———. 2000a. "Racialized Policing: Residents' Perceptions in Three Neighborhoods." *Law & Society Review* 34 (1): 129–55.

———. 2000b. "White, Black, or Blue Cops? Race and Citizen Assessments of Police Officers." *Journal of Criminal Justice* 28 (4): 313–24.

———. 2002. "Incidents of Police Misconduct and Public Opinion." *Journal of Criminal Justice* 30: 397–408.

Weitzer, Ronald, and Steven A. Tuch. 1999. "Race, Class, and Perceptions of Discrimination by the Police." *Crime & Delinquency* 45 (4): 494–507.

———. 2005. "Determinants of Public Satisfaction with the Police." *Police Quarterly* 8 (3): 279–97.

———. 2006. *Race and Policing in America: Conflict and Reform.* New York: Cambridge University Press.

Wells, William. 2007. "Types of Contact and Evaluations of Police Officers: The Effects of Procedural Justice across Three Types of Police-Citizen Encounters." *Journal of Criminal Justice* 35 (6): 612–21.

Whitaker, Gordon P. 1982. "What Is Patrol Work?" *Police Studies* 4: 13–22.

Whitaker, Gordon P., Charles David Phillips, Peter J. Haas, and Robert E. Worden. 1985. "Aggressive Policing and the Deterrence of Crime," *Law and Policy* 7: 395–416.

Willis, James J., Steven D. Mastrofski, and David Weisburd. 2003. *Compstat in Practice: An In-Depth Analysis of Three Cities.* Washington, DC: Police Foundation.

———. 2007. "Making Sense of Compstat: A Theory-based Analysis of Organizational Change in Three Police Departments." *Law & Society Review* 41 (1): 147–88.

Wilson, James Q. 1968. *Varieties of Police Behavior: The Management of Law and Order in Eight Communities.* Cambridge, MA: Harvard University Press.

———. 1989. *Bureaucracy: What Government Agencies Do and Why They Do It.* New York: Basic Books.

Wilson, James Q., and Barbara Boland. 1978. "The Effect of the Police on Crime." *Law & Society Review* 12: 367–90.

Wolfe, Scott E., Kyle McLean, and Travis C. Pratt. 2016. "I Learned It by Watching You: Legal Socialization and the Intergenerational Transmission of Legitimacy Attitudes." *British Journal of Criminology.* doi: 10.1093/bjc/azw038.

Wolfe, Scott E., and Alex R. Piquero. 2011. "Organizational Justice and Police Misconduct." *Criminal Justice and Behavior* 38 (4): 332–53.

Wood, Richard L., Mariah Davis, and Amelia Rouse. 2004. "Diving into Quicksand: Program Implementation and Police Subcultures." In *Community Policing: Can It Work?* ed. Wesley G. Skogan. Belmont, CA: Wadsworth.

Worden, Robert E. 1995. "The 'Causes' of Police Brutality: Theory and Evidence on Police Use of Force." In *And Justice for All: Understanding and Controlling Police Abuse of Force,* ed. William A. Geller and Hans Toch. Washington, DC: Police Executive Research Forum.

Worden, Robert E., and Kelly J. Becker, 2015. "Tip of an Iceberg: Citizen Complaints and Citizen Dissatisfaction with the Police." Paper presented at the Annual Meeting of the American Society of Criminology.

Worden, Robert E., Moonsun Kim, Christopher J. Harris, Mary Anne Pratte, Shelagh E. Dorn, and Shelley S. Hyland. 2013. "Intervention with Problem Officers: An Impact Evaluation of an EIS Intervention." *Criminal Justice and Behavior* 40 (4): 409–37.

Worden, Robert E., and Sarah J. McLean, 2014a. "Systematic Social Observation of the Police." In *Oxford Handbook on Police and Policing,* ed. Michael D. Reisig and Robert J. Kane. New York: Oxford University Press.

Worden, Robert E., and Sarah J. McLean, 2014b. "Police Discretion in Law Enforcement." In *Encyclopedia of Criminology and Criminal Justice,* ed. Gerben Bruinsma and David Weisburd. New York, NY: Springer.

———. 2016. "Measuring, Managing, and Enhancing Procedural Justice in Policing: Promise and Pitfalls." *Criminal Justice Policy Review.* Advance on-line publication.

Worden, Robert E., Sarah J. McLean, and Heidi S. Bonner. 2015. "You Can Observe a Lot by Watching: Contributions of Systematic Social Observation to Our Understanding of Police." In *Critical Issues in Policing: Contemporary Readings,* ed. Roger G. Dunham and Geoffrey P. Alpert. 7th ed. Long Grove, IL: Waveland.

Worden, Robert E., and Robin L. Shepard, 1996. "Demeanor, Crime, and Police Behavior: A Reexamination of Police Services Study Data," *Criminology* 34: 83–105.

Worden, Robert E., Robin L. Shepard, and Stephen D. Mastrofski, 1996. "On the Meaning and Measurement of Suspects' Demeanor toward the Police." *Journal of Research in Crime and Delinquency* 33: 324–32.

Wycoff, Mary Ann, 1994. *Community Policing Strategies.* Report to the National Institute of Justice. Washington, DC: Police Foundation.

Wycoff, Mary Ann, and Wesley G. Skogan. 1994. "The Effect of Community Policing Management Style on Officers' Attitudes." *Crime and Delinquency* 40 (3): 371–83.

Zaffron, Steve, and Dave Logan. 2011. *The Three Laws of Performance: Rewriting the Future of Your Organization and Your Life.* Jossey-Bass.

INDEX

Fig. refers to figures.

accountability. *See* management accountability; public accountability
administrative rules, 20, 28–29, 31, 33, 41, 156–57, 167, 183, 196
African Americans, 1, 34, 38, 47, 49. *See also* black community; Black Lives Matter movement; black police officers; blacks; racial disparities
age: citizen satisfaction and, 82, 84*fig.*, 86; citizens' subjective experiences and, 78; police dis/respect and, 211n4; procedural injustice and, 126–27; procedural justice and, 85, 86, 126–27; subjective outcomes and, 143*fig.*; subjective procedural justice and, 132, 138*fig.*, 139
Albuquerque (NM) Police Department, 29
American Civil Liberties Union, 19, 189–190
American National Election Studies (ANES), 44
armchair observations, 109, 110–12
arrests: audio/video recordings and, 212n13; blacks and, 200*fig.*, 206*fig.*; calls for service and, 59; citizen disrespect and, 120; citizen resistance and, 120; citizen satisfaction and, 72*fig.*, 73, 74, 77, 82, 84*fig.*, 85; citizens' subjective experiences and, 82; ethnicity and, 200*fig.*, 201*fig.*; females and, 200*fig.*, 201*fig.*, 206*fig.*; Hispanics/Latinos and, 200*fig.*; intoxication and, 121; legitimacy and, 82; males and, 200*fig.*, 201*fig.*, 202, 206*fig.*;

mental disorder and, 121; obligation index and, 67*fig.*; outcomes and, 59, 77; police-initiated encounters and, 119; police services survey and, 58, 59, 60, 150, 210n8; preliminary model of citizens' subjective experiences and, 213n1; primary citizens and, 107–8; primary officers and, 108; pro-arrest policies, 22–23, 28; procedural injustice and, 115*fig.*, 117, 129; procedural justice and, 50, 82, 84*fig.*, 85, 102, 115*fig.*, 117, 119, 212n14; procedural justice index and, 75–77; race and, 109, 200*fig.*, 201*fig.*; Schenectady (NY) Police Department and, 72*fig.*, 73, 75–77, 108, 109–10, 197–200, 202–3, 205–6*fig.*; search/frisk and, 81; sex and, 109, 200*fig.*, 201*fig.*; spouse assaults and, 28–29; subjective outcomes and, 143*fig.*; subjective procedural justice and, 132, 136, 138, 140, 141; Syracuse (NY) Police Department and, 72*fig.*, 73, 75–77, 197–98, 200–203; systematic social observation of police (SSO) and, 103; trust index and, 65*fig.*; trustworthy motives and, 115*fig.*, 116; verbal force and, 118; whites and, 200*fig.*, 206*fig.*
attitudes toward police: African Americans and, 1, 47, 49; blacks and, 47, 48; citizens' subjective experiences and, 46–47, 68; civil rights violations and, 47; Hispanics/Latinos and, 49; legitimacy and, 6–7, 44; media and, 47;

neighborhoods and, 79; obligation and, 42; police-community relations and, 47; police reform and, 5; police services survey and, 58; procedural justice and, 5, 179; public trust and, 42; race and, 47, 48; racial disparities and, 46, 48; urban neighborhoods and, 46; whites and, 47, 48, 49; youth and, 48–51. *See also* childhood legal socialization; prior attitudes

Attorney General's Task Force on Family Violence, 22

audio/video recordings: armchair observations and, 109, 110–12; arrests and, 212n13; Cincinnati (OH) Police Department (CPD) and, 190; deadly force use and, 3; Internal Affairs (IA) and, 187–88; King, Rodney and, 4; legitimacy and, 188–89; management and, 187–89; police behavior and, 187–89, 212n13; police-citizen interactions and, 101, 107; police performance and, 187–88; primary officers and, 111; procedural justice and, 188–89; Schenectady (NY) Police Department and, 11, 101, 107, 108, 111–12, 131, 181, 204–8, 215n7, 215n8; supervisors and, 187–88; traffic/stops and, 107. *See also* body-worn cameras

Augustyn, Megan Bears, 50

Australia, 49–50

authority, 49, 63, 69–70, 88, 102, 185–86. *See also* police authority

authorizing environments, 19

bad press. *See* media

Baltimore (MD) police, 3, 55, 56

Barnett, Richard, 36

battered women's movement, 22. *See also* domestic violence

Bayley, David H., 195

Bechky, Beth A., 167

best practices, 27–28

Bittner, Egon, 59

black community, 3, 4

Black Lives Matter movement, 3

black police officers, 5, 34, 40

blacks: arrests and, 200fig., 206fig.; attitudes toward police and, 46, 47, 48; Cincinnati (OH) Police Department (CPD) and, 189–191, 193; citizen satisfaction and, 78, 84fig.; citizens' subjective experiences and, 78, 185; fairness and, 47; Ferguson (MO) Police Department (FPD) and, 3; Kerner Commission/National Advisory Commission on Civil Disorders and, 4–5; procedural injustice and, 127–28, 179;

procedural justice and, 85, 127–28, 179; procedural justice index and, 78; riots and, 56–57; Schenectady (NY) Police Department and, 34, 77, 79, 202, 206fig.; subjective outcomes and, 143fig.; subjective procedural justice and, 132–33, 138fig.; Syracuse (NY) Police Department and, 38, 79; traffic/stops and, 201fig. *See also* African Americans; individuals

body-worn cameras, 111, 187–88, 212n12. *See also* audio/video recordings

Bond, Christine E. W., 49–50

Boston police, 210n2

Bradford, Ben, 44

Bradley, Tom, 4

Brandl, Steven G., 194

Bratton, Jason, 43

Bratton, William, 30, 187

Brown, Michael, 1–3, 4, 191

Brown, Michael K., 15, 16, 29, 155, 182, 183, 188

bureaucracies, 15. *See also* police bureaucracies; Weberian bureaucracy

Bureau of Justice Statistics, 59. *See also* Department of Justice (DOJ)

calls for service: arrests and, 59; citizen disrespect and, 120; citizen dissatisfaction and, 88; citizen satisfaction and, 74, 77, 79–80, 82, 83–85; citizens' subjective experiences and, 78, 79–80; failure to respond to scene and, 96; interpersonal conflicts and, 199fig., 200fig.; Lipsky, Michael and, 210n7; obligation index and, 67fig.; outcomes and, 77; police services survey and, 58–59, 60, 150, 153; preliminary model of citizens' subjective experiences and, 213n1; primary citizens and, 107–8; primary officers and, 108; procedural injustice and, 115fig., 117, 119, 180; procedural justice and, 82, 83–85, 115fig., 117, 119, 129; procedural justice index and, 75–76, 185–86; Schenectady (NY) Police Department and, 71–73, 75–76, 109, 197–200, 202–3, 205fig.; subjective outcomes and, 143fig.; subjective procedural justice and, 138, 140–41; Syracuse (NY) Police Department and, 71–73, 75–76, 197–98, 200–203; time of day and, 80; trust index and, 65fig.; trustworthy motives and, 115fig., 116; violent crime and, 199fig., 200fig.

care/concern, 89, 92–93, 104, 116–17, 146, 150

Case 6-1, 122

Case 6-2, 123–24

www.ingramcontent.com/pod-product-compliance
Lightning Source LLC
Chambersburg PA
CBHW050345270326
41926CB00016B/3607